Reprints of Economic Classics

AGRICULTURE

AND THE TRADE CYCLE

AGRICULTURE
AND THE TRADE CYCLE

THEIR MUTUAL RELATIONS
WITH SPECIAL REFERENCE
TO THE PERIOD 1926-1931

BY

JOHN H. KIRK

[1933]

AUGUSTUS M. KELLEY · PUBLISHERS
CLIFTON 1972

First Edition 1933

(London: P. S. King & Son Ltd., *Orchard House, 14 Great Smith Street, Westminster S. W. 1,* 1933)

Reprinted 1972 by
Augustus M. Kelley Publishers
REPRINTS OF ECONOMIC CLASSICS
Clifton New Jersey 07012

I S B N 0 678 00887 6
L C N 68-30531

PRINTED IN THE UNITED STATES OF AMERICA
by SENTRY PRESS, NEW YORK, N. Y. 10013

PREFACE

THIS book falls into two parts. First of all, I describe and analyse the effects upon agriculture of disturbances to the world economy, especially in their cyclical bearing. This is straightforward. In the second part I have plunged into the theory of the trade cycle, and emerged—quite out of breath—with what may turn out to be some novel conclusions. For the present, I sincerely hope they will not be taken too seriously. Until it becomes possible to test and elaborate them, my only excuse for publication is the unlikelihood of finding time for further work in the near future. Criticisms will be gratefully received, and since I have not arrived at any final formulations, I am almost ready to adopt them in advance.

It is my pleasant duty to offer a general acknowledgment to the monetary theories of Mr. Keynes. From them I have drawn my principal inspiration in the analytical portions of this work. Without the spectacles of savings and investment the picture of agriculture's part in world trade was a blur.

Mr. R. F. Kahn has made some very useful suggestions, and Mrs. M. Hollond was kind enough to read and comment on Chapter VII. To both I am exceedingly indebted.

I have finally to record my obligation to Sir Oswald Stoll. The scholarship at Christ's College, Cambridge, which bears his name, gave me facilities for a year's study of which this book is the result.

J. K.

CHRIST'S COLLEGE,
CAMBRIDGE.

CONTENTS

vii

PART II

THE RESPONSIBILITY OF AGRICULTURE FOR
TRADE CYCLES

CONTENTS

LIST OF TABLES

LIST OF TABLES

LIST OF DIAGRAMS

xiii

PART I

THE EFFECTS OF TRADE CYCLES ON AGRICULTURE

CHAPTER I

INTRODUCTORY

AGRICULTURE is the largest group of industries of appreciable uniformity of structure, and it is the largest group serving anything like a uniform market. A wide similarity of experiences and problems is encountered from crop to crop and from agricultural country to country. It so happens that during adversity the experiences of agriculture are more embarrassing and the problems more acute than commonly confront other industries. Conversely, when trade is buoyant, agriculture tends to be more than normally prosperous, and agricultural countries flourish and grow. In short, agriculture shares in the cyclical movements of trade in an exaggerated degree ; and by virtue of the scale of agriculture, the dependence of the bulk of the world's population upon its fortunes, and its most intimate connections with the solvency of governments, it is fair to say that one of the most urgent descriptive studies of the trade cycle is of its impact on agriculture.

An attempt at such a study forms the first part of this work. We require to discover why cyclical movements in agriculture are unduly severe, despite the staple nature of its products, and what are the laws that govern the adjustments which farming makes to its fluctuating economic prospects. This naturally leads on to a consideration of the particular distress which agriculture is suffering at the present, in the vicinity of the trough of the severest depression of recent times. The conditions of supply and demand —the workings of the marketing organisation—the steps which can be improvised to relieve agricultural depression—all these when studied at the extreme indicate with admirable vividness the nature of agriculture's normal problems.

3

In this section of the study the causes and normal development of trade cycles are regarded as given. It is assumed for convenience in exposition, in order that the data should seem to cohere, that the trade cycle has one grand cause, operating externally to agriculture. The phenomena studied become the pure consequences of cyclical fluctuation. But as we shall see later, the relations of agriculture and the trade cycle, even if more or less spontaneous fluctuations in agriculture itself can be excluded as causes, are at least mutual or circular. The vast agricultural expansion which has preceded the present slump is almost certainly not guiltless of the subsequent collapse.

It is necessary, of course, when interpreting facts in the light of some theory of the trade cycle—and only the least interesting facts ever interpret themselves unaided—to make clear what theory is entertained, even as only a provisional hypothesis. It is supposed for the time being that the greatest single cause of the present depression is the decline that occurred in 1928-9—and which has since proceeded to an extreme—in capital expenditure, conveniently known as "investment," in conjunction with the failure of the world to redress this deficiency—which it could not be expected to do—by enlarging its consumptive expenditure. The working out of the decline in investment will conveniently form part of the following brief summary account of recent events.

During the upswing of the cycle (here measured in periods of about nine years) which began in 1924, and indeed earlier in the immediate aftermath of the 1914–18 war, agriculture was being inflated by intensive technical reform. With the aid of the combine (harvester plus thresher) in wheat farming ; with the aid of new, cheap, and improved fertilisers ; on the introduction of many varieties of mechanical appliance, agriculture, with cereals well to the fore, began a course of expansion. Even before the turn of the cycle in 1929 the expanded output was forcing down prices to levels only profitable to those countries and producers who were in a position to apply the new methods. Nevertheless, the old producers—peasants in two continents and small family farmers nearly everywhere—could not be expected at three years' notice to commit suicide and yield place to the new. Abstractly, their governments might approve of mechanisation, but such a custom would corrupt the world. The hand-labour high cost capacity, whether in wheat, dairying, or silk, responded with an increased output in order to neutralise falling prices and maintain its income. Thus at the outset of the 1929 slump many commodities were faced with a " statistical problem," the accumulation of stocks in the face of slender prospects of reduced supply.

The results of technical change were aggravated during the upward phase of the cycle, as such, by the establishment of new capacity at all levels of cost. More sheep were bred, more rubber trees planted, more forests cleared, more land put under irrigation. A few years later this capacity matured. New supplies came on to nearly every market in time to be confronted with the rival supplies of mechanised output, and shortly afterwards producers of all grades of efficiency found themselves swimming in the mill-race of the slump. The demand receded, and prices fell still further, continuing to do so until a restriction scheme succeeded, or consumers had reached their minimum requirements remaining despite wage cuts and unemployment. Nor could farmers find compensation in the fall in the prices of manufactured goods. The exchange problems created in the raw produce countries by the collapse of their leading exports, and aggravated by the cessation of new borrowing, required the restriction of imports by tariffs, exchange regulation or depreciation of the currency. The prime difficulties of agriculture, inelastic supply and inelastic demand, were transmitted to manufacture. And as employment and trade in the manufacturing countries further declined, so accumulated the problems and losses of the agriculturist. It might almost seem the fittest subject of study, why the vicious spiral was not endless.

Furthermore, we have not yet noticed that when agricultural suppliers and holding concerns are in financial distress they are often obliged to sell weak. They sell in fear of the price collapsing further, and on such occasions banks and other creditors become insistent. The whole community clamours for ready money and presses its debtors. At the same time, buyers, either for trade or normal speculation, hold back waiting for prices to reach bottom, and off-load their existing stocks.

In the production of most raw commodities money prime cost, like the wages of hired labour, is but a small proportion of the total. Thus the lower limit of prices beyond which new production ceases is small in relation to normal remunerative price. A host of causes operates to make descent to the lowest limit as breathlessly rapid as can be.

This is the summary sketch of agriculture's cyclical embarrassment. The problems involved can be viewed separately from the angles of supply and demand. From the side of supply there arises the possibility that some cyclical rhythm in agriculture, governed possibly by the weather, contributes to the generation of the trade cycle. Alternatively, from the angle of agriculture, granted that cyclical disturbances are initiated on the side of demand, there is the probability that the inelasticity of supply and demand makes the fluctuations wilder. Were agricultural adjustments simple and easy, the trade cycle, while still a public nuisance, might lose some sting. It is true that any general disequilibrium, impinging on different degrees of resistance, and working itself out through differing elasticities of supply and demand, will give birth to secondary and more particular disequilibria. This would be a mild evil were not the elasticities governing agriculture less, and the resistances more, than those which govern services and intermediate and finished goods. Perhaps as much as 40 per cent. of the world's money income is won by the direct exploitation of the soil. Any measure which smoothed that income would concentrate the trade cycle on countries where reserve resources are greatest, and on industries producing secondary goods of which the supply is not intractably inelastic.

We shall see that the slump of 1930 was not only outrageously severe, but that it had pronounced agricultural features distinguishing it from old-fashioned slumps like those of 1886 and 1893. Grave over-production was one. Unquestionably the production of many raw commodities had exceeded the capacity of the market. True, it was not raw produce alone that had outrun the constable. But the over-production of raw produce was more extensive, more obvious, and much less tractable. Compared with luxury and finished goods the raw products are staple and, one by one, are traded in greater bulk. Their durability in several lines of supply, and the inelasticity of that supply, have—as it were—crystallised out surpluses as redundant stocks.

The saturation of the whole world market is still a reasonable explanation, if not of the depression, then of the crisis. Mr. Robertson, for instance, supposes that markets become gorged, and should be purged. Dr. Sprague, who finds that toxins of waste and inefficiency have entered industry, prescribes bleeding it.

In the medical world to-day, lowering treatment, by either aperients or leeches, is not as popular as it was in the early nineteenth century. Nevertheless, though strong measures with the patient may be no cure, it does not follow that the diagnosis of satiation is faulty. It would hardly be possible to contemplate the early emergence of " statistical positions " without bursting into the question whether redundant supplies have not precipitated, if not caused, the slump.

Without the complication of over-production, analysis of the agricultural slump would be greatly simplified. It would almost be possible to outline it in a paragraph, and write :

During the upward phase of the cycle, domestic investment [1] and that investment more specially associated with foreign lending, both increase. In the aggregate there is a cumulative wave of optimism in investing and lending for investment. The investment schemes, in which constructional work bulks large, directly increase employment.

---

[1] For a full treatment of investment the reader is referred to Keynes, *Treatise on Money*. Appendix I gives a summary of what I consider the essentials of the theory of savings and investment, and relates changes in either to changes in the quantity of money.

The purchasing power of the employed, and of all other wielders of productive resources, then circulates, perhaps many times round, producing secondary employment in every type of ancillary enterprise. But when the total of investment propositions capable of a yield at the current rate of interest becomes used up, or when the limits of the banking system's expansibility have been reached, the boom ceases. Purchasing power and demand are now in deficiency relative to the new level of production. Prices fall, a cumulative pessimism emerges, investment and foreign lending cease. This sudden chill freezes up the debtor countries, whose native investment resources are necessarily small. Since these debtor countries are in the main agricultural, the credit crisis is superimposed on a commodity crisis, made severer by the inelasticity of demand for agricultural and other raw produce. The demand is inelastic because foodstuffs are a large proportion of these products, and because the purchase price of the remainder, raw materials, is but a small part of total manufacturing cost. Again, the rawer the products of the debtor countries, the greater the burden of fixed or semi-fixed charges for handling, transport and distribution. Hence the severest pressure of a slump is on the agricultural countries, and this aggravates their misfortune as debtor countries. Then, once more, the vicious spiral.

But the vicious spiral is probably not endless. During the slump several palliating factors are released. It will be necessary to notice some in detail. Here the immediate question is whether the loss to the industrial countries of their markets in Brazil, Malaya, etc., robs them, either through the unemployment of factors of production or the fall in export prices, of an equivalent power to buy from Brazil and Malaya. Or is there some dispensation which supports, relatively, the volume of manufacturing employment ?

At first sight it would seem that if the prices of coffee and tin slumped, everyone (taken collectively) other than the producers of coffee and tin would be the richer. They would have more to spend on buying everything else.

Evidently that is formally correct. The consumer's bounty palliates the slump. Nevertheless, a large part of the gain is absorbed by merchants on the way, and partly for this reason much of the " saving " on coffee and tin is in fact saved—not spent on copper wiring and rubber tyres. The final consumer himself may very well save as well.

Again, if we suppose some branches of production to be specialised to the supply of raw produce industries and countries, then unemployment directly results from the impoverishment of the raw produce community. If despite the gain on coffee and tin, industry is generally depressed, then conditions cannot be favourable for the reabsorption of the unemployed specialised to supply Brazil and Malaya. The existence of that unemployment creates secondary unemployment in two ways : first, the loss of the purchasing power of the unemployed factors of production ; secondly, the loss of orders for raw material and other auxiliary goods. Then secondary unemployment produces tertiary unemployment, and so on.[1]

Thirdly, particular distress in the raw material countries, and in industries especially supplying them, discourages investment in these directions, and will diminish the total of investment. The collapse of general confidence then depresses the temperature of industry several degrees more.

Thus we see that Brazil's difficulties have their echo in England and Germany. Yet so far as the immediate tendency is for England and Germany to be enriched (at Brazil's expense) there is a compensation. When in those industries (and their satellites) that supply Brazil, unemployment is at its maximum, the adverse tendency is exhausted and will leave the compensatory factor in possession of the field. This arrests the course of the landslide. Such a brake (together with those checks internally operating within each country) is sufficient, it seems, to prevent the distress of the raw material countries from running away with the whole economic machine. If there is an endless

[1] Mr. Kahn has calculated that the direct unemployment of one man in Great Britain will cause the indirect unemployment of three-quarters of another (*Economic Journal*, June, 1931). This is a very small fraction, and the ratio is much larger elsewhere.

series of mutual or circular adverse reactions, the series is probably convergent.

Much of this is debatable matter, to be further argued in due course. For the time being, having accepted the view that cause and effect are inextricable among the phenomena of agricultural depression, we proceed, without misunderstanding, to consider in detail those elements of distress which can be regarded as simple effects of a relapse in trade experienced by agriculture initially from without. The first task is to study the elasticities of supply and demand for agricultural produce and the behaviour of the marketing system in boom and slump. These are the fundamental determinants of the levels reached by agricultural prices during a trade cycle of given amplitude.

CHAPTER II

THE CONDITIONS OF AGRICULTURAL SUPPLY

Adjustments to Instability.—The initial disturbance to price caused by a change in supply works itself out through the elasticity of demand. But the elasticity of supply also enters into the determination of the final price, after the completion of a production period. The same is true where the original disturbance was a change in demand. Accordingly, the elasticity of supply is a matter of some importance in deciding what are the limits of fluctuation in the producer's income when either the demand or supply are unstable. If supply were reasonably elastic, in the face of a recession of demand or of the impact of an inelastically demanded increase of output, the higher cost producers and the marginal departments and outputs of all producers would rapidly withdraw or be withdrawn. The lower limit of prices would be relatively high and the surviving production would not be unprofitable. However, in most circumstances, the lower limit in agriculture is remarkably low, and prices have been known to fall by 60 per cent. from levels which could not on historical grounds be judged inflated.

Given inelastic supply, an instability of price initiated either internally or externally to agriculture is violently intensified. This tendency to amplification may occasionally be relieved when the disturbance is external, by allowing for expected changes in demand. But the opportunities for anticipatory action are less for internal fluctuations in supply, which are more random and cannot be predicted and offset. For all practical purposes the behaviour of the weather is at random, and there is a random element in the programmes of any million uninformed farmers.

Perhaps the possibilities for reasonable forecasting of the condition of the market have always been exaggerated.

It is noteworthy that in those organised markets where attempts are made to assess prospective demand, that that demand is nearly always highly inelastic ; and the amount demanded is a fairly even function of visible trade conditions, or deducible from the experience of the immediate past. Anyone who knows the wheat consumption of one January can guess the demand of the next. These possibilities of good guesswork are quickly exhausted when we reach more elastically demanded commodities (whatever be the reason for elasticity), and the difficulties of forecasting become comparable with those that attend supply. For instance, at the price levels of wheat which ruled in 1931, the Chinese market began to stir, but no one could gauge the extra quantity that China would take. On the side of supply, crop forecasts have been extensively used for the discounting of prospective changes, but their utility is highly limited. Careful work on, say, wheat, by American authorities may be nullified by inaccurate estimates from India or the Danube.[1] Nor are the estimates of aid to current producers, except those in a hemisphere whose growing season does not begin until that of the other hemisphere is ended. The predominance of the Northern Hemisphere in the leading field crops makes this anticipatory inter-local compensation, or the possibility of it, quantitatively small. The scale of production, in general, is set for a year. Then at the expiry of the year, when the rigidity of current commitments has disappeared, the rigidities both of technique and of physical conditions of supply come into play. We may contrast with agriculture the happy situation of the United States Steel Corporation, which in the autumn of 1932 had managed to work down production to 13 per cent. of capacity.

Adaptation to Minor Changes.—The characteristics of elasticity of supply in agriculture may be generalised as follows : for small changes in price the supply is moderately flexible, and the readjustment in production which takes

---

[1] The American method is to issue monthly sampling reports estimating the condition of the crops at so much per cent. of normal. If I recollect rightly, errors of 20 per cent. at two months' distance from harvest-time have not infrequently occurred.

place is generally sufficient to cause a substantial reversal in price at the conclusion of a production period, or, equivalently, a " liquidation " period. But the limits of flexibility are quickly passed. Large changes in price cause no quick adjustments in output greater than those caused by small changes, until the new level of prices has been sustained some years. There appears to be, in response to minor price changes, a continual minor adjustment perpetually in progress ; and putting aside the major movements, which are usually due to changes in demand, we may discuss the opportunities which agricultural industries enjoy for continuous adaptation. This sort of development naturally takes place at the margin of most existing production at nearly all times, and is also to be found, more clearly, in the complete programmes of new producers, either at the outset of their career or when enlarging their responsibilities. It is open to most farmers from year to year to revise their ploughing and breeding programmes, vary their outlay on fertiliser and seed, make minor changes in the labour force, and change from less profitable lines of production to more profitable. The last known prices will be taken into account when increasing or renewing equipment, ploughing in new land, purchasing breeding stock, or buying farms.

Very often these adjustments are made impulsively, and many of them are large " lumpy " undertakings, so that while some producers are just tempted to make quite sweeping changes, others will delay. Thus the responses made to changes in price are not uniform functions of those changes, and they are not always far-sighted or nicely adequate from farm to farm. Yet taking the agricultural industries as a whole, it is fair to conclude that a moderate change in price will be followed by a reverse change a few years later, when an altered output has had time to emerge. An initial departure from normal in either prices or production is followed at the appropriate interval by a further departure in the opposite direction. This is commonest when an instability on the side of supply in the form of diminished output has first raised the price, and then, by leading to expansion in inelastically demanded lines of production, caused in turn the occurrence of a glut.[1] The history of the pig industry in the British market is a leading case. Generally speaking, the supply of agricultural produce is elastic enough to permit the emergence of a rhythm in most forms of output. The rhythms in the production of most separate commodities keep together by virtue of the tendency of substitutions both on the sides of supply and demand to keep most agricultural prices in step.

An idea of the quantitative importance of the minor adjustment to price changes that agriculture displays, together with the tendency for these adjustments to be overdone, may be gained from Professor Day's index of the physical production of twelve leading crops of the United States (1879–1920, trend eliminated).[2]   (See next page.)

In the United States agricultural production seems to have varied considerably from year to year and displayed a rough periodicity around periods of two, three and four years.   At first sight the variations appear to be due to the weather.   Weather probably does explain part of the year to year changes, but various evidences, considered in more detail in Chapter VIII, suggest that climate hardly accounts for the rhythm.   Although there seems to be a periodic change in barometric pressure at intervals of three and a half years, no such periodicity attaches to the same interval in rainfall.   It is not to be expected that any one component of the weather, such as rainfall, for which alone is there evidence of appreciable congruence of changes throughout the United States, will affect most districts and most crops in the same sense, being a limiting factor throughout, and changes in rainfall are not usually the uniquely operating climatic factor at any time.   Although the weather can by no means be excluded as a constituent cause of variability in agricultural output, the rhythmical changes seem to be

---

[1] In practice, many agricultural commodities behave in this fashion together, leading to trade relapse and an intensification of the agricultural price cycle (see Chapters VIII and IX).

[2] From *Review of Economic Statistics*, 1921, quoted by Professor Pigou, "Industrial Fluctuations," p. 62.

TABLE I.—PHYSICAL PRODUCTION OF AMERICAN AGRICULTURE

Year.	Crude Index.	Two Years' Moving Average.	Year.	Crude Index.	Two Years' Moving Average.
1879 . .	106·2	—	1900 . .	100·3	101·3
1880 . .	110·8	108·5	1901 . .	88·5	94·4
1881 . .	86·8	98·8	1902 . .	108·0	98·3
1882 . .	107·1	97·0	1903 . .	97·5	102·8
1883 . .	102·0	104·6	1904 . .	105·6	101·6
1884 . .	106·7	104·4	1905 . .	104·8	105·2
1885 . .	104·5	105·6	1906 . .	109·1	107·0
1886 . .	96·8	100·7	1907 . .	96·5	102·8
1887 . .	91·6	94·2	1908 . .	100·2	98·4
1888 . .	101·5	96·6	1909 . .	97·8	99·0
1889 . .	103·5	102·5	1910 . .	100·1	99·0
1890 . .	89·0	96·3	1911 . .	94·0	97·1
1891 . .	108·4	98·7	1912 . .	108·3	101·2
1892 . .	90·5	99·5	1913 . .	94·2	101·3
1893 . .	90·0	90·3	1914 . .	102·6	98·4
1894 . .	87·9	89·0	1915 . .	106·3	104·5
1895 . .	99·1	93·5	1916 . .	92·3	99·3
1896 . .	103·4	101·3	1917 . .	98·6	95·5
1897 . .	102·7	103·1	1918 . .	96·1	97·4
1898 . .	109·0	105·9	1919 . .	98·2	97·2
1899 . .	102·2	105·6	1920 . .	100·3	99·3

The two years' moving averages smooth out fluctuations due to random elements in the weather.

primarily due to variations in the scale and intensity of farming. These are variations operated within the limits of the elasticity of supply in response to previously ruling prices. The table given above also displays longer waves, corresponding to periods nearer eight years, which are probably the reflection of cyclical perturbations in demand. Generally the longer cycle in output has the larger dimension. The normal amplitude of disturbance on the side of supply is probably not greater than 15 per cent., but the recession of money demand, if we can judge it from statistics of national income, not infrequently attains a compass of 30 per cent.—from boom to slump. If the relapse in demand is sustained over two or three years (for instance 1891–4) it may very well lead to marked subnormal supply in the years following (cf. 1892–5 in the table above). It is with these fluctuations in demand, and their effect on the prosperity of agriculture, that we are primarily concerned in this chapter. Relative to the dimension of price change commonly found in the trade cycle of eight years, supply is considerably less elastic than in response to minor price changes. The ingredients of this inelasticity will be examined under various heads.

Since it is comparatively easy to demonstrate inelasticity by way of describing reasons for it, while similarly to demonstrate elasticity is almost impossible, it may appear from the cogency of the various reasons that agricultural supply is always and inevitably inelastic, for small changes in price as well as large. Accordingly, it is necessary to preface the succeeding sections with the remark that the conditions of supply examined are in most cases taken at the extreme. The conditions of inelasticity which we shall so consider no doubt generally apply also to cases much more moderate—in the absence of which supply would tend towards perfect elasticity—but the degrees of inelasticity which we shall find to apply to extreme cases apply to them only. We shall have in mind principally those obstructions to readjustment now operating.

The following are the principal crops with which we are now concerned. According to the League of Nations Secretariat [1] they are the principal world crops, and most of them are staples of international trade :

Maize	Potatoes	Rubber	Rice
Wheat	Tea	Barley	Cane-sugar
Cocoa	Oats	Coffee	Wool
Rye	Beet-sugar	Cotton	

We also have in mind, more generally,

Tobacco	Hops	Raw silk
Flax and hemp	Oil nuts and seeds	Jute

[1] *Memorandum on Production and Trade*, 1923–8. In this chapter I have also borrowed from the following accounts : Belshaw, " The Profit Cycle in Agriculture " (*Economic Journal*, March, 1926) ; O'Brien, *Agricultural Economics* ; Rowe, *Studies in the Artificial Control of Raw Material Supplies* ; and other publications of the League of Nations Secretariat, notably *The Agricultural Crisis*, Vol. I.

The following are analogous to crops :

| Beef | Mutton | Pork | Bacon |
| Milk | Eggs | Cheese | Butter |

Fruit, vegetables and timber will be counted in from time to time, where statistics are available. In that area of agricultural production where crops are regularly marketed, livestock products count in total values nearly as highly as field crops, but for the world as a whole the cereal group is by far the most important. Annual crops account for about three-quarters of world value under conditions of normal trade.

Obstacles to Rapid Expansion.—In the first place, the vagaries of the climate may wreck the farmer's estimates, and he is tempted not to vary his output until a changed level of prices promises in his view to be permanent. Secondly, the liability of land to diminishing returns causes a variation of yield per acre inverse to the number of acres worked, and similarly with intensive cultivation. A fairly drastic expansion of process produces a smaller variation in total supply. Thirdly, many crops have a long gestation period. The coffee plant takes four years, a beef animal two. Even a year's lag in the output of cereal crops increases the risks of weather and change in price, and therefore contributes to inertia. This would not matter so much if the bulk of money costs had not to be incurred many months before harvest. Something between fourteen and eighteen months is the true gestation period of an annual crop.

There is a certain amount of inelasticity in the supply of labour. The supply is limited of labour known to the farmer and accustomed to work in a team, and new hands have, of course, to be trained. The existing labour force is likely to have been used up to the hilt, at least at busy times of the year. When the cost of variable factors of production like labour is small in relation to the cost of fixed factors, like equipment, the variable factors tend to be used up to the limits set by the optimum capacity of the fixed factors. Thus there is not normally an unexploited residuum of productive opportunities which labour could have been profitably turned to, as might have been more the case had labour costs been the limiting factor. The same relations of capital and labour cost will have tended to check the formation of a pool of spare agricultural labour, at least of skilled agricultural labour.

At any time when farmers have an inducement to expand, the cost of most incidental aids to production will be rising, for most of the resources used in agriculture are specialised to that use. The upper reaches of the price of fertilisers, seed and feedstuffs, and of seasonal and casual labour, are primarily determined by the farmer's demand. If the prices of these items of outlay are a function of farm prosperity, they also after a while limit it, and thus limit expansion.

A good many of the incidentals are themselves agricultural produce—seed, hay, maize, lean cattle, etc.—and in respect of these the argument given above does not apply to the agricultural industry as a whole. The deterrent effect of rising costs in the latter stages of the industry appears as an encouragement in the earlier, where these costs are selling prices. Labour and fertiliser are exceptions, of course, and so are some artificial feedstuffs. The price of land is particularly important in this connection. At a time when prices are so attractive as to encourage extended cultivation, rents are likely to be rising. Rents and capital values appear to vary with net farm incomes with about a year's lag, but the lag is probably a phenomenon of observational error. Although rents are but a fraction of total costs (not often more than 10 per cent.), and though they are the result of profits rather than a deduction from them, there is nevertheless some deterrent in rising rents. In countries of owner tenure the rise of capital land values is often an even greater deterrent, especially to new farmers. The precise effect of rising rents at any time will depend on the number of new rent contracts that are being made, and thus on the rate of turnover of farms. The turnover is usually the more rapid the more that prices rise (or fall).

Some of these arguments that production is not greatly expansible, compared to manufacturing industry at least, apply also to contraction, but there are also a number of special difficulties in curtailing production which have no counterpart in expansion.

Obstacles to Rapid Contraction.—Most important perhaps is the tendency of a number of branches of production to display a negative elasticity of supply, especially among poorer and small-scale producers. When prices rise these producers may not slack off very much, since the upward elasticity of their effort demand for income is usually quite high ; but the elasticity of effort demand for income becomes very low when prices fall. Producers respond by increasing their hours of work and the vigour of it. The object is to equalise aggregate receipts as far as possible, and it is achieved the most easily when the producer's own labour, and that of his family, is the largest item in the immediate cost of production, and where money items in the total cost are small. Where no accounts are kept it is not un-common for farmers to increase their activity despite a higher burden of money outlay, and in that way achieve a loss.

Negative elasticity of supply, or a tendency toward it especially when prices are low, is common among peasants, smallholders, and native collectors, as of rubber. The money prime cost incurred by producers in these classes is negligible. By peasants and smallholders hired labour is not generally used : the use of fertiliser is rudimentary and often abandoned when selling prices no longer permit recovery of this cost [1] ; one's own seed will suffice for four or five years without badly damaging the quality of the crop ; bought feedstuffs are not of importance, except for poultry ; and no money prime cost items of any size are left. The limiting factors in production are physical diminishing returns coupled with the disutility of labour.

These considerations suggest that the elasticity of supply among peasants and the like is at least extremely low.

[1] Eventually this practice diminishes the crop, but it is only artificial nitrates that are exhausted in one annual crop, and the others have a decided hang-over.

Family farms differ from peasant holdings in these respects only in degree. But the importance of negative, zero or very low elasticity in production destined for markets does not necessarily follow from the frequency of these conditions of supply in production as a whole. Quite apart from the mere subsistence cultivation of most of China and similar inaccessible regions, a substantial part of production by peasants is for direct consumption. It is hard to decide how far this sort of production enters into the determination of prices. On the whole one would not lay stress in a world study on inelastic subsistence production, except where, as in Europe now, the protection of the peasantry forms ground for prohibitive tariffs that limit the world market. Normally, however, the peculiar conditions of subsistence production are comparatively unimportant, and by no means the whole of peasant production is of this character. Perhaps as much as one-third, in most of the European countries, is habitually marketed. Then if peasants may be defined as persons occupying not more than 20 acres, we may guess that about 40 per cent. of the world cereal crops is peasant-produced, of which one-third enters the market and contributes to the establishment of a general inelasticity of supply. The materials for forming some sort of estimate of peasant production—subject, of course, to wide possibilities of error—will be found in the regional statistical reports made to the International Institute of Agriculture.[1]

These particular ingredients of inelastic supply just considered are in their pure form the peculiar properties of peasant production, production from smallholdings, and production by small family farmers. Yet analogous conditions are found through the whole field of agriculture. The subdivision of the industry among hosts of individual producers, their remoteness from centres of information, and the relatively undifferentiated nature of the units of any one staple crop, all tend to perfect the market. Each producer is tempted to regard the price at any time as constant despite the addition of his own output.

[1] Rome : Annual Reports.

Next, the comparative smallness of labour and other prime costs gives the farmer a considerable ability to continue production without being embarrassed for ready money—more than farmers usually are—however low prices may be within reason. As we shall see, the typical short period costs of agriculture (0–1½ years) amount only to 30–35 per cent. of total costs including normal profit ; and the middle period costs (1½–10 years in respect of most items) are 50 per cent., of which only one-half are urgent (1½–3 years).[1] Thus there is a margin of postponable costs corresponding to a price fall of 40 per cent., or more if the costs themselves are declining. The principal postponable costs are profit, interest on own capital, depreciation, repairs, part of fertiliser bill, rent, part of own living expenses, interest on hired capital, part of own wages, and something on bought seed. It is not argued that these outgoings are indefinitely postponable, or that they all are postponed simultaneously at any time. More often, it is the postponement which the farmer makes of his own due remuneration for labour or capital that permits him to continue payments to bondholders and landlords. The same kind of relief is also available to manufacturing industry, but in farming the possibilities are larger. Capital costs are greater in agriculture generally than in manufacture generally. In agriculture, also, it is fairly easy to supplement the non-remuneration of the owner's own outlay of capital and labour by running up long debts without damaging the undertaking's credit. Farmers usually have the privilege of paying when they can.

At times of depression, hay, seed and fertiliser merchants commonly expect to find themselves enlarging their credits to farmers (unless perhaps the operations of some Agricultural Credit Bank are diminishing their security), and they rely for repayment on a subsequent recovery. These variations in temporary credit have the effect of stabilising output.

Adjustments to Sustained Price Movements.—Thus far we

---

[1] Appendix II examines farm costs in some detail, and offers evidence for the above conclusions.

have examined the principal ingredients of inelasticity over fairly short periods in response to small or moderate changes in price.   Now, when we turn to the limitations to large-scale expansion when prices are rising steeply, we meet not only the preliminary limits already noticed, but once more, in a different sense, the difficulty of capital costs.   The requirement of a heavy outlay on machinery, implements, breaking in new land, outhouses, drainage systems, and the provision of about fourteen months' working capital for the new output, usually comes up against a scarcity of liquid capital among the farming community, which is not distinguished for accumulations of wealth.   It is necessary as a rule to contract a mortgage.   Periods of agricultural prosperity and expansion are associated with a net increase in the volume of credit in the hands of farmers, and the growth of mortgaging to finance expansion is the principal reason.   But at the same time it is in periods of prosperity that old debts are expected to be repaid, and temporary credit contracted.   Generally speaking, high prices require to have lasted some time before farmers come into a position to borrow for the purpose of expanding.   Perhaps it should be mentioned that the supply of agricultural land to the industry as a whole is not very elastic, and most of the expansion must fall within the limitations of intensive usage.

Of rather more interest at the present time is the difficulty that agriculture meets in revising its commitments downward.   Even when the prices of farm produce have fallen catastrophically for profits, it is still possible to take up most of the shortfall out of postponing the discharge of capital costs.   This is the principal constituent of inelasticity even at the height of a general slump.   But in some agricultural industries prices are now so low that the recovery of even prime costs is threatened.   Except where producers have been able to change over to some less afflicted crop, they are now subject to even more ultimate inelasticities of supply.   We shall notice first that set of conditions of supply which prevents or seriously hinders curtailment of output ; and second, the obstacles to ceasing production altogether.

In the first place, it often happens that the burden of rent and interest leads the farmer to continue producing for the sake of procuring ready money, even if in order to produce he must borrow from his suppliers, or run up debts on personal account, or seriously let the land down. This scramble for ready money is particularly rough in countries where the laws of tenure do not put great difficulties in the way of obtaining compulsory sequestration and dispossession. It does not follow, of course, though the scale of production is maintained for the purpose of paying rent and interest out of the proceeds, that a surplus over prime outgoings actually is secured. If all farmers behave in the same way, they merely depress prices further. The policy tends to be its own undoing, and rents and interest in arrear are a regular feature of agricultural slumps. Whatever the struggle to be punctual, these capital payments to creditors must in greater or less measure be abandoned or postponed. Eventually, therefore, the price may fall to the level of those prime costs which are inescapably incurred on each unit produced. In some instances the price may fall even lower than this, if the producer is able to borrow or defer payment of prime cost. He may do so in the expectation that the price will rise during the growing period of the crop, or because it costs too much to cease production and resume later, meanwhile keeping up the condition of the land and plant.

A good farmer hates to let his land or stock deteriorate. If he retains the labour necessary to maintain the hedges or the sheep he may as well use it for harvesting or shearing. Land left fallow and neglected for a year may require three years' weeding before it really becomes fit for further arable use. Customary or specially apt labour once dismissed may not be easily re-engaged. On all these counts it seems worth while to continue producing.

No producer in any industry afflicted by a slump is very eager to abandon his established capital, at the prices likely to rule in such circumstances for land and plant; but in the case of agriculture the reluctance to dispose of a farm is aggravated by the fact that the farm is the home.

If the crops do not fetch the price expected, part will be consumed on the farm in replacement of commodities formerly bought from outside. On the sort of family farm where home consumption absorbs a large part of the produce, the use of family labour reduces prime cost almost to the mere cost of fertiliser and seed.

If matters are desperate the question of the farmer's staying power arises. Many have personal reserves or less impecunious relatives. In plantation industries most firms will have placed some sums to reserve. In most cases the banks will be asked to come to the rescue, and even if credit is being rationed it will at least be necessary to support such debtors as are already in arrear. Among limited companies operating in agriculture it is not uncommon to find a deflation of capital, even of debentures, and in extremer cases the concern may be sold for a song to someone who expects to cover prime cost and has only a small capital outlay to remunerate. In all cases the question arises, where is the distressed producer to go, and what else can he do ? If he can cover his barest direct outlay, then to continue producing is the only feasible course. Even if the price at the moment does not justify continuing, there is always the possibility that before harvest-time it may. In some instances it may be a condition of carrying on that the farmer's creditors lend him the wherewithal for his prime outlay. If the prime loss on cultivation is more than the amount of rent and interest, then it would seem to pay these creditors to re-lend the current debt rather than lend for production. But the interest of creditors collectively is not the interest of each individually, and some absurd cases have arisen of farmers sandwiched among rival creditors speculating on the prospects of the market on behalf of them all.

The views and behaviour of the farmers themselves are not irrelevant in this connection. Their opinions and motives, as is well known, cannot be deduced from conversations, and still less from proceedings at farmers' meetings. Apparently a career of battle with nature sours the manner of one's communications, and the public is always presented with a picture of agricultural ruin and decay. Evidently not completely disillusioned, the farmer stands as perpetual supplicant for tariffs, bounties and almost free credit. So far as these appeals are not a form of speculative outlay they seem to indicate an absence of self-reliance, except in the actual conduct of farming operations. Pending assistance the farmer, in the rôle of dependant of the State, continues woodenly with his routine activity.

It is true that co-operative efforts at self-help, to say nothing of State or joint schemes for protection, credit or marketing reform, are not infrequent oases in this wilderness of plaintive defeatism. More generally, the farmer's reaction to the trade cycle is to accept a rising level of prices as the merely just, natural and inevitable condition for the continuance of his professional existence. Very few people in any walk of life do adjust their commitments to the expectation of trade relapse, for the principal good reason that to predict the timing of trade movements is too intricate a task for even most professional economists. Nevertheless, it is usual for commercial and manufacturing undertakings to make provision for a rainy day to come some time. Nor is public relief expected except as another marking up of the tariff. The farmer, on the other hand, is usually caught unprepared and for many dangerous months unaware.

It is true that in no ordered society would the working farmer be expected to concern himself with the vagaries of the market. He has very frequently the valid excuse of isolation and the absence of useful crop and market forecasts. Whatever the explanation, when the slump comes the farmer is found up to the neck in debts and other engagements. Though adversity may breed schemes of rural reform, of co-operative marketing and the like, these eventuate later and cannot be rapidly improvised. The individual farmer's only recourse is to turn back to the only stable phenomenon in sight, his acres themselves. Burying himself in the activities and problems of his calling—showing what the land can do—he concentrates on maintaining, if not improving upon, his normal output, whatever value the world may attach to it. So alone can a man keep his self-respect.

If the price of his product has already fallen to a half or a third of the remunerative price, he may as well be indifferent to it, so long as he can finance production for the time being.   He draws on whatever reserves he may have or pledges his remaining assets, of which, in the eyes of many country storekeepers, his personal integrity is not the least. It is convenient in some connections to present the picture of farmers selling for a fall or being driven to sell by banks and other creditors.   Something may be said for this view when applied to estates, plantations, farming companies, marketing organisations, crop pools, and so on—to any organisation whose future credit depends on its present solvency, or which is accustomed to act on calculations. But the family farmer is not well represented either as a speculator or as the tractable tool of his creditors, unless they have—what is rare in distressed agricultural countries— an easy remedy in evicting him.   Thus we are left with a man who for the time is beyond economic behaviour, and to that extent agriculture ceases to obey economic law.

Quantitative Studies.—Now we pass from descriptive generalisations, necessarily based on limited personal experience, to statistical indications of the degree of elasticity of supply.   First of all we are concerned with the elasticity appropriate to small or moderate changes in price.   This is most easily measured by aggregating a large number of observations, so that the larger movements cancel with the negligible.   We shall consider five crops over periods of about twenty years, and find the coefficients of correlation between the prices ruling in the one year with the recorded production for the successive year and the year after that. If supply had zero elasticity, there would tend to be a complete absence of correlation ; and though when the measure of correlation is significantly larger than zero no certain indication of the elasticity is therein given, it is still probable that low correlations will be associated with low elasticities.   In ordinary time series the factor making for low correlations is predominantly the alternation of direct and inverse relations between deviations in the two series

—in this case representing an apparently uncertain elasticity of which the derived empirical value is likely to be low.[1] The coefficients are as follow :

	Oats United States (1890–1910).	Potatoes United States (1890–1912).	Maize United States (1890–1910).	Hay United States (1890–1913).	Wheat World (1890–1912).
1 year lag	·676	·578	·360	·081	·351
2 year lag	·069	·199	·001	·277	·305
Mean	·480	·384	·254	·204	·329

It is best to consider the results at one and two years' lag together, as either result separately may have been unduly influenced by the weather, particularly the result for one year's lag. After a large crop of one year, caused by good weather and which has depressed the price, next year's crop is likely to be less, due to a relapse in the weather or temporary exhaustion of the soil, but appearing as the result of the preceding year's low prices. The result for oats is slightly anomalous, but comparing maize and hay with wheat, we find, as will have been expected, that the supply of producers' goods, grown by the producer for his own use, is less elastic than that of a cash consumption crop. Taking the five crops together we may say that the supply is not intractably inelastic.[2]

For purposes of comparison we may notice that the correlation between pig iron production and prices in the United States during 1870–1912 was ·541.[3]

Now having come to the subject of elasticity of supply in the direction of expansion, when the movement in prices is rapid, we may summarise the war-time experience of the

[1] Since I am in doubt whether my series are strictly continuous I have removed trend by converting the data into link relatives, then dividing each relative by the mean of the relatives. The source for oats, hay, potatoes and maize is the United States Bureau of Agriculture, whose tabulations are summarised by Professor Moore, *Economic Cycles*, and by Professor Mills, *Behaviour of Prices*. The prices are December farm prices. The source for wheat is Stanford University, *Wheat Studies*, Vol. VIII, No. 1. The prices are of Chicago May futures. The " mean " of each two coefficients presented in the table is the square root of the mean square.

[2] Over those ranges of price change represented by standard deviations (from 100) respectively for the five crops of 20·7, 56·0, 22·9, 15·1, and 24·9.

[3] Trend removed as with the crops, i.e. correlation of first differences divided by their mean. It was not necessary that any of these coefficients be " significant " in the sense of warranting predictions.

United States.   When in 1920 the price level of field crops in the United States had reached 239 (1911–13 = 100), and of livestock 168, the output of raw produce of all kinds had reached only 118.[1]   To achieve this 18 per cent. increase in production, an increase of 9 per cent. in acreage proved necessary.   But it makes no immediate difference whether this inflexibility of agricultural supply (compared with the 29 per cent. increase in raw materials and 34 per cent. in manufactures) was due to land shortage, a rising cost level, or physical diminishing returns.

The aggregate costs of production, adjusted for the increase in output, rose 200 per cent., and outstripped the rise in prices.   Much of this inflation of aggregate outgoings represented new capital expenditure, and it is interesting to notice that the aggregate expenditure on plant, implements, automobiles and horses increased more than four-fold.   Even deducting the perhaps suspicious item of automobiles, there was an increase of 150 per cent.   We may conclude therefore that the limiting factor in the American war-time expansion was capital outlay.   This suggests two conclusions.   At the outbreak of the war the existing plant was being used to capacity.   The need to expand it is an indication that, given the existing equipment, diminishing returns on land worked by the old methods set in quickly. And despite the heavier capitalisation the yield per acre increased only 8 per cent.   (It is to be noticed, however, that in respect of livestock products land is only a remotely limiting factor.)   The limitations imposed by whatever diminishing returns were operative were reinforced by rising unit costs of auxiliary circulating capital.

The element of time seems to be indirectly responsible for a greater elasticity of supply than if new production were practically instantaneous.   The effects of the expansion are not visible until the production period is over.   During this period a large amount of new capacity is laid down by all and sundry, and if the period is long, there will be no

---

[1] Price statistics from U.S. Statistical Abstract, 1923, and production statistics from publications 2 (ii) and 14 of the National Bureau of Economic Research.

output emerging to drive down prices and call a halt to expansion. This is of some importance in the matter of expansion by means of new plant, new breeding programmes, and the reclamation or subjugation of new land—all features of the war period in the United States. The United States, as a matter of fact, was a leading contributor to the agricultural over-supply which soon followed the war. Everyone had overshot the mark. The time element also has direct application in that even in normal times it takes two years to increase most forms of agricultural output. But except in periods of rapidly rising prices the time factor also delays expansion by increasing risk.

So far there have been three leading periods of drastically falling agricultural prices which have strained and possibly exhausted the industry's capacity to readjust downwards— first 1890–6, then 1920–2, and finally 1929–32. The relapses in prices experienced were respectively in the neighbourhood of 30 per cent., 40 per cent., and 50 per cent. In the 1890–6 period the years of subnormal output in the United States were 1890 and 1892–5—1891 being a year of abnormally good weather. Even when this year be omitted, the average recession in output was only 8 per cent., or 11 per cent. if 1895 be further omitted. The major part of this decline was produced by a contraction of yield per acre.

During the 1920–2 slump the utmost contraction of output in the United States reached only 6 per cent. of the 1919 figure, of which 2 per cent. was due to a decline in acreage and 4 per cent. to a decline in yield. The depression did not last long enough to cause a permanent change in expectations.

The effect of the present agricultural collapse upon quantities produced is shown in Table 2, compiled for a number of representative field crops.[1]

Purely American figures carry us up to a later date,[2]

---

[1] Acreage and yield data from Annual Reports of the International Institute of Agriculture. Price data likewise, except where indicated.

[2] *Yearbook of Agriculture*, 1932. We might notice here that cotton, tobacco, and some maize and sugar-beet are produced on semi-peasant or small tenant holdings, and normally tend to display negative elasticity of supply for moderate changes in price.

TABLE 2.—WORLD PRODUCTION IN 1927–30 OF SEVEN CROPS
(1927–9 = 100)

	Price.	Acreage.	Yield.
		(World Production ex. U.S.S.R.)	
Wheat [1] :			
1927	109	99	99
1928	104	102	106
1929	87	99	95
1930	97	104	102
Rye :			
1927	120	100	93
1928	106	100	104
1929	72	100	105
1930	57	105	101
Maize :			
1927	86	98	102
1928	100	101	97
1929	115	101	100
1930	86	105	86
Rice :			
1927	103	98	100
1928	98	102	101
1929	99	100	100
1930	91	102	102
Potatoes (Berlin price) :			
1927	120	99	97
1928	91	101	96
1929	90	101	106
1930	96	97	107
Sugar beet (British price) :			
1927	104	101	99
1928	98	100	100
1929	99	100	100
1930	93	105	117
Cotton :			
1927	106	92	100
1928	103	104	100
1929	92	104	100
1930	50	103	94

and are given in Table 3. The same method of presentation is used, with the average of 1927–9 taken as 100.

Although for the world there are numerous indications

[1] Including Russia in the case of wheat.

TABLE 3.—AMERICAN PRODUCTION IN 1927–31 OF EIGHT CROPS

	Price.	Acreage.	Yield.
Wheat :			
1927	108	98	103
1928	93	97	108
1929	100	105	90
1930	58	102	97
1931	42	93	112
Rye :			
1927	100	105	120
1928	100	100	90
1929	101	95	89
1930	45	110	100
1931	46	98	81
Maize :			
1927	96	100	103
1928	100	102	103
1929	103	99	95
1930	87	103	75
1931	49	107	89
Oats :			
1927	104	102	90
1928	95	101	111
1929	100	96	100
1930	74	100	109
1931	54	100	95
Barley :			
1927	115	77	106
1928	93	108	108
1929	91	114	86
1930	66	107	100
1931	59	97	72
Cotton :			
1927	109	92	100
1928	100	104	100
1929	91	104	100
1930	63	103	96
1931	32	93	129
Sugar beet :			
1927	106	105	100
1928	97	94	102
1929	97	101	98
1930	97	103	96
1931	81	105	102
Tobacco :			
1927	106	87	101
1928	101	104	97
1929	93	109	103
1930	65	115	105
1931	49	111	105

of what has happened to production, acreage and yield of the various crops since 1930, no complete statistics that can be arranged comparatively are yet available. Since 1930 the prices of each of the crops considered has continued to fall, and at last, in 1932, contractions of acreage became visible, after three years' hesitation. The largest contractions have appeared among the cash export crops, particularly where alternative crops could be cultivated in the same region. For instance, the acreage sown to jute in Bengal in 1932 was hardly more than half the acreage of 1929 ; and the cotton acreage of the United States fell 19 per cent. between 1930 and 1932. The cereal sowings of the United States have also been contracted, and there is evidence of a switchover to potatoes. And so the story could be continued—in 1931 and 1932 declines of roughly 10 per cent. have been repeated through the world in nearly all commodities—in some cases more than 10 per cent., but generally less than 20. It is too early yet to prophesy how far the movement will continue. The most significant part of the story is not the attempts made by producers to restrict acreage and outlay, but the delays that have occurred in so doing. The fall in prices in most of the staple crops began in 1927 or 1928,[1] but by 1930 hardly any adjustment had taken place. Not until the slide in prices, which was gathering momentum each month, became a landslide, were steps taken to adjust the scale of production.

Some of the contraction is the work of separate individuals who have left their marginal acres fallow or put them to grass, but a greater part seems to have taken the form of economies on outlay. Thus between 1929 and 1932 the world's consumption of Chile nitrate is reported to have fallen by two-thirds, and only a small part of this collapse is due to the substitution of other fertilisers. In several countries hay and straw are becoming unsaleable.

In some agricultural industries it appeared early in the slump that the possibilities of contraction under *laissez-faire* were inadequate, and where feasible, organised restriction

---

[1] Due in part to falling costs, for which I can make no specific allowance.

schemes have been introduced, notably for sugar and tea. Similar restriction schemes may yet turn out indispensable for coping with inelasticity in other crops, like cotton or even wool. But administrative and financial difficulties, to say nothing of political obstacles, limit the circumstances in which these schemes can be successfully introduced. It will probably be found impossible whatever becomes the price of the cereals to apply restriction to these industries. Production is scattered about the world and largely in the hands of family farmers.[1] Surplus stocks will therefore continue to accumulate, and the agricultural crisis will not only be intensified but protracted.

[1] Yet there have been sporadic attempts to limit production or sale. A scheme for restricting the world production of wheat is being put together, and at the time of writing the farm strike of the American Middle-West is an interesting reality. All the same, isolated attempts at restriction seem doomed to failure.

CHAPTER III
ASPECTS OF THE DEMAND FOR AGRICULTURAL PRODUCE

THIS chapter collects together a number of points bearing on demand,·which are either of interest in themselves, or which form the raw material of later conclusions.

The Importance of Demand.—In this chapter variations in money demand are treated as important proximate determinants of trade fluctuation. This may seem somewhat novel. It is more common to assign demand to a subsidiary or passive rôle. In one group of trade cycle theories the slump is supposed to be proximately procured by monetary contraction which starves industry. Then via unemployment, bad debts, and the rest, demand is accommodated to a new level of production.

This small emphasis on demand apparently draws support from the fact that consumption in physical volumes, as contrasted with production, is fairly constant.[1] This is especially true of that consumption which gets into the statistics. Commodities can be stored for longer than

---

[1] Mr. Keynes reports an estimate of Dr. King that the American amplitude of variation in consumption is only 7 per cent. compared with 13 per cent. in output. These are average amplitudes over a series of cycles —some of them very minor movements. These estimates seem very plausible, but there are a few difficulties—which Dr. King has probably overcome—in making them. First of all, most of the available consumption statistics pertain to cheap standardised markets which improve their position in the slump relative to expensive markets. Secondly, to obtain an index of physical quantities it is necessary to divide an index of aggregate turnover by an index of retail prices. Almost any such index overweights inelastically supplied commodities, the price of which is exceptionally variable through boom and slump, simply because particulars are readily available. In Great Britain, both food and clothing are somewhat overweighted in the Cost of Living index, and the remarkable declines in price which have occurred in many lines of each, have led to a general admission that the index has varied more than the true cost of living. The effect of using a sensitive index as divisor is to create an impression of stagnation in physical turnover.

staple wants can be postponed, and hence production can cease while stocks are being liquidated. If this is the principal reason why consumption varies less than production, it alone does not show that changes in demand are a mere sluggish echo of changes in supply. Both production and consumption are variable, and production varies more freely. But it does not follow that production is the original variant. Moreover, in calculating the variation in physical output the more stable distributive services are usually underweighted. There is little reason for separating the physically creative side of production from the distributive.

If the importance of total demand may be thus rehabilitated, it follows that the importance of displacements among different types of demand is established. This reinstatement can be supported by a few further observations. First of all, the value of money demand is a better indicator of what is happening to consumption than physical volumes.

There are of course many contexts in which physical volumes are relevant. But if we may suppose that the production of consumable goods is controlled mainly by demand and not by difficulties placed in the way of production, the relevant aspect of demand becomes its money value. For instance, a 20 per cent. fall in money demand makes 20 per cent. on turnover the magnitude of the problem with which producers are confronted. They must make a joint adjustment of output and selling price requisite to this magnitude. To the extent to which output is uncontrollable, physical volumes both of production and consumption will appear unaltered. Since output does resist abridgment in some degree, the decline in physical volumes in the given case may be no more than 13 per cent. for production and 7 per cent. for consumption, despite a 20 per cent. fall in demand.

It would first seem as if displacements in demand, in their bearing on industry, were confined to this modest compass, 7 per cent. But it is now evident, since the ratio between the decline in prices and volumes will be different in each industry, as the elasticity of supply is different, that we must refer to the original 20 per cent. decline in demand to perceive the true compass of displacement.   Thus the importance of displacements may be more than double of what physical volumes indicate.   If the demand for agricultural produce is one of the more variable sections of demand, the standard of comparison is far from being virtual constancy.

Displacements among Incomes.—If in this chapter we retain the assumption stated in Chapter I, that agriculture is purely submissive to fluctuations imposed upon it from without, the elasticity of demand is of no immediate importance. The fluctuation in agricultural prices is a function of changes in demand in conjunction with the elasticity of supply. It would be erroneous to suppose that inelasticity of demand for agricultural products had directly contributed to the present debacle in agricultural prices.

Nevertheless, when demand is relapsing, it suffers displacement both by classes of commodities and by classes of consumers.   Hence relative elasticities—or their analogues, flexibilities of demand—among the commodities and consumers, come into play.   In the first place, for instance, when demand is falling it falls very little for an inflexibly demanded commodity like bread.   Secondly, the fall in demand will be unequal among different sections of the market characterised by differences of income.   If the price of the commodity fall equivalently to the average fall in demand it may have fallen too little for the more impoverished sections of the community and too much for the less impoverished.   Whether this inequality conduces to a larger or smaller consumption, compared with a homogeneous decline in demand, depends on whether the more or less impoverished section has the greater elasticity of demand. If the richer section has suffered least, and if elasticity is the smaller in this section, the displacements of incomes diminish demand on balance.   This is especially likely to be the case of agricultural foodstuffs, for which the demand of the rich is almost certainly very inelastic.

That the rich have suffered less in Great Britain during the current slump does not emerge from the available statistical evidences carried only up to 1931.   But since the middle of 1931 wage cuts have been extensive, and unemployment has further grown, so that later figures may well show that wages have suffered more than the national income a a whole, just as they appear to have done in other countries.[1]

We have now to notice that displacements among incomes are mitigated by unemployment relief. In Great Britain until September, 1931, unemployment generally wiped out 40–50 per cent. of a wage-earner's income. In the United States the proportion will be larger, but not so in France, Germany, Belgium or East Europe. In low-wage countries it is not feasible for incomes to fall by much more than 50 per cent. without producing widespread starvation.[2] In Germany, for instance the real " dole " of a man with wife and two children in 1932 even after the emergency decree of 27th June, 1932, was still worth as much as 40 per cent. of his wage when employed in 1929. If we take the support given to working-class incomes by unemployment relief in all its forms to average 40–50 per cent. of normal income, this relief is of great importance both in keeping up demand and diminishing the displacements.

Most of the commodities we deal with find their largest markets among the working class. They are widely consumed in most parts of the world, or are " universally " consumed in some large and important country. A considerable consumption is reached by all whose incomes will satisfy the standards of urban Western Europe. When in receipt of their normal incomes such families are buyers of wheat, sugar, potatoes, tea or coffee, cocoa, meat, soap, blankets, leather footwear, and occasional fine fabrics. It is improbable that any of the staple commodities, other than rubber, satisfies any want less urgent, or any need less

[1] I have not worked over the American figures, but I am authoritatively told that the computations for 1932 will disclose very clearly that wages varied more than any other class of income except farmers' earnings.

[2] The common supposition that real wages in Great Britain increased fourfold during the nineteenth century seems to me fantastic. It makes the wages of 1800 impossibly low and conveys the suggestion that current rates of unemployment relief could be halved. In the first place, the wholesale index has been used to correct nominal wages ; secondly, the calculations are usually made from the peak of paper prices in 1815 to the trough of 1896 ; and thirdly, I doubt if enough allowance has been made for privileges and wage supplements since commuted for cash.

simple, than for common comforts. The nearest we encroach on luxury is in respect of raw materials entering into the production of confectionery or of more or less fashionable articles of wear. Hence the repercussions on the demand for staple agricultural produce both of unemployment and the methods chosen for relieving it will be quite pronounced.

If unemployment relief is accomplished by borrowings, probably the whole of it is an inroad upon savings (i.e. it represents negative saving), and in this case net purchasing power is increased. The unemployed are fed *en route*, secondary employment is generated, and finally the whole mass of the extra purchasing power fetches up once more as savings. The consumption of staple commodities is enlarged both in respect of the direct relief of unemployment and of the secondary employment. When taxation provides the finance, savings are to some extent invaded, but purchasing power is diverted rather than increased, and secondary employment cannot be large. Where the relief of unemployment and distress depends on charity, the secondary effects are likewise small, so that if the consumption of staple agricultural produce is increased, it is at the expense of other produce. There occurs not only a redistribution of incomes but a redistribution of wants. Those income displacements which diminished the total demand—by increasing the savings of the rich when prices fell sufficiently to represent the average loss of income of both rich and poor—are cut down by transfers of purchasing power to the unemployed, and such transfers have the effect of increasing the demand for staple goods at the expense of luxuries.

Displacements of Demand among Commodities.—We have considered the commodity displacements that arise out of income displacements, but even within any one class of income a growth of unemployment and a fall in money income injures some commodities more than others. This works out both through the relative flexibilities of demand and through the distribution of income losses among families and districts. Granted in the first place that money incomes have fallen 20 per cent., we find individual relapses of demand ranging maybe from nil for house room (rents being fixed) to perhaps 80 per cent. for butter and eggs. We can see roughly what these displacements will be if we can classify commodities according to the urgency of the wants they satisfy, and see how expenditure is distributed among them. Let us classify wants as follows : indispensables, conventional necessaries, comforts, social requirements, and personal luxuries—in a sequence ranging upwards from purely visceral sensation and culminating, if one continued so far, in saving, which is the means of one of Freud's most complex regressions. The gratification yielded by any one commodity will fall into several of these groups of sensation, and one can analyse it in that respect according to one's general knowledge. The distribution of expenditure in Great Britain we obtain from three sources, as follows :

(a) Bowley's Bare Physical Efficiency Standard ;
(b) Rowntree's Human Needs Standard ;
(c) Weighting of Ministry of Labour Cost of Living Index.

TABLE 4.—CONSUMER'S BUDGETS IN GREAT BRITAIN (i)

	(a).	(b).	Mean of (a) and (b).	(c).
Food	54	40	47	60
Rent	19	14	16·5	16
Clothing	11	17	14	12
Fuel	9	9	9	8
Insurance	3	2	2·5	—
Household sundries . .	4	5	4·5	}4
Personal sundries . .	—	13	6·5	
	100	100	100	100

The mean standard is probably better for our purpose than either of Bowley's or Rowntree's original standards, which are respectively too severe and too liberal, and is more inclusive than the Cost of Living standard. By considering individual food items according to their importance in the Cost of Living Index, we are able to divide food expenditure as a whole fairly confidently among want categories, and then to do the same for non-food items as best we can. The following table gives a picture of the distribution :

TABLE 5.—CONSUMER'S BUDGETS IN GREAT BRITAIN (ii)

	Food.	Rent.	Clothes.	Fuel.	Insur-ance.	House-hold.	Per-sonal.	Total.
Indispensable .	17·4	12·7	5·2	4·0	—	2·0	3·0	44·3
Conventional necessity .	14·7	—	1·1	1·0	—	·5	·5	17·8
Comforts . .	13·5	—	1·4	1·0	—	·5	·5	16·9
Social . . .	5·9	—	3·0	·9	—	·5	—	10·3
Personal . .	6·9	—	·9	—	—	—	1·0	8·8
Other . . .	—	—	—	—	1·9	—	—	1·9
	58·4	12·7	11·6	6·9	1·9	3·5	5·0	100

Now suppose 20 per cent. of the community's income is wiped out by the advent of general unemployment, and that expenditure is contracted according to the urgency of wants. Insurance payments and social and personal luxuries are cut out, leaving in necessaries (actual and assumed) and comforts. Corresponding to the 20 per cent. all round diminution in expenditure, there is a fall of 22 per cent. in foods, 34 per cent. in clothes, 13 per cent. in fuel, 14 per cent. in household sundries, and 20 per cent. on personal sundries.

Agricultural produce as a whole should show a rather more than 20 per cent. decline. Among individual items, on this method of analysis, will be found : bread 10 per cent., flour (for confectionery, etc.) 40 per cent., meat and fish 15 per cent., butter 60 per cent., milk 5 per cent., eggs 40 per cent., cheese 15 per cent., potatoes nil, sugar 10 per cent., and tea 30 per cent. The dispersion is roughly proportionate to the elasticity of demand, the most elastic-ally demanded commodities being contracted the most. Except for sugar, the figures above give a fair account of how relative prices have in fact behaved.

This scheme of displacement of demand among com-modities assumes that unemployment, wage cuts, or what-ever the cause of the fall in incomes is taken to have been, was suffered by everyone in the same measure. But income, employment and unemployment are by no means distributed evenly either among the whole community or any occupational categories of it, nor among families.   The disturbing factors are : (*a*) unequal incomes per head as between classes of persons both consuming staple commodities ; (*b*) unequal incidence of unemployment on the various income groups ; (*c*) unequal incidence of unemployment among industries ; (*d*) unequal incidence among families ; (*e*) unequal income/wants ratio among families ; and (*f*) the availability of unemployment relief.   We can only deal with (*a*) —inequalities between social groups—by assuming that the consumption of staples by non-wage-earners is, for our purpose, negligible.   The same assumption enables us to rule out (*b*), and ignore the bulk of rent, interest and profit.   For Great Britain comparison of the distribution of employment in 1928 with that of 1931, with reference to point (*c*), suggests that the prime incidence of a slump is upon constructional industries, including coal, shipbuilding, and public works contracting and building.   There has certainly developed an inequality between constructional and distributive industries.   The inequality of unemployment among families and of incomes in relation to needs—(*d*) and (*e*)—is primarily responsible at all times for the mass of luxury expenditure which the working class is able to afford. In the cyclical case it is difficult to suppose that the income/wants ratio is much disturbed, except by such factors as the concentration of unemployment in mining areas where large families still occur.   More important is the unequal incidence due to the geographical concentration of unemployment, following on the marked localisation of industry.

It would appear from a review of all these factors, as if most of their separate, and certainly their aggregate, effect was aggravatory in respect of staple produce.   The more sheer want that unemployment causes, through its uneven distribution or through inequalities of income, the more must expenditure be curtailed on the relatively more urgent categories of consumption in which staple products progressively bulk.   These inequalities also worsen the income/elasticity of demand ratio which we noticed above as an aggravatory factor, by concentrating poverty in the most elastic sections of the market. While unemployment relief, poor relief, pensions and the pooling of family incomes, relieve these tendencies, their general properties are still important.

When we turn from Great Britain to the world at large, the most important new features are the lessened extent of inequality, and in general, a lower standard of living. These are conflicting, for the displacements to which inequality gives rise occur only within the scope of the size of incomes ; and if the lower standard of living is more important than the diminished displacement, the invasion on staple produce made by world unemployment is greater than in the case of Great Britain. The smaller amount and lesser efficiency of unemployment relief, compared with Britain, operates in the same direction. In general we may say that the aggregate diminution of purchasing power directed to staple produce, in respect of a general fall in incomes of 20 per cent., is nearer 30 per cent. The major part of this is due to unemployment and wage cuts, since staple produce finds its greatest market among wage-earners : it is extended by inequalities of income and the unequal incidence of unemployment, by the presence of fixed prior charges like house rent and by the tendency of aggregate wages to be among the most variable constituents of national income ; but is mitigated again so far as staple produce is inflexibly demanded, and by unemployment and poor relief.

Savings on the Price of Agricultural Produce.—This section deals primarily with a consequence of over-supply, which by reducing prices provides an opportunity to consumers to save the difference ; but owing to the occurrence of income displacements it is also relevant to a recession of demand. We shall deal primarily with savings effected by consumers, though such circumstances as have diminished agricultural prices also give middle-men an opportunity to save. As we shall see, distributive monopolies are tightened, and whether the distributor is a monopolist or not, he is well advised to build up reserves when his buying prices are falling and cover a later reversal.   Any savings that occur, in the absence of parallel increases in investment, inflict equal losses on producers, which in turn generate a spiral of secondary losses.   It is arguable that savings made on agricultural produce in particular, since the fortunes of a number of countries and their ability of import and invest depend on agricultural prices, are exceptionally vicious. The fact that agricultural produce is the largest item of the world's expenditure makes any savings that do occur, unless they are negligible for each consumer, highly important in the aggregate.   Thus if the world spends one half of its income on agricultural produce, and the typical consumer normally saves 5 per cent. of his income, and if furthermore agricultural prices fall 40 per cent., half of which he saves, he then trebles his savings, and inflicts a primary loss on producers equal to 10 per cent. of world income.

In order that this saving should occur it is requisite that the demand for agricultural produce should be inelastic, and the demand for other produce comparatively inflexible.   We shall now attempt to show, in general terms, that the elasticity of demand for agricultural produce is below unity. We use the supposition that two thirds of expenditure on food and clothing can be assigned to the categories of indispensables and conventional necessities.   Now at any moment, incomes being fixed, the composite elasticity of demand for all commodities, including savings, in terms of commodity prices, is unity.   It cannot be supposed that savings are directly responsive to commodity prices, and the elasticity of demand for them, in terms of commodity prices, must be taken as zero.   This puts the elasticity of demand for commodities as a whole above unity.   Then deduct commodities for which the demand is limited by the human digestion, for which the demand is obviously in-elastic, and the elasticity of demand for the remainder is further raised.   But we are not concerned with the luxury categories—with very little more luxurious than common comforts—and deducting these, the elasticity of demand for comforts and ordinary conventional expenditure is back again in the region of unity.   Taking these commodities and food together, it is fair to presume inelasticity since the elasticity of all commodities is not much greater than unity. Even the elasticity of demand for twelve competitive lines of American crops, as zero correlations between output and farm incomes seem to show, is not above unity, despite the fact that most of these crops reached a wide or free market.[1]

If the price of an inelastically demanded commodity falls it provides an opportunity to save, and this opportunity is used according to the manner in which other commodities are demanded. Is there an unsatisfied margin of wants more urgent than the desire to save ? Since the impulse to thrift is inborn, the economies on agricultural produce are almost certainly divided between savings and other expenditure—not wholly devoted to expenditure. The original economies have the appearance of a windfall ; they fall first of all into the pockets of the housewife, who in most working-class communities preaches thrift ; if low agricultural prices contribute to general depression the prices of non-agricultural commodities are falling also, so that more of them can be consumed by all those still in work without encroaching on the windfalls on food ; the industrial horizons are dark at such times, and increased thrift seems especially desirable ; and if the fall in prices of agricultural produce has gone to its usual cyclical dimensions, the amount of the windfall, in relation to the standard of life, is more than enough to support all the enhancement of luxury expenditure that it seems prudent and respectable to indulge in. It would be foolish of course to write off the demand for non-agricultural produce as totally inflexible. But to draw off the whole windfall gain on agricultural stuff the demand must be infinitely flexible over the relevant range. It is unreasonable to expect to find this condition over a comparatively short period during which the standard of life is comparatively fixed. For all these reasons we should expect to find a substantial part of the windfalls on agricultural produce absorbed into savings deposits, the purchase of savings certificates, instalments on hire-purchase goods

[1] Appendix III considers in some detail the elasticity of demand for a number of agricultural products.

paid in advance, contracts for the deferred purchase of houses through Building Societies, the enlargement of insurance policies, and the discharge of old debts. If one accepts, as one must, the fact that a large volume of thrift co-exists with the existing scales of wages, heroic as it seems, it is only reasonable to judge that windfall gains are more than likely to be used as the means for thrift.

Let us now place these arguments on a statistical basis. The League of Nations Secretariat (*Statistical Bulletin*, 1930–1) publishes figures for small-scale savings in a large number of countries—figures for savings deposits and the like—and against these we can set the published indexes for the price of food. We are concerned with the leading consuming countries, those with a large commercial and industrial population. The details are presented in index form so arranged as to permit comparisons from country to country.[1] (See next page.)

In all of these eleven countries, except France and Italy, savings and food prices varied inversely. The statistics are so arranged as to make 79 pairs of cases susceptible to correlation. The coefficient is −·312. This result indicates that savings for which opportunity was presented by a fall in food prices more than offset the damage done to savings by unemployment and wage cuts in the latter part of the period. It is not necessary, in order to show that savings and food prices vary inversely, over such a period, 1924–31, to produce signs of a high negative correlation ; considering the dimensions of the fall in incomes that took place, it is strong evidence for the view that savings were supported by windfall gains on the cost of living, especially on food, that savings were remarkably steady though trade was declining.[2]

[1] I have corrected the new savings and the food prices for a changing value of money represented in the retail indexes, divided the series then by one-tenth of their respective standard deviations, and added the results to 100 in order to obtain the index shown below.

[2] I do not think it was necessary to weight the eleven countries taken by relative size or wealth, nor would such a procedure have been methodologically pure. The data and method were both too rough to warrant elaborations, but not too rough, I imagine, to convey the superior likelihood of inverse variations of savings and food prices over direct.

This inverse relationship probably fails to hold for all savings and the

TABLE 6.—SAVINGS AND FOOD PRICES, 1924–31

	1924.	1925.	1926.	1927.	1928.	1929.	1930.	1931.
Germany :								
Savings . . .	—	93	102	89	116	109	91	—
Food prices .	—	116	102	104	96	98	84	—
Belgium :								
Savings . . .	85	98	91	98	103	106	119	—
Food prices .	98	104	113	107	101	98	79	—
France :								
Savings . . .	84	93	91	109	110	102	111	—
Food prices .	83	96	110	105	96	114	96	—
Italy :								
Savings . .	113	99	85	87	100	101	110	105
Food prices. .	107	114	107	88	100	103	100	81
United Kingdom :								
Savings . . .	107	103	83	93	106	87	114	107
Food prices .	110	110	103	103	103	100	92	79
Sweden :								
Savings . . .	83	96	114	95	96	110	106	—
Food prices. .	112	115	102	96	99	93	83	—
Switzerland :								
Savings . . .	90	90	100	101	95	102	122	—
Food prices. .	118	107	101	101	97	91	85	—
Czecho-Slovakia :								
Savings . . .	92	87	94	105	108	96	118	—
Food prices. .	104	106	103	106	106	99	76	—
Canada :								
Savings . . .	114	100	112	107	102	71	97	97
Food prices. .	91	98	107	107	107	107	107	76
United States :								
Savings . . .	109	112	106	87	106	91	89	—
Food prices. .	78	98	109	98	98	114	105	—
India :								
Savings . . .	95	116	109	106	85	98	91	—
Food prices. .	79	91	106	106	106	106	106	—

Dr. Kuznets has worked out a similar problem in respect
of the trade movements of 1920–4, and his tables are set

general price level over a complete cycle, for the trade conditions
associated with the price level tend to determine savings, especially at the
peak of depression, when negative saving becomes common—and there
is probably a positive correlation for all savings with general prices. But
with agricultural prices and consumer savings, especially over the gestation period of a depression, for instance, 1926–30, an inverse relation is
to be expected. The two relations are compatible, not only through
being between different pairs of events, but also because agricultural
prices lead general prices. While agricultural prices are (say) falling,
consumer savings mount up ; afterwards, partly for this reason and partly
for others, a depression ensues, in which savings may fall off rapidly.

out in *Cyclical Fluctuations* (p. 136), going into monthly detail.   He compares saving deposits in the United States with a series composed of cumulative differences between wage disbursements and grocery sales, which is in effect a table of the ratio of income spent on groceries.   The conclusions he reaches for groceries should apply *a fortiori* to agricultural produce, which is demanded less flexibly than groceries *qua* groceries.

Savings appeared to oscillate within a range of 7 per cent., and the oscillations occurred simultaneously and were in the same direction as changes in the entries for cumulative differences.   Whenever a fall occurred in the amount of income spent on groceries a corresponding rise occurred in savings.

Dr. Kuznets' observations for the United States are supported by British figures for 1924–30.   Column (*a*) below gives an index of aggregate wages ; column (*b*) an index of food prices ; column (*c*) gives the differences between (*a*) and (*b*) ; and these should be compared with the entries in column (*d*), a table of differences (in millions of pounds) of each year's gross subscriptions to National Savings Certificates from the average for the period.   None of the entries is adjusted for trend.

TABLE 7.—SMALL SAVINGS IN GREAT BRITAIN, 1924–30

	(*a*).	(*b*).	(*c*).	(*d*).
1924	98	106	− 8	− 7
1925	96	107	− 11	− 4
1926	98	102	− 4	− 7
1927	104	99	5	− 2
1928	102	98	4	3
1929	104	97	7	3
1930	98	91	7	14
Average . . .	100	100	0	0

It is clear that in Great Britain savings moved in fairly close accord with the surplus of wage income available after buying food.   As already observed, this is of no great importance to the price of agricultural produce so far as poverty is the governing factor, as in a slump operated almost entirely from the side of demand. But hardly any slump has this character alone, and most are found in association with agricultural over-supply, one of the most disagreeable features of which is its promotion of savings.

CHAPTER IV

THE MARKETING OF STAPLE PRODUCE

Introductory.—One is aware in a general way that the marketing of staple produce is a vast roundabout business in which a considerable part of the world's population is engaged. But so far as I know, no attempt has been made to give a unified account of the cost of these operations. It is not infrequent for the value of a commodity to become doubled between the land and the wholesale market, and in many cases the predominating cost of production, seen from the angle of the final market, is distributive, not physically creative. The importance of these costs in realistic economics is perfectly clear ; yet only scraps of information are available, and then for particular commodities or particular stages of distribution. Very few firms in these trades know anything about the whole marketing history of the crop they handle, but merely of the immediately antecedent or subsequent stages. Where large firms undertake several stages of handling, secrecy sets in. Large firms often fear that their price lists will be copied or undercut by smaller opportunistic competitors.

To overcome these difficulties of secrecy and of the dispersion of sources of reference, the investigator requires to live in the commodity markets for several years. In this chapter the data submitted are not complete nor strictly accurate. The analysis of distributive cost is only a means to discovering the elasticity and other relevant conditions of the demand with which the original producer is confronted.

The general character of marketing is a steady and gradual convergence of the commodities upon the retail shops. This process is one of great labour, and often the services of some ten specialists are needed before delivery is brought to a triumphant conclusion.

The Disintegration of Function.—Let us observe who is concerned with cotton between Alabama and Blackburn. The farmer may sell to ginner, country merchant, factor or scalper. Next the commodity comes into the hands of an f.o.b. man, who gets rid of it quickly to an exporter (or importer's agent) who in turn deals with an importer at Liverpool.[1] Eventually, after a sale in which buying and selling brokers are employed, it fetches up with a spinner. In some cases one or more of these stages may be missed. Except for the brokers, all the functionaries named at some stage own the cotton. Others hardly less intimately concerned with it, who do not buy with the intention of owning, include futures brokers, futures jobbers, banks both in America and Britain, freight brokers, shipping lines, and insurance companies. All these live off the cotton. So too do those responsible for ginning, weighing, sampling, compressing, warehousing (three doses), loading and unloading, carriage, grading, recompressing, loading on ship, landing and delivery.

In the case of wool it is interesting to watch a journey from Queensland to Bradford, via country merchant, woolbroker, buying and selling agents in Australia, London importer, buying and selling agents in London, dealers and manufacturers. The processes involved are shearing, classing, temporary baling, dumping, re-baling, railway carriage, warehousing, cataloguing, auctioning, loading, freight, landing and wharfage, warehousing, mending, re-weighing, sampling, certifying, taring, piling, exhibiting, railage and delivery. Some of these could be further subdivided. But on the other hand a few consignments are handled more directly.

On the whole wool and cotton are efficiently handled by a comparatively small number of intermediaries. The standard for comparison is jute, where twelve middlemen and brokers may be interposed between the Indian peasant and the mill. Sugar has four intermediaries, coffee six, wheat seven. We do not include as intermediaries, banks, insurance houses, operators in futures, freight brokers, or persons engaged in physical operations on the commodity.

There has always been a controversy over the degree, if any, to which this specialisation of marketing function is overdone, particularly over the separation of those functions which the layman finds almost indistinguishable, e.g. buying and selling broking. Generally the conclusion is drawn that if all this segmentation and particularism were not necessary it would not have evolved. If this is true, " rationalisation " of marketing, by means of more direct selling, as many co-operative and integrated bodies undertake, is a redundancy. But if rationalisation has worked well, we must distrust the facile conclusion, to which *laisser-faire* premises inevitably lead, that the organisation of the moment is a working optimum. We must see specialisation as a mere alias for disintegration. The tendency to disintegrate is a familiar human weakness. Various activities are sloughed off on the pretext that it is more " convenient " to leave them to others. That indeed it may be when a growth in the trade permits the relinquishment of responsibilities without sacrifice of income. Very often this division of labour becomes accepted as a custom before competition can arise to challenge it. When the custom is well established a Leverhulme is needed to weed out the redundant functions and re-integrate the remainder.

On the whole it is improbable that a great many of the actual functions are redundant, other than certain occasions of buying and selling. The commodity must be moved, stored, processed and financed by someone. Nevertheless, specialisation, besides adding to the total of tolls for profits, salaries, wages, rents, taxes and bad debts, increases risks, and the margins required to cover them, by increasing the number of independent judgments liable to influence prices at various stages of distribution. Opportunities for rational price anticipation are diminished. The more the merchants, and the smaller the scale on which they operate, the more they must live from hand to mouth. The less competent are they to undertake a planned policy of holding stocks. We shall see that the erratic behaviour of stocks is an important source of uncertainty and disequilibrium, and that it adds to the general disorganisation in affording opportunities for questionable speculation.

Cyclical Movements in Distributive Costs.—The piling up of intermediate costs is particularly serious when they are charged on a flat rate per quantity of the commodity handled. As the price falls they become more burdensome. The less becomes the consumer's gain and incentive to buy in respect of any sacrifice the producer makes in the shape of diminished real income—for instance, in consequence of the almost inevitable depreciation of currencies in a slump. The same applies to the loss of real income suffered by a raw-material country which is obliged to deflate or subsidise its exports. For the larger the fixed costs standing between producer and consumer the greater is the proportional fall in the producer's income for any given fall in the final price necessary to carry off the total supply. On the other hand the producer gains when prices are rising. The extent to which this gain on rising prices compensates for the loss on falling, depends on the rate of decline in the marginal utility of income.

Most of the fixed charges are made for indispensable physical services. Nevertheless, a large number of financial and commercial services are also charged per bag, or per hundredweight, on a fixed margin. Country merchants frequently take their commissions per bag, and forwarders like to concern themselves with weights and volumes. Graders and inspectors often charge per lot, and so too some auction- eers. Specific duties on the commodity are another and notorious fixed chai ge. We have seen how these items pile up during a slump. These criticisms, however, do not apply to those items, like insurances and discounts, brokers' com- missions and *ad valorem* taxes, which vary proportionately with the price of the commodity. A further category of costs is intermediate between fixed and proportional—we may call them sliding costs. As they play an important part in the determination of raw produce prices, a few of the leading charges may be noticed separately.

Shipping freights.—The *Economist* index of freights fell

between 1929 and 1931 by 15 per cent. Some hard-hit staple commodities may have procured a greater relief than the average. The Rubber Growers' Association claims to have made successful pleas of poverty.

Bagging material.—There are no official quotations for the price of finished bags, but since the price of raw jute declined between 1929 and 1931 by 50 per cent., there follows some presumption that the price of bags and sacks also fell. The barrel and crate industries, as far as is known, are generally competitive, and packing charges have been somewhat abated.

Railway freights.—When railway companies were more competitive and less regulated than to-day, it was not uncommon for freights to fall, during mild slumps, in a degree commensurate to the diminished volume of trade. In the present slump, there may have been some local abatements of freight charges, but these are overshadowed by two contrary movements : (a) the permissions granted to North and South American railways to raise their charges in order to avoid bankruptcy, and (b) the efforts of State railways to balance official budgets in the same manner. Most State railways have raised their rates.

Dock and harbour charges.—The wages of dockers, lightermen, tugmasters, and so forth, appear to have suffered widespread reductions, but, generally speaking, dock charges are still much the same. The distances which separate harbours, and the element of statutory monopoly at many ports, have enabled charges to be maintained and the diminished costs of working be set against smaller volumes.

The rate of interest.—Interest as a cost is repeated over and over again in the distributive chain. It is especially important in the retail section, where the margin charged on the various commodities tends to reflect their velocity of turnover. Although the rate of interest on short term is not an even function of trade activity, it does undergo a cyclical movement, tending to a minimum toward the trough of a slump. In Great Britain this relief, on most bank loans, ceases at the 5 per cent. stop rate. In the producing countries, including the United States, the tendency for interest to fall during the slump is not very marked, either because rationing of credit is a more usual weapon of control, or at times because exchange problems accumulate when commodity prices are low. In India, for instance, the official rate rose 33 per cent. (from 6 to 8 per cent.) between 1929 and the second half of 1931, and did not fall again until devaluation had relieved the exchanges. Despite these considerations, there is probably a net gain on interest for distribution as a whole.

Wages and salaries.—There is no need to dwell on the wage reductions accomplished almost everywhere during a slump, and which affect distribution costs the whole way from producer to consumer.

These six items of sliding costs, under the headings of transportation, wages and interest, comprise more than half the distribution costs of most produce—perhaps three-quarters of some—and accordingly there is no need to consider in any detail such further charges as rents and wastage. Taking the big six as a whole, there is evidence for some positive correlation with commodity prices, but, clearly enough, the variations are by no means proportionate. During the slump, most of such savings as do occur, originate within the hands of individual distributors themselves. This raises the problem, already hinted at under the heading of dock charges, whether, and if so, to what extent, producers and consumers participate.

Distributive Monopolies.—In order to trace the distribution of this gain among producers, consumers and distributors, let us assume first the absence of monopoly among distributors. Then the distributors may be supposed to pass on the economy, which ends up among producers and consumers according to the elasticities of supply and demand. The smaller the elasticity of demand, the more does the final price fall as distributive economies emerge, in respect of any increase in the quantity taken. The greater is the benefit via lower prices to the consumer, compared with the producer's benefit in the shape of a larger market.

But the assumption of perfect competition is quite untenable. Quite apart from the existence of any formal monopoly among distributors, there exist chronic imperfections of the market due to transport costs, personal preferences, the use of branding, and so on. It is possible that any such monopolies might in the long run break down, but there is no reason why they should not survive through a slump. If a slump increases profit margins, presumably a boom depresses them, and they average out over a complete cycle to give no more than a normal profit. Similarly, competition in the retail trade not only takes time to develop, but it proceeds by aggregates of commodities, and not, generally speaking, by particular commodities. Falling buying prices may present an opportunity for an increase in the profit margins on a number of special lines—or for that matter, on goods sold to particular classes of less impoverished consumers. Again, retailers do not invariably pass on to the consumer odd fractions of currency denominations saved on the buying price, especially if they are smaller than the nearest convenient coin. It is common, also, in many distributive trades for what competition exists to use the channel of offering at the same price better qualities or superior incidental facilities. Competition in the tea and coffee trades usually takes this form, and it is not unknown in clothing shops. It is improbable that a better quality stimulates extra consumption to the same extent as a more attractive price. Both the form of such competition as does exist, and the insufficiency of competition in retail trade in general, have the effect of holding up distributive economies in the hands of the distributors themselves. The same applies to a fall in farm prices due to over-production, for this, too, is in a sense a distributor's economy. (Cf. Diagram I, below.)

It is not necessary to show, in support of this argument, that merchants and middlemen are enriched by a slump. The gain on margins is offset by a diminished quantity of trade, and some of the enhancement of margins will not have been absolute, but merely as a proportion of a diminished price. Whether on balance distributors have gained during the present slump is a matter for discovery by income statistics.

In all probability a slump provides conditions for the strengthening of monopoly. It is true that competition may become keener among merchants established in a trade, but slump times are unfavourable for the entry of new-comers, or for the laying down of bold competitive programmes. Again, as already noticed, the enlargement of merchants' margins is not accompanied by the emergence of enormous attractive profits, since the volume of trade is diminished. On the other hand, customers running accounts fall more and more into the power of dealers supplying them, as the slump cuts down their incomes and ability to pay off debts. Again, it is a feature of slumps that prices of raw commodities fall more than the money value of demand, especially since overproduction is a regular accompaniment. In such circumstances it is easier to exercise or institute monopoly without diminishing the volume of sales. The monopolist is in a position to absorb the gain on buying prices without hindrance except from the fear of under-cutting.

The increase in monopoly during a slump is evidently more prejudicial to producers than the mere existence of monopoly. By comparing the competitive and monopoly cases in the diagrams below it can be seen that the existence of monopoly is favourable to the maintenance of the volume of sales when demand is relapsing. This is some compensation for the greater fall in prices. It is even feasible that the producer might suffer less during a slump if his commodity has been customarily dealt with in an imperfect market. But if the slump increases the monopoly, it is almost certain that the producer loses : the market is curtailed, and unsold accumulations far back struggling for disposal depress the price. These considerations perhaps can play some part in explaining the gap that has arisen between wholesale and retail prices. Between 1928 and 1931 (up to the suspension of the gold standard) the *Economist* wholesale index fell 34 per cent., but the retail index (Ministry of Labour) only 12 per cent. It is hard to believe that fixed and semi-fixed distributional charges account for the whole of the dispersion of the price levels.

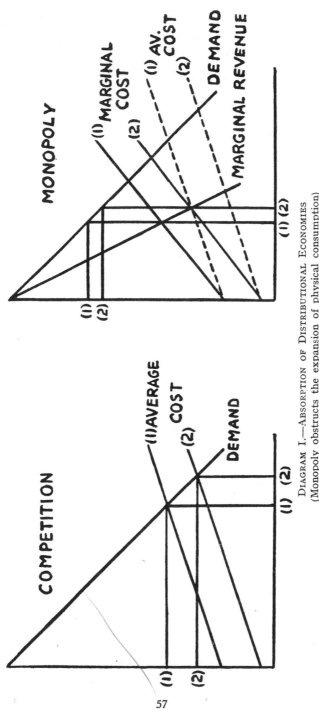

COMPETITION

(1) AVERAGE
(2) COST

DEMAND

(1) (2)

MONOPOLY

(1) MARGINAL
COST
(2)

(1) AV.
COST
(2)

DEMAND

MARGINAL REVENUE

(1)
(2)

(1) (2)

DIAGRAM I.—ABSORPTION OF DISTRIBUTIONAL ECONOMIES
(Monopoly obstructs the expansion of physical consumption)

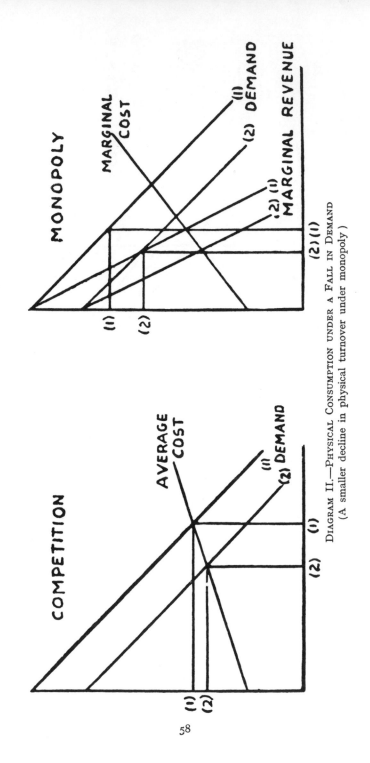

DIAGRAM II.—PHYSICAL CONSUMPTION UNDER A FALL IN DEMAND
(A smaller decline in physical turnover under monopoly)

Diagrams I and II illustrate the theoretical framework of the argument : [1]

Postponement of Demand.—So far we have seen that fixed distribution costs, monopoly and inelastic demand combine during a slump to drive raw prices to lower levels than the decline in final demand would seem to indicate. If any further explanations are necessary they may be found in the variation in merchants' stocks. The merchant has the opportunity to alter the volume of his stocks and to date his purchases according to his expectation of movements in price.

In a certain degree the final consumer has the same choice—that is, of refraining from purchase until prices appear to have touched bottom. Behaviour of this sort seems to be a feature of the trade in durable commodities. Some indication of its importance may be gauged from the following table : [2]

TABLE 8.—STANDARD DEVIATIONS IN U.S. SALES, 1919–25

	Values.	Volumes.
Retail :		
Groceries	10·6	4·5
Department stores	6·3	6·3
Shoes	9·6	9·9
Wholesale :		
Drugs	6·2	5·1
General	14·8	6·7
Groceries	14·4	7·6
Hardware	13·4	10·0
Dry goods	16·5	13·3
Shoes	18·1	14·6

The volume series indicates conclusively, and the value series only less so, that the more durable goods suffered the wider amplitude of fluctuation. These amplitudes suggest that the public at times refrained from buying—possibly because prices were falling or because their incomes

[1] In the use of marginal revenue curves to elucidate monopoly I follow Mrs. J. Robinson and Mr. R. F. Kahn.
[2] Reprinted from Dr. Kuznets' *Cyclical Fluctuations*, p. 114.

were less—and then bought unanimously.[1] If the retail series, corroborated by the wholesale, makes this clear about the public's behaviour, the fact that greater amplitudes are to be found in the wholesale than the retail section attaches a presumption of the same behaviour to retailers. This sort of discretionary buying is more of a commonplace among merchants, and the element of discretion, exhibited as a sort of negatively elastic intermediate demand, has quantitative importance.

Before we come to this perhaps it will be as well to notice the limits within which stocks should normally vary, apart from speculative anticipation. I shall adapt an illustration given by Dr. Kuznets,[2] which speaks for itself when we have understood that the merchant is taken to regulate his stocks as a fixed ratio to sales.[3]

	Stocks at 1st of Month.	Sales during Month.	Old Stocks at End of Month.	Stocks required to maintain Ratio.	Purchases required to maintain Ratio.
1st month	400	100	300	400	100
2nd ,,	400	100	300	400	100
3rd ,,	400	90	310	360	50
4th ,,	360	80	280	320	40
5th ,,	320	75	245	300	55
6th ,,	300	75	225	300	75
7th ,,	300	100	200	400	200
8th ,,	400	100	300	400	100
9th ,,	400	120	280	480	200
10th ,,	480	100	380	400	20

In this example the ratio of the standard deviations of the sales and purchases series is 1 to 4, approximately. So far as the illustration is just we have reason to suppose that the variation in purchases cumulatively magnifies itself fourfold [4] as it impinges on each successive merchant

[1] In case I may have underestimated the effect of diminished income, I may mention that Dr. Kuznets has found evidence of speculative intent in respect of footwear in July, 1919, and of apparel in January, 1920.

[2] op. cit.

[3] In this instance, a ratio of stocks to monthly sales of 4 to 1, representing a turnover of three times a year.

[4] The figure four has no direct connection with the stocks-sales ratio noticed above.

successively nearer the producer. The weaknesses of the illustration, in respect of these implications, are : (*a*) final purchases probably do not vary so rapidly ; (*b*) the ratio of stocks to sales is possibly too high, i.e. stocks may on the average be turned over more than three times a year ; (*c*) the upper limit of stocks is possibly not so high as indicated—e.g. space and interest charges ; (*d*) the lower limit is possibly not so low—e.g. custom and the convenience of clients ; (*e*) if the time unit in placing orders is less than a month, the variation in orders is smoothed out ; and (*f*) small changes in sales are not unlikely to go unnoticed, and perhaps purchases are not adjusted to them. These six considerations suggest that the magnification ratio is not necessarily so high as provisionally indicated, but nevertheless, any such modest ratio as two, even if only two merchants hold stocks, would impose violent instability on the distributive system by magnifying variation fourfold. The table of standard deviations in sales given above, in conjunction with some similar evidence, suggests that the magnification ratio appropriate to retailers is between 1·5 and 2. The wholesalers' ratio is not known.

Such evidence of the variability of stocks as we may obtain by comparing variations in purchases and sales, can be supplemented by a brief examination of the stocks themselves. The period 1919–25 is admirable for the purpose as it averages a major and a marked minor cycle, the former being closely connected with variations in working rather than in fixed capital. The effect of speculative anticipation, or even of prudent regard to the actual course of prices, has not been, and cannot be, abstracted from the series. The monthly variation in the first series—value stocks of United States' department stores—which there is no need to reprint—may be represented by a standard deviation of 8·5. We may compare this with the standard deviation for sales—6·3. Similarly the standard deviation, by volumes, for wholesale groceries (four products by months) was 12·6, and of sales, 7·6. Compared to sales, stocks, either by values or volumes, are the more variable, and the variation in wholesalers' stocks is very much greater than in retailers'. Consequently, if a decline in final purchasing power is either the original or proximate cause of a slump, the adjustment of stocks has the effect of aggravating the fluctuation of prices and incomes at the producers' end of the distributive chain.

If the part played in this fluctuation of stocks by adaptation of commitments to the expected price cannot be statistically separated, an illustrative example will demonstrate the possibilities. In the illustrative case given above a fixed ratio of stocks to monthly sales was maintained at four to one. The ratio of the standard deviation of purchases to that of sales, in the given instances of sales variation, was four to one. Now we may assume that the merchant reduces his stocks ratio to three and a half to one when sales are falling, and raises it to four and a half when they are rising. On this assumption the ratio of standard deviations in purchases and sales rises from four to seven. If the same behaviour as is assumed to attend variations in sales volumes is in fact prompted by price changes, it follows that those price changes will be greatly magnified even if customers' demand has remained unchanged. Evidently this observation applies as accurately to price changes wholly or partly conditioned on the side of supply as it does to price changes dependent on incomes. The limits to the aggravation are given by the minimum level of merchants' stocks. In 1922, wholesale grocery stocks in the United States, considered by volumes, touched a minimum of 27 per cent. below the mean for the period 1919–25, though even the value sales of groceries did not, even at the worst, fall below 17 per cent. of normal. Then, as we have seen, the variability of merchants' purchases is even greater than that of their stocks.

It is improbable that manufacturers vary their stocks of finished goods as violently as merchants do, since a rising and a falling price level are apt to indicate respectively a scarcity or redundancy of supplies emerging from the productive machine, rather than lead to accumulation and decumulation. If this is so, the efforts of manufacturers to adjust their finished stocks to prices will be alleviatory. A rise in demand is likely to be satisfied by drawing on stocks, and a relapse will lead to "making for stock." This compensatory behaviour is not so likely to apply to stocks of raw materials. A manufacturer will vary his raw stocks much in the ratio of orders received, as modified by anticipations of the future price. The permissible extent of speculative variation is given mainly by the time taken to procure and manufacture new stocks. On the other hand the variation in stocks which reflects variation in orders should reflect them quite faithfully—so far as the placing of orders is not spasmodic and capricious—since there is little fear of being caught with more or less stocks than can soon be profitably used. Hence the movement in wholesalers' purchases, which is more violent than the movement in their stocks or in retailers' purchases, tends to be transmitted, with little smoothing out, to the sales of the original raw producers.

On considering all these movements together, we may conclude that the letting down of stocks during a period of falling prices seriously aggravates that fall. It is rather difficult to decide whether staple agricultural produce suffers more or less than the average. On the one hand, the comparative regularity of demand should tend to equalise stocks : on the other, the nature of the produce is such that short stocks can speedily be brought up to normal if the movement in demand is suddenly reversed. The statistical sources suggest that on balance staple commodities are subject to greater variability, both in wholesale and retail areas of trade, but the evidence is not conclusive.

Speculation.—If semi-speculative anticipation of price movements is common to most branches of trade, it is primarily in raw produce that professional speculation assumes importance. The prevalence and nature of what is generally known as organised speculation in commodities is well understood. These remarks concern speculation which is comparatively intermittent—not regular inter-harvest speculation, but that for which opportunities are presented by the cyclical movement of prices. It is generally essential for this sort of speculation, as for most sorts, that the commodity should be storable and recognisable by description.   The fact that staple products are not made to suit individual tastes aids sale by description ; and storability is enhanced by the comparative absence of risk so far as the demand for such commodities does not vary unaccountably.   Staple products which more or less fulfil all the requirements include the cereals, the vegetable fibres, most organic raw materials, and the more valuable minerals.   It makes no important difference that the bear position frequently consists in the abridgment of normal buying.   The raw material of this speculation is the whole of the stocks in being other than merchants' minima. Generally the speculative market so behaves as to establish as rapidly as possible in the present a price equal, after making the adjustments noticed below, to what is generally anticipated for the future.

The willingness to hold stocks depends on three factors : (A) convenience of holding ;   (B) cost of holding ;   and (C) the excess ($+$) or deficiency ($-$) of future prices over present in respect of the period under consideration.   In equilibrium the factors so interconnect that $A + C = B$, or $C = B - A$. Now let us suppose that A (convenience) is diminished by a fall in demand.   C then must rise ; and that is, the present price must fall in relation to the anticipated future.   A situation of this sort arises—if the aggregate volume of speculative stocks is constant—when stocks are evacuated by merchants and forced on to professional speculators, who have no other than a speculative use for them.   When time has elapsed for the new prices to have restricted production and encouraged consumption the speculators are relieved of part of their burden ; but until then prices must have fallen by the value of the convenience formerly yielded.

Furthermore, C and B have now become equal—that is, the difference between present and anticipated prices must be at least equal to the cost of carrying stocks.   In the given conditions when stocks have been passed over to speculators, the cost of carrying has probably risen.   Risk is increased simply by virtue of the commodity having come into speculative hands, and the supply price of the speculators enters into cost, as that of the merchants did not. If the stocks are large the marginal supply price of the service may be considerable, and there is reason to suppose that this marginal supply price rises more than proportionally to an increase in the stocks to be carried. The present price must fall by enough to allow for these enhancements of cost as well as for the elimination of convenience. Hence the switchover from merchant to speculative carrying adds a further element of instability to the prices of staple produce. It is clear, however, that if stocks could not be carried speculatively, they would have to be disposed of at knock-down prices when demand declined, and thus the instability would be even more aggravated.

Carrying of Stocks through a Slump.—These considerations lead on to a study of the minima to which raw commodity prices may be expected to attain in a slump of given dimension.[1] We start from the proposition reached above that $C = B$, where B equals the marginal cost of carrying (including the supply price of the carrier), and C the spread between present prices and the anticipated future prices which the recovery of trade is expected to establish. The expansion of this proposition may be used in various ways, but for the time being the relation of minimum to normal price is the matter in hand. Although no numerical results are obtainable, except upon making numerical assumptions, it is still possible to achieve results expressible in formulæ simple enough to suggest further conclusions. It is convenient to assume (*a*) that the market is competitive; (*b*) that the final position is in all respects similar to the original; and (*c*) that stocks are disposed of evenly. Let p be a normal price in equilibrium to production and consumption each normally equal to k per annum. Let the amount of stocks at their maximum equal wk; the internormal period be r years[2]; and the annual cost of carrying

---

[1] The only existing treatment of this subject is to be found in the terse argument and arithmetical illustrations of Mr. Keynes (*Treatise*, Chap. XXIX). Considering the importance of the point, there seems to be room for amplification.

[2] The stocks wk are taken as in being at the beginning of this period; where we allow time for the accumulation, the period is designated r_2.

be tp.   The elasticities of supply and demand are m and n, that is, in respect of the prices established during the period of holding.   The buying price of the stocks is taken to be q, and hence p-q measures the fall in price necessary to evoke holding.   Whether all the stocks are bought at q, or whether q is a mere average, is not of importance.   It is easiest to suppose that all the stocks are bought at q, which price is immediately established as a result of oversupply or its equivalent.

Evaluation of $p - q$.   The fundamental principle used is that the difference between buying price and normal is to cover the cost of carrying.   Now the stocks are held for a total of r years and are evenly decumulated.   It follows that the average period of storage is $\frac{r}{2}$ years, and that the average cost of holding is $\frac{ptr}{2}$.   Hence

$$p - q = \frac{ptr}{2} \quad \cdots \quad (1)$$

Evaluation of t and r.—The stocks are liquidated as and when the price q makes appropriate adjustments to supply and demand.   If the quantities supplied and taken at price p were k, at price q they become respectively

$$k\left(1 - m\frac{(p - q)}{p}\right) \text{ and } k\left(1 + n\frac{(p - q)}{p}\right)$$

There is now an annual deficiency of supply equal to $\frac{k(m + n)\,(p - q)}{p}$.   Over the decumulation period this deficiency amounts to $\frac{kr(m + n)\,(p - q)}{p}$ and is sufficient to clear away stocks equal to wk.   Hence

$$\frac{kr(m + n)\,(p - q)}{p} = wk$$

$$r = \frac{wp}{(m + n)\,(p - q)} \quad \cdots \quad (2)$$

Now substitute for $(p - q)$ from (1), and proceed :

$$r = \frac{wp}{(m + n)\frac{ptr}{2}}$$

$$= \frac{2w}{tr(m + n)}$$

$$t = \frac{2w}{r^2(m + n)} \quad \cdot \quad \cdot \quad \cdot \quad \text{(3)}$$

Now when we take w, m, and n as constants, we find that t varies as $\frac{2}{r^2}$. That is to say, the longer the period, the less the cost (including remuneration) of carrying. The verbal reason is this : the longer the period the stocks are held, the less violent need be the contraction of supply and stimulation of demand, the less need prices fall to accomplish this, and the less is the cost of carrying which would just be profitably covered by a reversal of the price fall. We shall call this the profit relation of t and r. There is also a cost relation, consisting in the fact that the longer the period the greater is the actual burden of carrying. These two relations are respectively inverse and direct. It follows that each can only be true at one pair of values for t and r, and at these values profit and cost are in equilibrium. Considered graphically, the profit relation can be represented as a curve of t in terms of r, negatively inclined, and the cost relation as a similar curve positively inclined. The equilibrium values are given at the point of intersection.

To form some useful idea of the equilibrium values it is necessary to make some numerical assumptions. Let us suppose that the elasticities are together equal to unity, and that the surplus stocks are first equal to 80 and then to 40 per cent. of normal supply, and then take appropriate values of t to correspond in the cost relation to the amount of stocks and to a number of trial periods. (Table below.)

In the first instance r is between 2 and 3 years (about $2\frac{1}{2}$) and t 26 per cent., and in the second they are 2 and 20. Respectively prices would fall $\frac{(ptr)}{2}$ by 33 and 20 per cent.

80 Per Cent. Stocks.				40 Per Cent. Stocks.		
	Profit.		Cost.		Profit.	Cost.
$t =$	r	Per Cent.	Per Cent.	$t =$	r Per Cent.	Per Cent.
	1 year	160	20		1 year 80	16
	2 years	40	24		2 years 20	20
	3 ,,	18	29		3 ,, 9	25

The items in the second series are guesswork—especially as to the way in which costs vary with volumes and periods—but an attempt will be made to justify them in Appendix V, and they reasonably agree with the estimates of Mr. Keynes. If we take the sum of the elasticities to be one-half, the results become rather different :

80 Per Cent. Stocks.				40 Per Cent. Stocks.		
	Profit.		Cost.		Profit.	Cost.
$t =$	r	Per Cent.	Per Cent.	$t =$	r Per Cent.	Per Cent.
	1 year	320	20		1 year 160	16
	2 years	80	24		2 years 40	20
	3 ,,	36	29		3 ,, 18	25
	4 ,,	20	36		4 ,, 10	32

Here the holding periods are respectively $3\frac{1}{4}$ and $2\frac{3}{5}$ years, and the price falls 49 and 31 per cent.

By using the various formulæ given and making whatever seem reasonable assumptions as to the way in which carrying cost varies with the period and the amount to be carried, it is possible, since t and r are fixed by these assumptions as to carrying cost, to arrive at estimates of any of the three quantities, w, $(m + n)$ and $(p - q)$, provided the other two are known. These will not be profitable exercises when undertaken for the discovery of w and $(m + n)$, but some interest seems to attach to $(p - q)$. It is not without point to compare the price fall when stocks are held to that which would have resulted had the stocks been thrown on to the market, as those of some commodities must be.

We have considered four cases distinguished as to amount carried and as to the sum of the elasticities.   These may be summarised below in contrast with the relative price fall which would have occurred without storage, and supplemented by two more cases in which each elasticity is unity.   In calculating the price fall when storage is not practised, it is assumed that both production and consumption immediately adjust themselves to the fall in price, and that supply and demand have constant elasticities.   The difference of result which the removal of these assumptions would make could be worked out as special cases.

		Prices Fall.	
		Stocks 80 Per Cent.	Stocks 40 Per Cent.
$m + n =$		Per Cent.	Per Cent.
1	Storage . . .	33	20
	No storage . .	80	40
$1\frac{1}{2}$	Storage . . .	49	31
	No storage . .	—	80
2	Storage . . .	23	13
	No storage . .	40	20

These cases are only illustrative, for the elasticities given could not really co-exist with some of the price falls.   Also, the elasticities vary according to the volume of stocks, so that comparisons between falls in prices when stocks are 80 per cent. and corresponding falls at 40 per cent. are quite useless.   The greater the volume of stocks pressing on the price level, the greater the inelasticity of demand that is reached.

The price falls where no storage is practised are given as movements in the year when the excess stocks developed. If we took average price falls over the period that holding would have occupied had it been resorted to, there is then no difference in the magnitude of price movement as between storage and the absence of it.   Both are equal (as a percentage) to $\frac{ptr}{2}$.   Without averaging, on the other hand, the price fall that the absence of storage would have permitted was $\dfrac{wp}{(m+n)}$, or $\dfrac{ptr^2}{2}$ (ref. equation (3)). This latter is the significant quantity. The average fall in prices for a holding period, when stocks are not in fact held, is an artificial notion. Also, it is more interesting to discover the maximum oscillation of prices in both cases, stored and non-stored, rather than average variability over a period.

We have presumed so far that the excess stocks arose suddenly. If they take time to accumulate, rather different results are reached, and the price falls, in respect of a given maximum of excess stocks to be dealt with, are less in all cases. Let us suppose that the stocks take as long to accumulate as to be disposed of. This is another artificial assumption, but to remove it would involve us in a series of particular cases rather more complicated. The holding period is now denoted by r_2 years, $\dfrac{r_2}{2}$ years for accumulation, and the same for decumulation. T in the profit relation becomes $\dfrac{4w}{r_2^{2}(m+n)}$, and the price falls in six cases, arranged as before for different volumes and elasticities, become as follows :

			Prices Fall.	
			Stocks 80 Per Cent.	Stocks 40 Per Cent.
$(m+n)=$			Per Cent.	Per Cent.
1	With accumulation period .		24	16
	Without . . .		33	20
$\frac{1}{2}$	With		38	22
	Without . . .		49	31
2	With		16	10
	Without . . .		23	13

In both sets of cases, whether or not a period for the accumulation of stocks is required, the storing of commodities smoothes out prices compared with selling the excess supply for what it will fetch. This we already knew : the interest of the method, which we shall apply again in Chapter IX, is the way in which the period of stock holding can be deduced. The method also brings out that the degree of smoothing is occasionally trifling, and always small in relation to the volume of stocks ; but, after all, it is a virtue of the speculative system that some degree of stability is attained.

CHAPTER V

AGRICULTURAL " CRISES "

THIS chapter collates a number of topics bearing on the depths to which agricultural slumps may attain ; makes a comparison of past and present experience in this regard ; studies the relations of agricultural prosperity and adversity to the fortunes of agricultural countries ; and notes measures which may be taken to palliate an agricultural collapse.

The Violence of Price Fluctuations.—Of immediate and obvious importance in the determination of the gravity of an agricultural slump, caused by a recession in demand, is the degree by which the selling prices of agricultural produce fall, though, as we shall see, this is not the end of the story. We shall now summarise the arguments bearing on this matter which were considered in detail in Chapters II, III and IV.

When the demand recedes, the first and most important factor bearing on the fall in prices likely to be experienced at retail, is the magnitude of the decline. Measured in money, 10 to 15 per cent. appears to be not uncommon (from boom to slump), and between 1929 and 1931 it is arguable that 25–35 per cent. represents the true magnitude. It is built up out of the fall in the money incomes of the factors of production, particularly in wages (10 to 15 per cent. appears to be a reasonable world average for the wage cuts of 1929–31) ; out of unemployment (something like 20–25 per cent. was the world proportion of unemployment in 1931, as against 5–10 per cent. in 1929)—but here minus the alleviatory effects of unemployment relief and the clubbing together of members of the family ; and, finally, out of the increase in savings which seems to occur in the early stages of a slump. In all, it seems certain that a relapse in money demand for commodities in general

72

of the order of magnitude of 30 per cent. must have occurred. But lest agricultural produce, as it consists largely of food (in 1926–8 food, including colonial produce, accounted for 57·6 per cent. of the total of food and all raw materials), should suffer relatively little, let us reduce this 30 per cent. decline for commodities in general to 20 per cent., to give a picture of the fall in money demand specifically impinging on agriculture.[1] All these quantities are of course purely conjectural. But even the crudest quantitative analysis is more useful than the qualitative when dealing with matters that owe their importance to scale.

When this decline in demand made itself felt in the level of prices, it would be the natural response of manufacturing industry to restrict production and avoid losses on marginal output. Agriculture, unfortunately, is not in a position to make such adjustments to really large movements in prices. It is almost fair to say that the farmer can make his adjustments on only one scale, whatever be the fall in prices (within reason). The scale is mainly determined by the possibilities of economising in feed and fertiliser, cutting wages, diminishing acreage by 4 or 5 per cent.,[2] and dispensing with some casual and overtime labour—part of which economies are themselves economies on the end product of some other farmer. The scale in question seems to be fairly adequate to price movements up to 20 per cent., but is left in the rear when prices fall 40 per cent.

Now the price fall of 40 per cent. which we have just mentioned—as a conservative estimate of the all-round decline in agricultural prices during 1929–31—seems hardly consistent with a decline in demand by only 20 per cent. The main explanation of this discrepancy [3] is to be found in further developments, of a speculative or price anticipatory character, on the side of demand, in conjunction with the interposition of fixed or sticky costs between

---

[1] I do not believe that this reduction is necessary so far as I can judge from British data, but it may be that for the world as a whole the demand for food is less flexible than in Britain.

[2] Cf. the decline in American acreage, 1919–21, which amounted to 2 per cent. *Vide* King, *Wealth and Income in the United States.*

[3] Apart from the presence of over-supply.

producer and consumer. In the first place, when prices are falling, it pays middlemen and many alert consumers to diminish their purchases until prices seem to have reached bottom, and if possible, to work down the volume of their stocks. At the same time, if the demand happens to be, or has become, highly inelastic, the stocks in question can only be passed on to some other middleman. The latter looks for his recoupment of the costs of holding them to an eventual rise in prices to normal. Thus in order to educe the holding, prices are bound to fall considerably—in not exceptional cases by 50 per cent. In holding propositions of this type the element of business convenience, which had formerly offset the cost of carrying, is absent. When prices are falling, moreover, a given price fall at the retail end of the distributive chain is greatly magnified by the presence of more or less fixed distributive costs, which remain as a hardly altered lump sum to be added to a falling price at the farmer's end. Some of these fixed distributive costs are statistically separable from the general body of working and overhead costs together with profits that constitutes the complete spread between farm and retail prices. But generally speaking, statistical determinations cannot indicate whether some of these costs—the profit items—are not enlarged during a slump with the strengthening of distributive monopolies and semi-monopolies. There is a tendency for this to occur when the initial relapse in demand is not uniform throughout the market, either by classes of consumers or by commodities. Take first the element of heterogeneity in demand which is experienced when some types of consumer—e.g. the working classes—are impoverished by more than the average. Though the price fall at wholesale represents the average recession of demand, nevertheless the gap between wholesale prices and the prices which can be charged the less-impoverished customers is absorbable by middlemen. Analogously, though sufficient competition may obtain among middlemen to keep down their aggregate rewards to a figure not inappropriate to the general relapse in trade, yet in certain commodities for which the demand is rigid or inelastic, opportunities accrue for the enlargement of margins. This last circumstance is especially common in cases of over-supply, but occurs also in a relapse in demand when producers transfer their energies from hard-hit commodities to steadier ones. The element of monopoly in distribution, whether chronic or merely specific to a slump, is also responsible for the absorption by middlemen of the gains represented in economies in distribution on items other than profits.

These are all the principal determinants of the magnitude of a price fall in raw produce. The list could be extended, but as the points become nicer they yield diminishing returns in quantitative significance. It is not of great importance, for instance, that farmers themselves are often forced to sell weak (below prime cost), or driven to part with capital—e.g. livestock. Such events are symptoms of agricultural depression rather than causes, and striking in their nature [1] rather than frequent in their occurrence. They are found, of course, in association with severe losses, but losses are no uniform function of a given fall in price. Losses depend on the relations of prices to costs, and we shall have to see what is the character of these relations, especially with reference to the element of time.

The " Economic Lag " in the Clearance of Farm Costs.[2]— The farmer suffers his loss by virtue of his outlay antedating his receipts, together with the failure of costs to fall as rapidly as selling prices. The first ingredient of loss is by far the more important. It is present in production in general, but of rather more moment in agriculture, where the adjustment to falling prices is a slow process, taking 18–24 months as against the 6–12 months more common in manufacturing. Moreover, in agriculture a larger proportion of the total cost is incurred toward the commence-

---

[1] For example, the price of beef in South Africa, owing to the collapse of the meat and leather trade and the distress sales of oxen, fell more than 50 per cent. during 1931–2, even at retail.

[2] A matter treated statistically by Mr. W. C. Dampier Whetham, *Economic Journal*, December, 1925, whose quantitative estimates, together with the trend of his reasoning, have made a valuable contribution to farm economics. I follow Mr. Dampier Whetham's account of this matter in the text of this chapter, and reprint two of his tables as Tables 9 and 11.

ment of this period. In manufacturing, prime cost tends to be virtually immediate—only overheads representing outlay incurred substantially in advance : in agriculture, a large part of the working costs are also incurred at early dates. Again, the farmer has less opportunity of safeguarding himself by insurance and forward selling of his produce—to correspond to manufacture to order—although in the cases of cotton, wheat and a few other crops, sales three months forward are not uncommon. Thus if farm costs are incurred on the average twelve months before harvest, and if selling prices fall during that time, the farmer loses almost the whole value of the crop represented in that fall, irrespective of any decline in unit cost.

Mr. Dampier Whetham has worked out the average measure by which costs are predated on various types of English farm. The periods are calculated separately for each item of outlay, and then each period is multiplied by the proportion of that item in total cost—the reduced periods being then added. Accordingly we get the weighted mean " lag." Among the results obtained are the following :

TABLE 9.—WEIGHTED " LAG " OF FARM COSTS

A Light Arable Farm.

	Months.		Months.
Barley	14·3	Wheat	13·6
Oats	14·5	Cattle	17·7
Milk	8·3	Sheep and wool	15·0
Pigs	8·6	Roots, etc.	11·2
Hay and straw	14·0	Weighted mean	13·77

Dairy Farming on Heavy Land.

	Months.		Months.
Milk	7·65	Calves	6·95
Cows	8·5	Pigs	3·9
Poultry	3·0	Corn	13·6
Sundries	5·0	Weighted mean	7·01

Taking agriculture as a whole, it is probably fair to say that costs are incurred on the average a year before sales. The somewhat larger mean period found on the first farm was due to the use of elaborate systems of rotation. The period in question was computed on the supposition that costs were stationary. But actually if costs are falling, the " lag " lengthens out, as the farmer gets more benefit from the fall in costs incurred later than earlier. The amount of lengthening, however, is not quantitatively important.

Now, taking an average fall in prices over the year 1930 as 20 per cent., and assuming that the costs subject to a lag (working costs) amount to 50 per cent. of the whole, then we may take it that a lag of twelve months is responsible for a loss of 10 per cent. on receipts. These are the receipts calculated prior to the relapse in price, since the costs incurred during 1930 will have been based on the expectation of stationary prices. The contraction in the residual items—either profits or overheads—to be added to the loss on the lag of working costs (10 per cent.)—is of course equals to 20 per cent. of their proportionate share (50 per cent.) of receipts—10 per cent.—so that the total loss equals 20 per cent., or the amount by which the aggregate value of sales has declined. If any fall in costs has occurred, the producer has had no advantage from it.

The Decline in Farm Costs.—Even when costs do fall, they rarely fall proportionately to the fall in selling prices. For the present slump it is impossible to give a complete account of the fall in costs that has so far taken place— one only knows the following items :

TABLE 10.—FALL IN FARM COSTS, 1929–31

Type of Cost.	Period Studied.	Market.	Percentage Decline.
			Per Cent.
Fertiliser	1929–31	Various	0–32
Feed barley	1929–31	London	31
Oats	1929–31	London	33
Maize	1929–31	London	52
Labour	1929–31	U.S. and Canada	30–31
Feed rice	1929–31	London	30
Feed sugar	1929–31	London	32
Seed corn	1929–31	England	25–35

The average fall in price against which these savings on working cost should be compared is 40–50 per cent.

The decline in costs during 1921–2 is much better known. In Great Britain the following falls occurred :

TABLE II.—FALL IN FARM COSTS IN GREAT BRITAIN, 1920–3

	1920–2.	1920–3.
	Per Cent.	Per Cent.
An arable farm :		
Labour	30	41
Feeding stuffs	46	48
Fertiliser	43	52
Seed	40	54
Implements, etc.	47	54
Coal, stores, insurance, etc. . . .	50	49
Rent	4	4
Rates	—	50
Weighted total	34	42
Selling prices, weighted . . .	44	49
A dairy farm :		
Labour	30	41
Feeding stuffs	46	48
Fertilisers	43	52
Store pigs	41	40
Implements and tradesmen . . .	47	54
Coal, stores and sundries . . .	50	49
Rent	4	4
Rates	—	9
Weighted total	36	42
Selling prices, weighted . . .	40	43

The costs given above were probably more than 50 per cent. of total costs—nearly 70 per cent. They declined quite easily from the inflated levels of the war, and far more easily than recently. Most of the decline was naturally provoked by agricultural losses, in the main due to the lag in costs.

The Debacle in Agricultural Prices.—Before coming to the devastation that has been wrought by the present collapse in agricultural prices in the finances of the leading raw-material countries, we must notice by how far and how rapidly prices have declined in the leading commodities.

A great many particulars are now available for 1932, but

not all, so the price history is taken up to a uniform date throughout, 1931.[1]

TABLE 12.—PRICE FALLS OF VEGETABLE PRODUCE, 1927–31
(1927–9 = 100)

Commodity.	Market.	1927.	1928.	1929.	1930.	1931.
Wheat . . .	London .	109	105	87	97	52
,, . . .	U.S.A. .	107	94	99	58	43
Barley . . .	London .	97	107	95	82	63
,, . . .	U.S.A. .	115	93	93	71	65
Oats	London .	99	96	105	97	58
,, . . .	U.S.A. .	104	95	101	74	54
Maize . . .	London .	85	100	114	85	51
,, . . .	U.S.A. .	96	100	103	87	48
Rice	London .	104	97	99	91	79
Rye	U.S.A. .	99	99	101	45	46
Buckwheat . .	U.S.A. .	93	98	109	94	48
Sorghums . .	U.S.A. .	97	95	109	98	47
Cotton . . . (American)	U.S.A. .	109	100	91	53	32
Cotton . . . (Egyptian)	Liverpool .	104	114	83	45	41
Flax	London .	114	113	72	43	51
Hemp . . .	London .	108	96	95	62	54
Jute	London .	104	105	91	51	63
Silk	Milan . .	99	109	91	52	57
Flaxseed. . .	U.S.A. .	83	90	127	62	54
Linseed Oil . .	U.S.A. .	104	96	100	137	88
,, ,, . .	London .	82	86	132	65	43
Cottonseed . .	U.S.A. .	70	116	114	98	71
Peanuts . . .	U.S.A. .	99	101	93	65	49
Coconut Oil . .	London .	110	101	88	66	65
Potatoes . .	England .	123	97	79	71	97
Fruit and Vege-tables	U.S.A. .	106	100	93	108	67
Hay	U.S.A. .	95	103	102	106	76
Sugarbeet . .	U.S.A. .	105	97	97	98	80
Tobacco . . .	U.S.A. .	106	101	93	65	49
Coffee (Rio No. 7)	New York	100	92	107	73	42
,, (Costa Rica)	London .	106	96	98	73	68
Tea	London .	114	107	80	87	62
Cocoa . . .	London .	113	92	94	75	70
Sugar (raw) . .	London .	119	102	80	58	60
,, (crystal) .	,, .	121	94	86	79	77
Rubber . . .	London .	163	71	66	35	27

[1] American figures from *Year Book of Agriculture*, 1932.   Others from the *Economist*.

TABLE 13.—PRICE FALLS OF ANIMAL PRODUCE, 1927–31
(1927–9 = 100).

Commodity.	Market.	1927.	1928.	1929.	1930.	1931.
Beef Cattle . .	U.S.A. .	87	106	107	86	61
Hogs . . .	U.S.A. .	109	92	99	95	74
Sheep . . .	U.S.A. .	97	102	101	71	46
Horses . . .	U.S.A. .	97	103	100	100	81
Beef	England .	93	93	115	104	83
Mutton . . .	England .	97	103	100	81	58
Bacon (Danish)	England .	84	104	111	66	48
Milk	U.S.A. .	100	100	100	91	68
Butter . . .	Copenhagen	98	103	99	79	64
Cheese . . . (American)	U.S.A.. .	104	100	96	80	60
Cheese (Canadian)	London .	100	104	96	75	64
Oleomargarine .	U.S.A. .	98	99	103	96	59
Eggs	U.S.A. .	90	102	108	86	63
Poultry . . .	U.S.A. .	102	96	102	104	79
Wool . . .	London .	102	113	85	51	37
Hides . . .	London .	119	102	78	72	63
Leather . . .	London .	119	100	81	85	85

The least of these declines, 1931 compared with 1927–9, was 3 per cent. for English potatoes ; the greatest 73 per cent. for rubber ; the median 36 per cent.

Now we shall notice a few instances of the damage done to agricultural exporting countries by the collapse in their staple produce.[1] Some of the most glaring are these :

(a) Malaya : 47 per cent. of exports in 1929 consisted of rubber, of which the price fell 73 per cent.

(b) Ceylon : 77 per cent. of exports in 1929 were rubber and tea, of which the prices fell 73 and 38 per cent.

(c) Denmark : 63 per cent. of exports in 1929 were butter and meat, of which prices fell 36 and 40 per cent.

(d) Australia : 53 per cent. of exports in 1929 consisted of wool and wheat products, of which prices fell 63 and 48 per cent.

(e) New Zealand : 86 per cent. of exports in 1929 con-

[1] Data taken from League of Nations' *Memoranda on Production and Trade.*

sisted of wool, dairy produce and meat, of which prices fell 63, 40 and 40 per cent.

(*f*) Brazil : 71 per cent. of exports in 1929 consisted of coffee, of which the price fell 58 per cent.

(*g*) Argentina : 61 per cent. of exports in 1929 consisted of wheat, maize and meat, of which prices fell 48, 49 and 20 per cent.

(*h*) China : 41 per cent. of exports in 1929 were silk and beans (or nuts), of which prices fell 38 and 30–40 per cent.

(*i*) India : 63 per cent. of exports in 1929 were of cotton, jute, rice and tea, of which prices fell 60, 37, 21 and 38 per cent.

(*j*) Cuba : 70 per cent. of exports in 1929 were sugar, of which the price fell 40 per cent.

In most instances the prices are taken at wholesale, after considerable distributive costs have already been incurred. Hence the producers' price will have fluctuated more than listed above, usually about half as much again. The exact amounts are only on record in a few cases. The year 1932 in every case continued the story of decline, at least of decline in gold prices.

The cases chosen above are not so much those in which prices have declined extremely, but are of countries tending to specialise on a few leading lines of agricultural export. The greater the specialisation, even in exports alone, the greater tends to be the drop in the national income if the specialised commodity has suffered severely. But more important perhaps, in the immediate problems it poses, is the fall in total export receipts. It happens that a good many of the specialised exports, e.g. rubber, coffee, wool, and cotton, were commodities that sustained more than average damage. But also, for diverse reasons, many widespread staples are also to be found at the extremes of price decline—wheat, maize, rye, etc. There is no inclusive explanation of this state of affairs. The upshot is that impoverishment has been carried into all the agricultural communities, and many makeweight exports, apart from the leading categories, failed to average out the decline, but rather, as in Australia and Argentina, accentuated it.

Perhaps in many cases it was cash export crops that were particularly liable to price fluctuation, and therefore to overproduction during the boom, followed by an intensified collapse. Sugar, tobacco and coffee in specialised economies, and wheat and hogs in less specialised, are all crops of relatively unstable price in any case, due chiefly to marketing cost and in some cases specialised use. And then, because they are important cash export crops, instability of price engenders instability of production. When prices soar it is more than usually attractive to expand production and reap an immediately larger cash income. Machinery and other intensive technical reform have been an especial feature of cash export crops. And then when the slump ensues overproduction is found added to underconsumption. So in short, the more important a crop is for export, the wider its price fluctuations, and in turn the more damage they do.

It would be instructive to go on and compute the degrees in which the export receipts of the leading agricultural countries—or those most dependent on agriculture—have suffered, and then find the relative importance of export receipts in money national income. The first of these tasks is easy. But owing to the lack of national income statistics in many countries, the second is possible only over a most restricted range.

The table on page 83 gives an indication of what has happened to export receipts, measured in gold value.[1]

It all depends on the type of economy practised in the countries what proportion export receipts bear to national income, and in many cases that proportion may run as high as a half. In Australia, despite considerable industrialisation, the proportion is 20–25 per cent.[2] In this country the national income had already declined 20 per cent. by 1930–1. But into the ramifications of the decline, country by country, or crop by crop, we do not propose to enter.

---

[1] From League of Nations' *Statistical Yearbook*.
[2] The information on Australia used in this chapter is taken from Shann and Copland, *The Crisis in Australian Finance*, 1929–31.

TABLE 14.—EXPORT RECEIPTS OF AGRICULTURAL COUNTRIES, 1927-31 (1927-9 = 100)

Country.	1927.	1928.	1929.	1930.	1931.
Canada	96	111	94	69	48
Cuba	111	95	93	57	—
Argentina . . .	95	101	105	52	53
Brazil	95	103	101	98	55
Ceylon	108	94	98	75	55
China	96	105	99	65	47
India	98	102	100	77	62
Malaya	112	89	99	71	45
Denmark . . .	95	101	104	98	74
Greece	93	98	109	92	65
Hungary . . .	92	92	116	102	63
Ireland	96	100	104	99	77
Poland	96	96	108	95	72
Australia . . .	101	98	101	87	63
New Zealand . .	93	104	104	83	64

Reactions and Palliative Measures.—So far we have considered a fall in export receipts chiefly as contributor to a drop in total national income. But the consequences are more serious. It is out of export receipts that those of the agricultural countries that are debtors (and nearly all are) require not only to purchase their imports but discharge their indebtedness. Again, in most of these countries exports normally exceed imports, the balance representing interest, so that a given decline in exports necessitates a proportionately greater decline in imports. A portion of the imports, moreover, will usually have represented, prior to the decline, the receipt of new loans. This support to the exchanges and source of import dues ceases almost entirely with the breakdown of the country's capacity to borrow. In short, loan imports cease, debt service becomes excessively painful, normal imports wither away, and budget problems, accentuated both by the fall in exporters' incomes and the loss of import dues, become insoluble.

The case of Australia is interesting. Exports fell in 1928-9 to 1930-1 from £138 millions to £76 millions. To this decline of £62 millions add £28 millions for reduced foreign borrowing. Imports in one way or another had to decline £90 millions from £144 millions, or by vastly more absolutely and proportionately, than exports.

The chief methods of curtailing imports, and indeed of re-establishing equilibrium generally, are import restriction, deflation and depreciation.   Practically all of the agricultural countries have practised all of the three.

Import Restrictions.—Existing tariffs are raised and new ones imposed.   Australia, which early felt the slump, took the lead with four revisions of the tariff between October, 1929, and April, 1930.   Or perhaps all commodities are made subject to a special surtax (India, South Africa, etc.). If the tariff on any one commodity, to be effective, must verge on 100 per cent., a quota is usually used instead, and the volume of import is regulated by fiat.   This practice has gone furthest in Europe, France and Germany being notable exponents.

Finally the course of *ad hoc* import restriction tends to culminate in exchange restrictions.   Europe again, chiefly in order that Germany, Austria, etc., might protect themselves from the withdrawal of short-term funds, has taken the lead here.   The example has been copied in South America, and Chile and Argentina are regulating the withdrawal of foreign exchange.

All these methods are in themselves somewhat crude— though special circumstances may justify them—and the happiest of the agricultural countries to-day are those which chose some way of aiding exports as well.   Nevertheless, so long as a country like Austria is almost contractually bound to remain nominally on the gold standard, or finds it politically impossible to devaluate, import restrictions are almost the sole self-defence left.   It is impossible, in the given conditions of distress, to borrow to peg the exchange ; the internal level of costs is necessarily somewhat intractable ; and some important political interest clamours for protection.

Probably exchange restrictions are the most effective of the three ways of reducing imports, but they make the retention of exchange parities a patent farce.   And unless the restrictions are judiciously managed, importing becomes a race to take advantage of what foreign exchange becomes available. In fact the country has all the disadvantages of devaluating without its benefits—its foreign trade is disorganised, and the whole burden of exchange readjustment is thrown upon imports alone.

Quotas similarly are effective, but again are destructive of trade channels and inappropriate to a pure cyclical difficulty. When the quotas are block quotas and not a running proportion of home production, trade becomes a scramble among competing importers and a source of international dispute.

Tariffs are perhaps the least effective in coping with the immediate difficulty. But if the tariff takes the form of a surcharge, it is non-discriminatory, as the other methods of import restriction can hardly be, and stands a good chance of being removed when it had served its purpose. The ordinary method of raising tariffs, commodity by commodity, creates vested interests, and, as a matter of fact, the process of piecemeal tariff revision has often failed to cope with the pace of the decline. Australia, until depreciation was resorted to, found herself obliged to raise tariffs step after step in the effort to get even with falling external prices. But piecemeal tariff revision has been practised more commonly during the last three years than tariff surcharges. The protection of the exchanges is made to serve for the protection of particular industries and usually to aggrandise the politically important.

Deflation.—There are two types of deflation, either of prices alone, or of costs also. In the first case the operations of the banking system, either deliberate or reflex, perhaps in conjunction with a changed spending policy of Governments or peoples, procure a fall in selling prices but not in costs. The incidence of the deflation therefore falls on profits. Deflation of this sort is ordinarily to be regarded as a reflex action of the financial organism confronted with the early stimuli of a slump. Their confidence evaporated, banks ration credit stringently or call in loans, and the public at large refrains from new commitments either for personal luxuries or business expansion. At the same time the drop in export receipts has diminished the capacity of farmers to pay their interest, and made farm credit, and the whole pyramid of secondary credit depending on it, insecure. The farmers also have lost current purchasing power. Governments, too, find their credit weakened and their revenue receipts declining. The exchange situation deteriorates, and the Central Bank finds it necessary to guard its gold, or the commercial banks their London balances. Deflation is the expression of a general *sauve qui peut*.

Then this reflex or instinctive behaviour is rationalised into a cure. Thus the Australian bankers, 19th December, 1930 : [1]

Unless effective steps are taken by the Governments of Australia to balance their budgets and reduce costs, the time is coming when the banks and other financial institutions will be unable to assist the Governments to meet salaries, wages, and other commitments except at the expense of widening the gap already in evidence between the cost of and the returns from Australian industries.

And Sir Otto Niemeyer, July, 1930 : [1]

There is also evidence to show that the standard of living in Australia has reached a point which is economically beyond the capacity of the country to bear without a considerable reduction of costs resulting in increased *per capita* output.

The emphasis in these extracts is upon the need for cautionary finance and a fall in the standard of living, not so much to tide over the slump as to liquidate past extravagance. This last may well be desirable, but the cutting of costs is not the only method. And if the objective were simply to adjust to a temporary slump, cost cutting might well be too troublesome to be worth while. It provokes industrial strife, is usually unfair as between classes of income, and may require a later, and equally troublesome, reversal. Nor in fact do the purists usually consider in what way costs should and can be cut. Before any effective steps are taken to lower the cost level the deflation of prices is in full blast ; and the orthodox are still found complaining

---

[1] From documents collected by Shann and Copland, op. cit.

of unbalanced budgets while the decline in profits—chief contributor to the deficits—which the failure to cut costs occasions, becomes steeper. But at last, to some extent, costs must fall. Even if no concerted action is taken, entrepreneurs at length pass part of their burden to the other factors of production. If they encounter resistance in so doing, probably the fall in costs will never take up the whole loss, and the attack on costs will be an endless guerilla war, lasting till the slump is over. But if the authorities step in and decree a reduction of costs, price deflation can then be absorbed wholly into a deflation of costs, so that producers are restored to fair equilibrium. The machinery for such action exists so far only in Australasia. Australia and New Zealand are probably the only countries justified in having used cost cuts as a substantial contribution to the task of re-establishing equilibrium with the outside world. In Australia the Courts lowered the minimum wage by roughly 20 per cent., and the Governments induced or forced their bond creditors to accept an equal reduction in interest. Such was the condition of Australia that neither depreciation of the currency nor import restriction, alone or together, were feasible, within reasonable limits of either course of action, to redress the Commonwealth's unbalance without the support of internal cost reduction as well. But by combining three methods the objective was at length obtained without alarm or unnecessary inconvenience. But Australia is perhaps a somewhat special case. It is more usual for attempts to break the level of costs either to fail or to degenerate into an attack on wages alone.

Devaluation.—When a country causes or permits a depreciation of its currency, usually consequent on a departure from the gold standard, the result is to curtail imports into and stimulate exports from that country relative to others ; and the value of export receipts in local currency now becomes more adequate to meet the level of costs, until they have risen, which they may do slightly in time. A change in the value of the currency may take up most or all of the gap between internal costs and external prices ; and, in effect, all money costs are cut automatically and equally.

The exact extent to which the factors of production lose in real income depends on the degree of their dependence on import goods, which will have risen in price. Depreciation is sometimes represented as occasioning an aggrandisement of debtors as against creditors, since the external value of the currency is lowered. This certainly occurs in respect of external debts payable in the local currency, which are rare, but the point is scarcely relevant for internal debts, since external values did not enter into the contract. The general effect of devaluation is therefore to stabilise home prices, prevent a fall in incomes which was making debts more burdensome, and keep alive the country's competitive power abroad.

Within limits these advantages may be obtained automatically by using a currency which is free to vary in accordance with relative internal costs and external prices. For China, the price of silver represents the value of the currency and it is governed mainly by the exigencies of China's exchange situation. China is therefore always in exchange equilibrium ; and the fall in silver prices since 1926 has maintained a very stable price level and contributed to China's ability to avoid default.

There are three principal species—by countries—of devaluation or depreciation. First of all there are the countries whose hold on any definite parity has usually been temporary or precarious. They have glided out of one exchange difficulty after another by depreciation, only recovering part of the ground during a boom. Most of the South American countries go into this category, and Spain, Portugal, Greece and Japan have provided instances in the last decade. The present slump has given every excuse for a resumption of the practice.

Then there are the countries which have abandoned gold only in pain and remorse after a struggle. South Africa, which adhered to gold for about two years after her rival exporter, Australia, had abandoned it, is a leading case. In fact, South Africa had to be sold off the gold standard by her own nationals who exported gold in anticipation of a political upheaval. Australia and New Zealand, also, though they were early obliged to suspend gold payments, only did so after a black exchange market had developed in which the official quotations were undersold. (To-day black markets are developing in some of the countries of the first group, as Argentina, which have tried to arrest depreciation before restoring equilibrium. Japan, which also properly belongs to the first group, made a short effort to remain on gold, having returned to it after devious wanderings just in time to participate in the slump.) It is not reported that any countries in the second group have regretted that they were in the end forced to devaluate—had they been less conscious of their " honesty " they might have been glad to arrange the happy accident.

The third group of agricultural countries consists of those which followed the leadership of Great Britain, itself un-willingly forced off gold by a fortunate concatenation of curious circumstances. India, Ireland, the British colonies, and Denmark are the leading members of the group. Australia and New Zealand took the opportunity to add the measure of the British depreciation to the gap between parities and current quotations which they had already established. The primary objective of all these countries was to keep themselves linked to sterling. They wished either to facilitate capital transactions or to retain a large English market which the British depreciation had other-wise curtailed.

These countries, including several not distinctively agricultural, like Sweden, have managed to follow quite faithfully the wanderings of the pound. They have evidently not used depreciation as a weapon in itself. But New Zealand and Denmark are exceptions. New Zealand added a third instalment of devaluation early in 1933, in order to invade the Danish market in Britain, and Denmark, of course, retaliated in kind.

Defaults.—The failure to contrive the continuance of public external debt services is now a commonplace of the slump. Sometimes it is the budget which breaks down—or rather the people refuse to tax their impoverished selves for the benefit of overseas capitalists—but more often the obstacle is one of transfer.   In this case the funds already appropriated for debt service are placed in a block account inside the paying country.   They are pledged to remain intact until the value of the currency shows an upward trend.   The immediate transfer difficulty may be, and has usually been, the exhaustion of gold reserves or the fear of depressing the currency further.   But the low value of the currency already resulting from depreciation has also contributed to the burden of payment, since most of these (agricultural) debts are in terms of the creditor's currency.

In view of the gravity of defaults by states professing adherence to the capitalist ideology, it is a moot question whether devaluation, since it increases the size of the current debt in terms of the debtor's currency, can be regarded as defensible.   But since the occasion for devaluation has usually been the disappearance of any favourable balance of trade that may have existed, default was inevitable in any case.   Indeed, devaluation has been used to procure a favourable balance out of which at least some part of the payment might be made.   Again, devaluation increases tax receipts.   It may generally be assumed that for any one country the elasticity of demand for exports and imports is sufficient for devaluation to increase the former and diminish the latter, each way stimulating home industry, so that, furthermore, extra tax receipts take care of the enhanced money burden of payment.   On modest assumptions as to the typical proportion of foreign trade to national income, proportion of national income falling to the public revenues, and proportion of debt payments to the budget, elasticities equal to unity should satisfy the condition that devaluation does not raise the real burden of the debt.   The assumptions given above seem to be justified by the statistics of Australia, for instance.

Taken far enough, the policy of devaluation as a method of accomplishing the transfer of debt might fall into a vicious circle—or rather resolve itself into an endless race between a mounting debt charge and a rising trade balance, with the former gaining, and the currency at length reaching wall-paper values.   But no such circumstances are yet in sight, except perhaps in Japan for reasons connected with the Asiatic war.

But these arguments in favour of devaluation have more or less postulated individual action by a single country. The benefits of devaluation, not only for debt service but more widely, similarly accrue to their full extent only to individual states striking out from the ruck of their competitors. But when quite a big bloc of agricultural countries devaluates, and to much the same extent from country to country, it is clear that none of them has gained much advantage at the expense of others. None, for instance, is guaranteed the discharge of its debts if the means of payment are to be secured only by invading the markets of a rival country operating similarly. But the devaluated bloc as a whole has scored at the expense of the non-devaluated. So far as these blocs divide on debtor creditor lines—some creditors being also agricultural—it is a merit of devaluation as a policy for the debtors, that the creditors are forced to facilitate payment by receiving their debts in goods even at the expense of home industry. In so far as the reluctance of creditors to accept the only feasible form of payment is at the root of defaults, devaluation on the part of debtors becomes almost indispensable.

We now come to the brief enumeration of several minor types of defensive reaction by distressed agricultural states. None of them can pretend to strengthen the position of agriculture as a whole to any very useful extent.

Export Subsidies.—Naked subsidies have been paid to exporters in South Africa and Australia, and in South America, notably Colombia. Subsidies are also paid via valorisation corporations like the Canadian wheat pools or the Federal Farm Board, when they pay their farmer clients more than the market value of the crop.

Agricultural Debt Readjustment.—Moratoria on farm debts have appeared in Central Europe—in Germany for instance—and notably in Rumania. In the latter country most comprehensive measures have been taken for the relief of the peasantry from the pressure of landlords, mortgage holders and rural loan sharks. The Rumanian scheme is admittedly deficient in detail,[1] but since the deflation of rural debt is in any case inevitable now that the return to pre-slump crop values is out of the question, it is as well to have it undertaken in a concerted campaign.   The alternative is a war of attrition.   Creditors foreclose and evict the farmer, only to find that they have a bankrupt and deteriorating farm on their hands.   Or when the farm is put to auction the debtor's friends with the connivance of the police have rigged the market.   Matters are improved somewhat when, as in the American Mid-west, facilities are provided for the orderly composition of the debts.   But even here the final adjustment owes too much to the relative bargaining power of the parties, and too little to a settled view of what agriculture can now afford.   Also, as it is inevitable that the bulk of the world's present farm population will remain on the land, the arrangements that will secure this ultimate result should not include a wholesale reversion to tenancies as farms are lost on foreclosure, nor the muddle and waste of forced sales.

Storage of Surplus Supplies and Restriction of Output.— These subjects are examined in the next chapter in special reference to problems of overproduction.   Of some interest in this connection are the American proposals, now going through the legislative mill, to subsidise farmers in respect of certain leading crops if they will contract to reduce their acreage in a specified proportion.   It is questionable if the American scheme has much prospect of administrative success, but the principle, granted that the farmers must be kept alive, has undoubted merit.

Regional Agreements to Limit Competition.—Germany and Poland have concluded a treaty of this sort in regard to rye, and the south-east European states have begun the preliminaries for other crops.   The agreements get rid of a certain amount of weak selling.

Protection.—Apart from import restriction undertaken in the interests of exchange equilibrium, farmers in many of the agricultural countries have claimed and received special

---

[1] See Sollohub, " Agricultural Debts in Rumania," *Economic Journal* December, 1932.

protection. Tariffs are the traditional method, but quotas are making an increasing appearance. Germany and France are now notorious for the obstacles they have placed in the way of trade in foodstuffs.

Co-operation, etc.—The slump has destroyed many established co-operative organisations as members become increasingly dissatisfied with the prices that the agency has obtained for them. But at the same time it has become increasingly realised in official circles that the rationalisation of agricultural marketing is overdue. An interesting development is the endowment of co-operative organisations with privileged export rights and facilities, and even the erection of these and analogous bodies into monopoly buyers. Poland, Jugoslavia, Bulgaria and Java have made experiments along these lines, the last-named in connection with an attempt to valorise sugar. Similarly many Governments confronted with problems of local over-supply have found themselves obliged to construct storage capacity on behalf of the farmers or to set up organisations to carry the surplus. Argentina has had difficult problems of carrying wheat and maize and has arranged for the building of warehouses and elevators.

Tax Suspensions.—Several countries have granted rebates on farm taxes or shown a very accommodating attitude to farm tax delinquency. Greece has gone so far as to exempt farmers from taxes.

Farm Loans.—In most countries the existing agricultural credit agencies have been reinforced by the grant of State funds to tide the farmers over. Sometimes the money is granted as direct relief, sometimes as loans on doubtful security, sometimes as seed loans secured on the prospective crop, sometimes for the purpose of converting more burdensome debt contracted in the past, sometimes to help the farmer avoid eviction, and sometimes to reimburse the agency for continuing to carry the farmer who cannot pay his interest.

Reorganisation of Farm Methods.—In times of slump most attempts at improving farm organisation, since they involve increased outlay by the governments for agricultural education or extra capitalisation of the farm, fall into abeyance. But not so in Italy, where the Government has forced upon farmers a host of small adjustments designed to increase the competitive capacity of the nation. Cartellisation in England, under the Marketing Act of 1931, so far as it also involves rationalisation of marketing method and the elimination of superfluous middlemen, is a step in the same direction.

These are a few of the leading efforts that have been made to protect or relieve the farmers of separate countries. The remainder, a host of minor expedients, are also more or less pitiful by comparison with the dimensions of the collapse.

Past Agricultural Depressions.—Agricultural depressions are known from earliest history, but most historical expositions begin with the crisis that followed the Napoleonic Wars, especially as it offers some resemblances to the present emergency. But perhaps even more similar to the depression which began in 1928 is the depression of the eighteen-nineties. The resemblance holds even outside the agricultural sphere.

First of all, each depression originated largely as a reaction from over-investment—in 1924–9 in public works and railways, automobiles, instalment goods, and mechanisation generally—and in 1889–91 in land, railways, tramways, telephones, gold, and oil wells. In both cases the overinvestment was most marked in South America and Australia, which had overborrowed. In the reactions occurred notable financial crashes, which were the triggers of general crisis —in 1890 the Baring crash, and in 1929 to 1931 the debacles of Wall Street, Insull, Kreuger, Hatry, etc. Following on the panics came protracted courses of decline and financial congealment. Foreign lending virtually ceased. In the nineties England, which reached her panic early, made a temporary financial recovery and began to hoard gold. In the beginnings of the present slump the withdrawal of France's balances from other countries in conjunction with a failure to lend abroad, also locked up gold and accentuated its maldistribution. Both depressions, furthermore, were associated with a stage in the progressive demonetisation of silver, which lowered the price of that metal and curtailed

the purchasing power of the East.   Both, again, were superimposed on a falling trend of prices.[1]

Both depressions were associated with agricultural overproduction.   In 1890–3 the production of both wheat and
rye—world statistics for other crops are scanty—were
running much above their usual levels.   In 1894 wheat
carry-overs exceeded the normal by 40 per cent.[2]   Except
for 1890 the American production of some twelve crops
combined was also above normal.[3]   Corn, oats and hay were
all in excess.   Partly on account of the overproduction and
partly on account of the falling off of demand in the slump,
prices fell steeply.   Wheat declined 40 per cent. between
1891 and 1894, and rye 50 per cent. at Liverpool prices.[4]
The whole of vegetable foods in the United Kingdom fell
21 per cent. in price between 1891 and 1893.[5]

The causes of the overproduction are usually given as the
development of virgin lands in the New World and the
emergence in the 'nincties of Russia as the leading exporter
of cereals.[6]   Australia also contributed.   The greatest single
cause of the development was the extension of railways.
Agriculture had been running a prolonged course of expansion, and the crisis of the 'nineties was only one of a number
which afflicted the latter half of the century.   It seems that
at times the increasing productivity of farming ran ahead
of the growth in population and demand.   Especially so,
since during this period, a combination of shortage in gold
supplies and the tendency of Victorian thrift to outrun the
available investment outlets was continually depressing the
non-agricultural world's capacity to buy.   That agriculture
was able to grow at all in such circumstances shows that
much of what investment and development did take place
directly conditioned the prospects of farming.

The depression was at length liquidated by the discovery

[1] Mr. Keynes' analysis of the financial history of the period will be found
in Chapter XXX of his *Treatise*.
[2] Estimate taken from tables quoted by Robertson, *Industrial Fluctuations*.
[3] From Professor Day's index set forth in Chapter II.
[4] From the Wheat number of *Index* (Svenska Handelsbanken) by Mr.
Broomhall.
[5] *Statist* index.   [6] See the *Agricultural Crisis*, p. 21.

of new forms of investment—electricity, communications, chemicals, and non-ferrous metals, for instance—all encouraged by abundant supplies of gold and cheap credit. Agriculture shared in the revival and nothing much more in the way of farm depression was heard of until after the Great War.   There was of course a sharp recession in 1907–8, when purchasing power was broken in the industrial and financial collapse.   Farm prices in the United States fell precipitately by 18 per cent.   But this loss was wholly recovered within the next three or four years.   A certain amount of overproduction from 1904 to 1906 may have been responsible as well, but the condition was not chronic.

Although the depression of the 'nineties had its moments of rapid decline, its general character was one of slow deflation—a gradual submergence of profits under falling prices.   Compared to this the slump of 1920–2 was a cloudburst.   From a condition of trade in which American farmers received a gross income of $1,700 millions in 1919, they descended to $900 millions in 1921 ; [1] and net receipts fell from nearly ten millions to four and a half. [2]   Prices of field crops in the United States fell 58 per cent., and of animal products, 37 per cent. [3]   In England the respective declines were 45 and 40 per cent. [4]   The rest of the world repeated the story.

On the side of agriculture a leading cause of the debacle was, as usual, overproduction.   America and the neutral countries had increased production in order to supply the belligerents, whose agricultural output was seriously reduced by the war, and which did not at once recover.   The output of the United States by 1920 had increased 18 per cent. over 1911–13. [5]   Such countries as Australia also reached peaks in output.   But by 1920 Europe was beginning to recover, and in that year it became evident that the total supply was in excess of the world's capacity to buy at current prices.   But the overproduction that took place was in the

[1] Estimates from U.S. Bureau of Agriculture Bulletins.
[2] Estimates of Dr. King in *National Income and its Purchasing Power*.
[3] From U.S. Statistical Abstract.
[4] Quoted from Dampier Whetham, op. cit.
[5] From U.S. Statistical Abstracts.

nature of the case, since it occurred so rapidly and without the stimulus of new methods, comparatively small compared with the overproduction with which the world was faced in 1893 and 1929. More important as a precipitating cause of the 1920 crisis was the conclusion of the replenishment of stocks of food and raw material which followed the Armistice. The pressure of demand during the war had stripped stocks, more especially of raw materials which are normally carried longer than foods, and the process of rebuilding stocks constituted an enormous addition to demand. In these circumstances the gradual recovery in European production failed to lower prices ; indeed, demand outran agricultural prices, which continued rising until the eve of the collapse. But when at length stocks were restored the extra support to demand was withdrawn. This event was rapidly succeeded by a collapse in final purchasing power due to the conclusion of a working capital boom in general.[1]

Just as the world found it necessary or desirable to replenish its stocks of food and agricultural raw materials, so it was necessary or desirable to re-create working capital in all its forms. Manufacturers' and dealers' inventories both of finished and intermediate goods had to be brought up to a long-delayed normal. And the putting of a vast volume of materials and labour into process was the necessary preliminary to restoring a normal level of final output. The normal volume of stocks and goods in process probably approximates in value to half of a year's national income in most countries, and if we may take it that the level of stocks, etc., had fallen one-third by December, 1918, the world had two months' extra work to do. If the extra quantity of factors of production that could be mobilised for the purpose was not more than 10 per cent. of normal supply, the boom would run about eighteen months, which it did.[2]

[1] I have followed Mr. Keynes' account of the post-war boom in Chap. XXX of his *Treatise*.

[2] Or rather two years if we allow that the U.S. was expanding stocks prior to the Armistice, and that stocks continued growing after the 1920 price collapse had already begun. In Chapter IX I argue that thirty months is a reasonable estimate for the production period, but of course a shorter period is in order if sadly depleted stocks provide an incentive for overtime work, and if the building up begins in most commodities almost simultaneously.

When stocks were at length repleted and goods in process began emerging in finished form, prices must suddenly decline and heavy unemployment would commence.   This was especially so since very little fixed investment, except in houses, was going on,[1] and savings were high since the public was making good its drafts on savings during the war.[2]   Once the decline in prices had begun, stocks were then allowed to run down again, in order to avoid losses on inventories, and through fright, so that the decline was carried still a stage further.   Hence, among other phenomena of the collapse, an agricultural crisis.

In Europe the disequilibrium liquidated itself rather gradually.   Distressed trade became uncomfortable subnormal trade, and then later passed into the mild and uneasy upward phase of the cycle that reached its peak in 1928–9. In the United States, on the other hand, 1920–2 had a quick reaction in the activity of 1923–4, during which a second attempt was made to build up working capital.   By that time the whole apparatus of post-war American prosperity was in motion, accompanied by a variety of technical innovations ;   and good trade continued until 1929 with only a minor intermission in 1926–7.

The ultimate collapse of 1929–30 was of course due to a variety of causes, not so susceptible to an inclusive explanation as the slump of 1920.   Perhaps the two principal reasons were the necessarily temporary, because artificial, investment boom of 1925–8, and, once more, agricultural oversupply under the inspiration of technical reform.   The pace of fixed investment, expressed very largely in foreign lending to agricultural debtor countries, was quite out of relation to the rates of interest that the war had left as legacy ;   and it was only a question of time before the investment collapse should expose agricultural oversupply. The relations of these two disequilibria are a topic of the next chapter.

---

[1] Ref. the *Economist's* total of new London issues.

[2] e.g. the American percentage of time to total bank deposits began growing from 23 in 1918 to 35 in 1923.

CHAPTER VI

PROBLEMS OF OVERPRODUCTION

Limits of Study.—The overproduction of agricultural staples may ensue from cyclical changes in supply or demand or from either a permanent decline in demand or technical improvement in the conditions of supply. The cyclical elements in overproduction are examined elsewhere. Here the most important subject for study is of technical change in production. Our concern is with those tendencies to, and facts of, post-war agricultural overproduction which have put agriculture out of gear with industry. It is conceivable perhaps that there is some ideal relation between the two—some optimum ratio of interchange that is a condition of maximum productivity in both spheres. The search for this optimum, as such, is not our task, except so far as the optimum ratio is also an equilibrium ratio. Of all the methods of approach to this equilibrium, we must select, in order to permit of topical illustration, the method of supposing the exchange values of manufactured goods, and of all the factors of production, to be constant. Then we may deal in isolation with changes in the exchange value of agricultural products, as affected by changes in the methods of combining or utilising the factors of production engaged. It may be as well also to study such physical conditions of demand as the number of the world's bread-eating mouths. That is to say, our immediate objectives are technical improvement in supply and the general changes that have affected demand, of which the size and distribution of world population are not the least important.

It is probably an important first approximation to equilibrium that technical and technological improvement in agriculture should not outpace population, which, broadly speaking, governs demand. Similarly, it is desirable that

99

technical advance in agriculture and in other industry should so far proceed at the same rate as not to cause congestion in established channels of trade. If all productive resources were very mobile, changes in the ratio of agricultural and industrial interchange would probably have no important secondary consequences. As it is, the problem of overproduction has immobility and rigidity as its prime constituent, and the pyramiding of dislocation, via spreading unemployment, as a good second.

Productivity and Population.—Whereas the world population in the decade preceding the war increased at the rate of 1 per cent. per annum, the post-war rate of increase has been only half. That the population has increased at all seems at first sight to widen the market for agricultural goods. But the new population may be of agricultural producers. It is a matter of some importance whether population has grown most in agricultural areas. As it happens, the fastest growth of population has been in South and North America, in lands where not only is the expansibility of agriculture greatest, but where the output/labour ratio is greatest. The growth in population has largely taken place in those countries and in association with those circumstances in which agricultural operations might extend even more. Whatever the growth in population has been due to, whether or not it has been controlled by economic opportunities, it has been associated with improvement and increase in the means of transport and communication, of irrigation, fencing, and all those other developments which comprise the opening up of areas in some sense virgin. The extension of wheat cultivation into the Arctic Circle, and of crops and stock in general into areas of drought or former impenetrability, are not an unimportant part of the recent agricultural expansion.

Most of this expansion has been accomplished by systems of farming in which the output/labour ratio is rather high, or systems in which labour has not been a limiting factor.

Roughly the same condition has governed expansion on existing acreage—indeed, it has been a governing factor in the introduction of mechanisation that the land was being extensively exploited. There is no room for machines on peasant holdings. So it was in areas of large productivity per head that mechanisation and other technical developments have further increased production. This in itself would tend to produce disequilibrium between productivity and population. It is an aggravation that much of the technical improvement has been labour-saving, as witness the migration of nearly a million people from the soil of the United States between 1924 and 1929. The new productivity has made population superfluous. Perhaps some day the cheapening of food and clothing will stimulate its own neutralisation in the shape of extra mouths to feed and backs to clothe—or at least, it may, if that cheapness does not involve sustained disequilibrium and unemployment. For the time being unemployment has diminished purchasing power.

Similar developments in industry, equally labour-saving, have added to unemployment, and contributed a further quota to the congestion of agricultural supply. Some estimates of unemployment in the Western World prior to the slump [1] seem to indicate that pure technological unemployment may already have reached an average proportion of 10 per cent. If this curtailed the total demand for marketed staple crops by as much as 5 per cent. directly, to say nothing of further repercussions, the quantitative importance is obvious.

Probably more important is the decline in the rate of increase in world population. The fairly nice adjustment of agricultural expansion to demand which was an agreeable feature of the nineteenth century depended very largely on an ever-expanding population, for population is the main regulator of demand for staple products. Naturally the equilibrium ratio between productivity and population was not constant, as there were other variables, such as the standard of living. Whenever the mechanism of equilibrium was functioning adequately, an increase in the standard of living could take up the slack of technical advance in production. Among the conditions precedent to such an

[1] J. Hilton, *Real Wages and Unemployment.*

increase in real incomes were, first, that man should have been made efficient rather than redundant ; secondly, that most of the leading industries should advance in step, and preserve some constancy in the various ratios of interchange ; and thirdly, that the means of productive advance should largely have consisted of capital creation, like railway construction, in order to use up those extra savings which a rise in real incomes will promote.

The Latent Maladjustment.—In the post-war period none of these conditions has been adequately fulfilled. Technological advance, wherever it has occurred, has tended to save labour, and in agriculture, capital also. Tractors, to say nothing of better seed and fertiliser, have absorbed less capital than, for instance, the railway building which would have been necessary equivalently to expand output in earlier days. Again, agriculture has gone ahead of the ruck of industry and commerce as a whole. The demand for raw produce being inelastic, the terms of trade have gone against raw produce countries and, among other consequences, magnified their external debts. In terms of money, there has been a fall in the gross income of agriculture available for purchase from the non-agricultural community. The consumer may have saved on his raw produce bill, but he has not used the proceeds to buy more raw produce, except in special lines like fruit and eggs, and to a less extent meat. On the whole there has been a diversion of purchasing power from the familiar staples to luxury goods, and indeed from commodities as a whole to services and " service."

Possibly the extent of the new adaptations, or attempted adaptations, has not in itself been beyond reason, but the period for assimilation has been too brief. Had the period been longer there might have been the possibility of using the unlimited diversity of human wants to turn away resources from saturated industries and establish reciprocal trade relations in respect of pairs of new commodities. This possibility is much limited, however, in the context of agricultural over-supply, by the specialised nature of agriculturally used resources.

When a technical revolution in supply coincides with a diversion to new varieties of demand ; when latent productivity per head, apart from technical gains, outstrides the growth in population ; and when all these changes and events disperse themselves unevenly among industries and countries, it would be a miracle if the disorganisation did not proceed so far as to fall into a vicious circle.   Not only are the conditions unfavourable for a translation of augmented productivity into an improved standard of life, but there is a certainty that maladjustment will impose a fall in total production so soon as the economic structure begins to disintegrate.

Ever since the beginnings of the agricultural revolution, from 1923 onwards, there has been at least a latent disorganisation.   Apart from the fact that technical reform did not reach alarming intensity and extent until the latter years of cyclical upswing, the upward phase itself neutralised over-productivity and plastered over all those cracks in the structure which made their due appearance when the boom ended.   The boom, such as it was, provided sources of demand.   Millions of labourers were employed in constructional works all over the world ; incomes per head were high, and rising ; and general unemployment fell to fairly manageable proportions.   The day of reckoning was postponed.

That much might have been written about industry as a whole, for manufacturing industry was also working up for overproduction, and shared in the gain, if it was a gain, of postponement.   There are nevertheless abundant special sources of maladjustment peculiar to agriculture.   The worst excesses of rampant protectionism have been applied to agricultural produce.[1]   Continental Europe surpassed

---

[1] The cereals have been especially afflicted.   Tariffs of 200 per cent. have made their appearance, and so have bounties, export subsidies, guaranteed prices, import quotas, and " home-grown " quotas.   To take wheat as an example, the German tariff, to say nothing of supplementary measures, was quintupled between 1928 and 1931, and in France and Italy, more than doubled.   The German specific duties are now more than three times the price.   It is easy to see, granted the constant aim of excluding American imports, that the tariffs must move in a vicious spiral.

itself in the grossest forms of fiscal shamelessness, which only a few years previously would have been accounted open indecency. This example was not lost on other continents. Almost all countries of any agricultural importance protected their high cost capacity from the onslaught of the cheaper output of regions where the former limiting factors were overthrown by the technical revolution. Again, there was a series of misconceived or misdirected restriction schemes (rubber, sugar, etc.) which merely led to an increase in productive capacity. The surrender of hard labour to machines diminished men's needs of bulky foodstuffs like bread, and habit, as such, has probably switched over for good to meat, fruit and dairy produce. The horse as a consumer of cereal crops is also on the decline.

" Technological " Disequilibrium.—Of all these special agricultural difficulties probably the more important arise out of the agricultural revolution itself. All rapid technical changes lead to over-expansion and to the assumption of extravagant commitments by individual producers, as if they alone had cheapened their cost. The rate of liquidation of these commitments depends on their duration, and that is, in practice, on the life of leases contracted, machinery installed, trees planted, stock bred, new acres broken up, fertiliser put down, outhouses built, and so on. The evil of over-commitment in these directions is particularly severe, when, as is usual, the new activity synchronises with the tempting price level of a general trade boom. Supply by established methods of working may be inelastic enough, but no such rigidity applies to the institution of new methods and appliances which would soon diminish working cost. As Mr. Robertson has pointed out,[1] there is an element in normal inelasticity of supply which aggravates the tendency to over-expand in response to new technical opportunities. During the gestation period of working by new methods, no enlarged output emerges such as would depress prices and call a halt to expansion. Again, given the highly competitive nature of the leading agricultural industries,

[1] *Industrial Fluctuations*, Chap. II.

the institution of new methods and appliances on farms to which they were suited would necessarily force some other sort of expansion on other farms, even by the development of older methods, and their more intensive application. In the special case of European-grown cereals, competition, if it can be so called, was effected collectively, by protection. But fiscal protection by no means exhausted the efforts of the higher cost capacity (or of the respective governments) to maintain a place in the market.

The world story of agricultural borrowings during the boom period makes it clear that new capacity was being financed even in areas where the new technology was not or could not have been applied. Not the whole of this, however, would represent an effort to cope with the gradually falling price level. It is also a regular phenomenon of the upward phase of the cycle that monetary and other financial conditions favour productive expansion. Mr. Rowe made this especially clear in his studies of Brazilian coffee, and traced the connection between foreign loans, a buoyant exchange, a liberal domestic bank policy, and the planting of surplus coffee trees. To some extent, nevertheless, agricultural expansion must have been inspired by the falling price level on the principle of equalising gross receipts or of diminishing unit overhead costs. It is not otherwise possible to explain the increased output of a number of European countries which have never known cheap money. Furthermore, the export programmes of Russia, particularly of cereals, appear to have been framed with the market price in view, in order to maximise gross receipts, more or less irrespective of domestic costs. Apart from the importance of negative elasticity of supply, from Russia or elsewhere, it is a matter of quantitative importance that the Five-Year Plan followed, and did not precede, the technological revolution in agricultural method. Russia, in consequence, had the opportunity of nearly doubling her more normal expectation of increased physical output.

One other commercial aspect of the technical developments, particularly in arable farming, deserves some special attention. Normally, when producers have come into a position to reduce their unit cost, they have the alternatives of taking the immediate profit either by increasing output or by diminishing aggregate cost. The final equilibrium position usually embraces a blend of the two. But it was a special feature of many of the technical developments with which we are concerned, that larger output was essential for their efficient utilisation. A tractor working at low capacity is less economical than no tractor at all. Furthermore, the optimum capacity of a tractor is vast in relation to that of the animal labour which it displaced. Only such characteristics of relative potential scale could justify the purchase of self-propelling machines, which are initially expensive per unit of the former limiting factor, horse-power. Similar considerations apply to combines, threshers, drying machines, mechanical milking appliances, sanitary cowsheds for intensive " grazing," concrete silos, and so forth. The institution of plant increased output irreversibly. Moreover, the plant, by saving labour, increased the ratio of output to men. The more production for which a man is directly or indirectly responsible, whether as labourer or supervisor, the larger, and usually impossibly larger, becomes the curtailment of output which would justify dispensing with a man. In terms of successive men, output has become vastly discontinuous. Lastly, there is this special feature of expansion by means of machinery, that the machinery itself is available as a security for loans to support the general agricultural activity.

The Agricultural Revolution.—Although the installation of agricultural machinery has been one of the most characteristic features of the period, it stands by no means alone in responsibility for the unprecedented enhancement of productivity. We may as well notice the several leading developments separately.

Botanical : Seed Selection.—Quick-maturing and drought-resisting cereals, especially wheat, have made remarkable progress. When the former limitations are overcome, all the valuable qualities of seed and environment have full play. Other successful seed experiments have been made on disease resistance and on the overcoming of mechanical and chemical imperfections of the soil. · There is also nowa-days a greater readiness among farmers to select seed more carefully. Other botanical and allied improvements have been registered in the fields of mycology, insect control, and the closer adaptation of methods of cultivation to the requirements of plant nutrition. Some distinguished gains in mycological and bacteriological control have been achieved in cold storage and canning, which diminish the waste on large annual crops.

Veterinary.—More selective breeding, the evolution of new strains, control of insect-borne and other microbic disease, and economies on feedstuffs without injuring the animal. The modern cow is only allowed a few per cent. more carbohydrates, proteins, etc., than she can profitably utilise. A wider variety of artificial feedstuffs is now used, and hours of milking have been re-arranged. In sheep farming a notable reform has been the standardisation of types of wool, followed by breeding and rearing for those types, with minimum waste.

" Agrarian Reform."—In the Old World there have been many and various attempts to foster production by splitting up large estates ; settling smallholders ; augmenting security of tenure ; making available cheaper and more appropriate credit ; instituting grading and inspection ; establishing experimental farms ; providing facilities for testing and advice ; and in some countries by efforts to elevate the physical and economic condition of the farm labourer. Other collectively provided advantages, more particularly in the New World, include elevators, pre-cooling stations, branch railways, special railway cars for perishable and refrigerated produce, and co-operative method in buying, selling, consigning, storing, grading and marketing.

Fertilisers.—The prices of some typical fertilisers fell by 20 per cent. between 1924 and 1929. This encouraged a more widespread use, and with use came experience and education. The use of fertiliser was in any case on the upgrade, and it is gradually displacing farmyard dung, even on mixed farms.

Mechanisation.—The utility of mechanised method is not

exhausted in the increased output of cereals, where such methods are fairly widespread, but extends to animal farming wherever the current practice is to market crops on the hoof. Nevertheless, the prime importance of agricultural machinery, most of it petrol-driven, lies with cereals, and wheat farming has benefited or suffered the most. In the special case of wheat, hardly any secondary consequences impinge on animal farming, and the mechanical appliances, particularly the combine, are not well adapted for handling straw, nor is straw the most valuable part of the crop as it frequently is in Europe. Accordingly, mechanisation is characteristic chiefly of extensive arable farming. Its main economic impact has been on labour.

Mr. Enfield,[1] in a survey of the world wheat situation, 1931, quotes statements that the number of hours of labour per acre in reaping and threshing has been reduced to one hour or less, from 35 or more with pure hand labour, or from four to five with the semi-mechanised methods in use only a few years ago. At a low estimate the average gain on full mechanisation has been 80 per cent. of the labour formerly used in these operations. This gain has been supplemented by dispensing with overtime and casual labour, which was always the most expensive; and, as Mr. Enfield points out, it is no longer the peak requirements of harvesting that determine the size of the labour force, or productive layout and programmes as a whole. The combine is the greatest labour-saver of all, but its full use has awaited the commercialisation of the petrol engine on a mass-produced scale, and in humid areas, awaited also the invention of methods of drying the grain, so that it might be reaped and threshed in one short continuous operation. Mechanical methods are also in use for ploughing and sowing, and, as a whole, have promoted large-scale farming, with its incidental economies. Tractor-drawn drills, ploughs, harrows, and so forth are also available for the other cereal crops, and some of them can be reaped and freed from straw or leaf by mechanical means only less

[1] *Economic Journal*, December, 1931. I have taken the liberty of summarising some of his valuable material.

economical than in the case of wheat, though continuous operation is still hard to apply.

The suddenness of these mechanical developments may be illustrated by mention of the quadrupling of the annual output of tractors in the United States between 1917 and 1929. Whatever be the extent of the efficient utilisation of the tractor in Russia, it has been achieved with even greater speed. The number of tractors in use in the U.S.S.R. rose twelvefold between 1924 and 1929.[1] As for combines, two-thirds of the 1923-9 sales of the United States were made in the last two years. Canada increased her use of them nearly tenfold between 1927 and 1929, and the Argentine bought about as freely.

The exact savings made by the use of mechanical appliances, or any of them, are difficult to compute, but the order of magnitude can be gauged from the fact that in the United States output per man rose by an average of 25 per cent. between 1924 and 1929. Another item of saving was the release of arable land whose product was otherwise required to feed horses. This was a consequence both of tractors and of automobiles, whether used on and about the farm or in towns.

All these, then, are the leading events in the agricultural world prior to the slump, and they collectively represent an expansion of power to produce that has never before, in modern history, been compressed into so brief a period. At the same time there has been a steady evolution of economy and efficiency in established lines of activity, coupled with the introduction of a host of minor novelties in method, too tedious to notice separately. Furthermore, farmers are adding to their purely professional interests the commercial outlook, and many well-known economies, formerly the prerogative of manufacture, are now to be found on the farm.

Liquidation under " laissez-faire."—In various contexts the general consequences of these technical changes have

---

[1] From the League of Nations' publication, *Course and Phases of the World Economic Depression*. This contains much useful information, on which I have freely drawn.

already been examined, especially with respect to equilibrium. A continued examination in general form, of the various consequences and problems, can now be conveniently combined with a study of restriction of supply. Granted that new conditions for equilibrium in international interchange cannot be improvised, it is in restriction of some sort that we shall find, if it can be found, the cure for the immediate ills of overproduction. Restriction schemes may be full of obvious faults but, compared to tariffs and doles, they are more than palliatives. They are not unlikely, in some instances, to culminate in international action aimed at a permanent cure. Contrasted with most of the alternative nostrums recommended for easing the problem of the farmer, restriction, since international co-operation is generally requisite to a sound scheme, tackles its problems on a more adequate scale. Most of the nationally prescribed remedies have repelled agricultural depression, or attempted to, by passing it on to the nationals of some other region.

Restriction schemes, though less open to that objection, have encountered a good many more. Most people, particularly when the world is impoverished and hungry, look on the curtailment of production, or even the withholding of surplus realised supplies, as blasphemy, absurdity, irony, capitalist conspiracy, the failure of private enterprise, or whatever else excites them. If the controversies aroused by restriction and valorisation have been somewhat inconclusive, and the reproaches, though indignant, a trifle nebulous, the fault has usually been a confusion of dissimilar circumstances. We must distinguish between schemes intended to ward off (permanent) overproduction and schemes instituted to cope with (cyclical) underconsumption, between which the essence of the distinction lies in time.

Let us first deal with overproduction up to the point where its consequences merge with those of underconsumption. For most commodities the root of the difficulty is that old high cost capacity has refused to make its bow and its exit in the face of the entrance of new lower cost capacity. According to theory the fall in price resulting from overproduction should first extinguish marginal activity and then go on to extinguish marginal producers themselves. This exit of high cost capacity would undeniably take time. It would bankrupt most of the reluctant outgoers and cripple the remainder during the struggle. A measure of the total loss would be found in the time taken for the elimination of the surplus capacity, but, after all, it would only be a matter of time. As one by one the outgoing producers disappeared prices would gently ascend to a level that would remunerate the survivors. Eventually an equilibrium would be established at which the average cost of the firms remaining would equal the price obtainable for the aggregate of optimum quantities produced by each. The balloon would gradually deflate itself until in equilibrium with the pressure of the air, but never pop.

The significant theme of this picture is the orderly retirement of redundant producers one by one, as released from their labours by the progress of science. But clearly such a pattern of behaviour requires that the redundant producers enjoy or are afflicted with evenly unequal reserves. They resign in an order of exhaustion of resources, as modified by the character of their private expectations. But the bearing of these spare resources on the behaviour of the producers is not the same for all scales of individual production. If the structure of the industry is oligopoly, a few large-scale undertakings are all likely to possess initial reserves so vast as to be practically equal. The copper producers are of such a kind, and so too the heavy fertiliser producers, many of the tea estates, and the typical Cuban sugar *centrals*. In a sense the wheat pools and other co-operative storage agencies are large producers, capable of giving up the ghost in a large way. Thus the struggle may continue until in despair or poverty several producers, almost equally anguished, retire together. In the case of copper, the retirement of even one of the large-scale units, if that involved the final supersession of the capacity it controlled, might directly lead to a scarcity of the product. Similarly, if the expectations and hopes entertained by a considerable number of largish producers are roughly the same, they may make something of a simultaneous exit.

Even small-scale producers are liable to behave as a body, and this is not unlikely to be the end of the native rubber producers.

It is only fair to say that these remarks, made in some scepticism of *laissez-faire*, envisage the possible rather than the probable, though the probability of debacle in some industries is by no means negligible. Agriculture is less likely to see large-scale retirements than mining, it is true, but the unorganised condition of agriculture enhances the danger of disorderly contraction. It needs no elaborate demonstration to show that abandoned farms cannot be easily reoccupied and re-equipped should the exit of high cost capacity go too far.

Unfortunately also, it is not necessarily the high cost capacity that will be forced out. Mr. Rowe has already noticed that the distress of such producers will not for certain lead to a disappearance of capacity but merely to a metamorphosis of ownership. The former producers may sell their businesses at low valuations on which others can make a profit. Or, after writing down capital, the original producers may be in a position to earn tolerable dividends, or at least expect to do so. The consequence is that price must dip below prime cost before the surplus capacity will go. When that happens, small producers, and any others whose reserves are small, no matter how efficient their production, will be forced out, possibly suddenly and in large numbers. In such matters, at extremes of despair, one may behave as in a herd. So long as the price was above prime cost, though below equilibrium, the adjustment of supply to demand might take place fairly gradually. No one was drastically squeezed at the moment. But when price falls below prime cost, particularly in industries where supply is physically inelastic, an immediate and widespread devastation is almost certain. This could not benefit the industry, and might lead to famine. During the period of subnormal prices the technical equipment of the industry might fall into disrepair, and so accentuate shortage in the event of a crash.

Both where the high cost capacity has the largest reserves

and where it deflates capital, it is probably fair to presume that the outgoing producers will not be the least efficient so much as the poorest.   The ultimate supply price may become that of the old-established and sessile but rich or protected section of the industry.   Thus the survivors of the wheat war will probably be the peasantry of Europe, protected from the efficiency of America.   The survivors in rubber are as likely as not to be the old profiteers of the 1926–8 restriction ramp.

In times not remotely past, where the less resistant producers, as in Cuba, have been the backbone of the nation's social economy, not only has the Government been forced into policies of doles and discrimination, but found itself confronted by chronic incipient revolt.   Except for coffee loans, the political volcanoes of Brazil would never have been supposed almost extinct.   India, too, when her competitive power in wheat, cotton and sugar is depressed, finds new reasons for discontent ; and China, when tea and silk are down, almost invites the excursions of opportunist imperialism.   Even if the world pays no more for its staple produce, it trades in the face of crisis and uncertainty.

Overproduction and the Consumer.—The cases where the consumer has to fear shortage as a later consequence of overproduction may be few and extreme.   But the consumer is not the only party whose comfort and prosperity should be our concern ; his direct and indirect interests do not necessarily coincide ; nor does he necessarily receive the benefit of any lower price that may immediately or permanently result.   Let us consider the last possibility forthwith.   The retailer has no obvious motive for marking down particular commodities which have become cheaper at wholesale, even if the costs of marketing and processing are relatively so light that a given fall at the producer's end is visible at the consumer's.   It is true that the retailer, and other middlemen, may add a conventional percentage to each product sold, rather than make a separate calculation of demand.   But this conventional practice is only a provisional convenience   Estimates of elasticity of demand, however crude, are made as well, even if only subjectively.

It is usually in the sale of those commodities judged to be demanded elastically that keen price competition occurs, and in which retail prices follow wholesale with appreciable speed or fidelity. Some of the commodities in question are demanded elastically, because, like bacon, they are on the fringe of working-class luxury, and others are competitive because they are important enough in the budget of the housewife to warrant her transferring her custom when a price discrepancy occurs. Tea and coffee do not enter these lists in Great Britain, nor to any great extent, sugar or bread. So the middleman may very well be the gainer on the given commodity, whether or not he makes a concession on some other. Whether or not this particular analysis, which must be admitted to be speculative, has hit the mark, the width of the gap between numerous farm and shop prices, and its widening during the slump, are now notorious.

Wider Consequences of Overproduction.—Next we have to study the divergence between the consumer's immediate and ultimate interests. In this connection we shall ignore the possibility that the consumer may be nothing but a consumer, but identify him with the whole non-agricultural population, which is also concerned in production.

Now if many agricultural commodities are overproduced, or even some few commodities on which specific national economies vitally depend, a vicious spiral of secondary disorganisation will almost certainly be generated. This disorganisation first afflicts industries specialised to supply primary producers, and then their satellites and clients, directly and indirectly. Then there arises a temptation to over-save, prompted by windfall gains at the producer's expense. Further, there develops a general reluctance to invest, both in the distressed industries themselves, and at large in the countries that depend on them. And finally let us consider the exchange and financial difficulties that afflict debtor countries specialised to agriculture. They may be forced into deflation, which cuts costs and leads to forced sales, or export subsidies or devaluation, or any or all of them. These practices or consequences may be necessary for individual countries and are correct national policy. But they cannot help agriculture as a whole— they assist merely those debtor countries which are enabled to undersell the creditor agricultural countries, if the creditors themselves do not devaluate or erect impassable barriers to trade. So far the debtor countries have reaped some advantage—in particular, the American market for raw produce has been undermined and inroads have been made on France, Holland and Belgium. But in order to solve the agricultural problem by all-round devaluation in mainly agricultural countries, with compensating subsidies for agricultural production in other countries, it would be necessary that the market for agricultural produce be elastic. Or alternatively it would suffice if devaluation served to curtail weak selling by raising incomes in the national devaluated currencies. But neither elasticity of demand above unity nor negative elasticity of supply are commonly found at the price levels which rule during a severe depression.[1] In the absence of these two circumstances favourable to devaluation such a policy is advisable for debtors only—when both creditors and debtors resort to it, in order to relieve agricultural distress, they are more likely to achieve only a further fall in gold prices. This result will embarrass the debtor countries all the more. It will probably go on to force them into import restrictions

---

[1] Mr. Keynes, I believe, has expressed a rather contrary view. He supposes that in the given case (devaluation in producing countries) gold prices will rise, as the gain in local values will diminish anxiety to sell. Producers will hold back for a further rise, and creditors will relax their pressure. It is a condition of this behaviour, on the part of creditors, to begin with, that local prices should have risen. The proportion of the devaluation which is taken out this way is given by the fraction of elasticity of demand divided by elasticity of supply. It is most unlikely to be the full amount of the devaluation. I question whether local prices have yet risen, or that they are likely to rise, in the given circumstances, by enough to make a serious difference to the expectations of creditors, who can only hope to be reimbursed spontaneously when profits begin to emerge. When prices rise a sensible creditor is the more likely to renew his demands for payment. As for the producers themselves, those who withhold realised crops are rarities indeed. Nor have the collective storage agencies, like the Canadian wheat pool, yet behaved as indicated. Although agricultural supply is in many circumstances negatively elastic, those circumstances, as suggested in Chapter II, rarely include the depths of the slump. As a matter of fact, after the devaluations of September, 1931, gold prices went on falling.

which will diminish the market for manufactures, so that prices fall all round and intensify the general slump. If valorisation and restriction are alternatives to large-scale devaluation, they are not industrial expedients alone.

These financial problems, or problems of secondary disorganisation, belong most properly of all to cyclical underconsumption. But they have also a relevance to permanent excess capacity. The distinction between the two types of maladjustment is, as before, merely one of time and accentuation. Whatever the degree of agricultural distress, and however long it lasts, its existence vitiates the whole industrial climate, and obstructs the course of investment and development in the more backward world. Some of the long-drawn-out agricultural depressions of the period 1873–96 were of sufficient scope to generate general economic malaise. Perhaps the deflationary trend of the period was primarily responsible, but there was also at fault the overexpansion of several export crops, following on rapid settlement of new lands and technical change. Although rapid population increase was a standing relief, the mark was overshot. In these days the trend of population is no help : on the contrary, technological unemployment the world over continually tends to depress demand. While these evils last they require something analogous to the remedies that might relieve the specific symptoms of a slump, and then, after palliation, a skilled amputation. These two treatments, in ordinary medical practice, frequently conflict : the patient refuses drastic measures if the preliminary care has relieved his pain. We must see if valorisation is too easy.

Valorisation by Storage.—There are two principal species —the withdrawal of supplies from the market into elevators and warehouses, and arrangements for restricting new production. Neither of these measures eliminates any part of the capacity to produce. If the demand is inelastic, which is usually a principal constituent of the difficulty under treatment, the effect of either method is to augment the aggregate receipts of the industry. Where supply is curtailed there is also the presumption that costs will be diminished.   On the other hand, if storage is the chosen method, it requires that the storing agency possess funds both to buy up the surplus and hold it.   If the funds are co-operatively supplied, for the time being producers will probably, on balance, be out of pocket.   But as a rule the storage authorities manage to finance themselves out of bank loans guaranteed by the Government.   Such, in effect, is the method of the coffee valorisation schemes, and recently, of the Canadian wheat pools.   The Federal Farm Board, and its subsidiary, the Grain Stabilisation Corporation, have likewise been publicly financed.   The final market price must be such as to ensure repayment together with the recoupment of accumulated costs of storage.   These costs, if the average period of storage is two years, will probably amount to about 40 per cent. of outlay.[1]   But whether the capital required for buying up stocks is provided by the State or not, it is usually one of the *raisons d'être* of the scheme that the outlay is swollen by payments to producers above market price.   If 20 per cent. above market price is paid, the final price must have climbed 70 per cent. before complete liquidation can be achieved.[2]

If the commodity valorised is a raw material being cyclically under-consumed, such a recovery is not impossible. Seventy per cent. of the depressed price need not be more than 40 per cent. of the normal price.   The relapse of demand (from normal) therein represented may be found by multiplying 40 per cent. by the elasticity of demand, which is probably a fraction less than one.   If the elasticity is one-half the relapse suffered becomes 20 per cent., which is not abnormal.   If, as seems more probable, the elasticity of demand at wholesale for most raw materials is less than one-half, an even slighter improvement in demand than 20 per cent. will suffice to recoup all costs.   This expected recovery by 20 per cent., on the assumption of elasticity

---

[1] I have found no reason but to accept Mr. Keynes' estimate of 10 per cent. as a typical carrying cost, together with another 10 per cent. for risk.

[2] Forty per cent. to costs and 20 per cent. to subsidies :

$$100 \times \frac{140}{100} \times \frac{120}{100} = 170 \text{ (approx.)}.$$

equal to one-half, which would make the scheme solvent, is only sufficient, however, on the supposition that the stocks are bought when the demand has in fact relapsed just 20 per cent. If on the average stocks were bought in before the full limits of downward fluctuation were attained, the commodity, to satisfy the given conditions, must be subject to a full fluctuation of more than 20 per cent. If the average price were the mean of the normal and the lower limit, the necessary full fluctuation would become 40 per cent. Yet even while still retaining this liberal estimate of elasticity of one-half, and the same supposition as to average buying price, there are two reasons for thinking that a requirement of 40 per cent. in fluctuation is nevertheless too severe. First, when the average buying price is above the low limit of market price, there is less likelihood of supplementary payments to producers—e.g. the 20 per cent. allowed in the above computations. And secondly, the largest single item in carrying cost is the allowance for risk, say 10 per cent. If the valorisation is so thorough as to amount to monopoly the risk item falls away, if indeed it was ever relevant to storage transactions not undertaken with the hope of profit. On the other hand, the estimate of an average period of only two years of storage, even though this is consistent with a period of five years or more for storage as a whole, may be too little. But it is impossible to generalise as to the date by which the stocks are likely to have cleared themselves, as it depends on the degree of overproduction which may be associated with underconsumption. If we accept two years as the average length of storage, and then dispense with risk and supplementary payments, but retain the other assumptions, the necessary fluctuation in demand to which the commodity must be subject is only 15–20 per cent. In all reasonable probability a fluctuation of that order of magnitude would warrant a storage scheme. Or if the elasticity of demand were less than one-half, a smaller fluctuation would do. Fifteen to 20 per cent. is probably a safe minimum, and most storable raw commodities, other than staple foodstuffs demanded with some constancy, would fulfil the condition, if the slump were of at least normal intensity. Wheat should probably be excluded from the list of eligible commodities. It is hard to believe that the elasticity of demand is so low as to justify overlooking the rigidity of it. The possibility of error to which all these judgments are liable is obvious.

The judgments made in practice by those who initiate valorisation schemes are commonly clouded by another sort of error—undue expectation of future short crops. In actual fact three or four years of bumper crops are as likely as a slump in demand and the consequences may be as serious. Overproduction of the order of magnitude of 15 to 20 per cent., on the average of three years, is not unknown. If the next three years or so turn up short crops, equally below par, the scheme is self-liquidating, except for risk and the cost of carrying. But valorisation schemes do not always fairly face the risk that the short crop may be delayed, nor take into account the concurrent growth in capacity. These errors lead to over-sanguine price-fixing.

Although individual valorisation schemes have not infrequently over-estimated the rate at which their commitments were likely to be extinguished, over-estimations and like errors of judgment are not inherent in these schemes. The British Australian, Wool Realisation, and the rubber, coffee, and tin schemes of the 1921 slump, were not combined with any serious gambling on the date of recovery, and were brought to a successful conclusion. But other schemes, even if they have avoided the rocks of speculation, have wrecked themselves on the shoals of overpayment to producers. Such overpayments encourage the entrance of new capacity, or the survival of old redundant capacity, as the case may be, and will overburden the scheme's finances. If the valorised producers are a monopoly, the entrance of new capacity is likely to be the greater evil, as monopoly revenues can be applied to the aid of valorisation finance. But many storage schemes, like those of the Federal Farm Board or of the Canadian wheat pools, have never controlled the market. These, above all, since the chances of successful valorisation are slender, should avoid paying producers more than the market price, or much more than it, especially if they have withheld sufficient stocks already to raise the price. It is true that non-payment of bounties, when prices have not been substantially raised, makes the scheme look futile to the producers, as indeed it always was, but futility should not end in bankruptcy. State doles in these circumstances are preferable by far : to mix up valorisation with subsidies brings both into discredit. The actions of the Federal Farm Board probably had other objectives than subsidy in view, and the inflated prices in part represented payments to farmers at pre-harvest prices, and at prices which had not yet felt the full effect of the current year's crop. The Canadian wheat pools did not escape the same dangers of buying in well before the slump—indeed they bought quite near the boom—and also have acted in effect as a channel for subsidies.

The problems of monopoly valorisations are slightly different. If the price is well under control, there arises a temptation to store too much, especially if the high cost capacity has been active in the arrangements. If the wheat schemes ever had any useful purpose, it was to take over the functions of the merchant speculators, on the ground that large-scale public undertakings were better able to resist the temptation prematurely to sell, and could afford to wait longer to recoup themselves. Here the keenest problems of policy concern buying price and estimates of final or equilibrium price—the same problems that trouble an ordinary vulgar speculator. But when effective monopoly power is enjoyed and the price is determinable at will, the limiting factor becomes the possibility of permanent deterioration in the statistical position. Too rigorous a use of monopoly power may lead to an enlargement of capacity if monopoly revenues are not directed to extra-industrial uses. If chronic over-capacity is generated, the monopoly may crumble from within, or the size of the stocks to be carried may exhaust the valorisers' capital and credit. Exhaustion of capital funds is at the root of the difficulties of Brazil. Coupled with these twin dangers of breakdown, and consequent on them, is the further danger of bear speculation in outside markets. To some extent visible stocks always depress the price, but as Mr. Rowe in his coffee studies has shown, the depression is least, and may be but small, if the stocks are held at a great distance from market, and, if possible, masked. Nevertheless a continuously deteriorating statistical position cannot be disguised for long, and, especially if the market loses confidence in the scheme's capacity to finance itself, speculative selling might yet undermine the whole operation.

Restriction of Production.—Since visible stocks, which are reckoned as potential liquid supply, always weaken the market, curtailment of output appears preferable to storage. It would be rash to dismiss as a mere figment, the common expectation, especially in cases of cyclical slump or bumper crops, that demand will increase or future crops fail, or both. In practice, however, over-optimistic dispositions are not infrequent, and storage drags on indefinitely. In these circumstances, a restriction of output, at least as a supplement to storage, seems indispensable. Such a measure is supremely desirable for the regulation of those commodities of which cyclical overproduction is merely superimposed on a long-period maladjustment. In practice, a combination of storage and restriction, practised concurrently, has not been seen in a pure form. It is more frequent for restriction to follow on the realisation of accumulated unsaleable stocks. The policy then chosen is to stabilise stocks for a year or two, by restricting output to the level of computed demand, and then continue restriction, although the market has improved, until the stocks are absorbed. Such is the essence of the tin and sugar restrictions, and it was the policy of the Rubber Growers' Association in the early days of the Stevenson scheme. Had restriction been practised earlier, or more intensively, the stocks would not have become unmanageable, nor necessitated a continuance of restriction so long into a period of high price and potential profit.

Restriction, needless to say, is infinitely less popular than storage, unless maladjustment is so acute that drastic measures are the obvious only cure. Restriction has the appearance of diminishing the individual's income, possibly a just appearance if stocks are to be worked off before prices can rise, but not a welcome apparition. Storage policies are more usually arranged so as to support the producer's income. Restriction is also an unwelcome intimation of over-capacity, and the thin edge of who knows what wedge. Individuals suppose either that they will be allotted an unfair quota, or that countries outside the scheme will take advantage of it. The American cotton farmers refused to curtail their sowings, and rejected a proposal that they should plough in one out of every three growing furrows. On the other hand, the more commercially minded rubber growers of Ceylon and Malaya found no great difficulty in accepting either the principle or practice of restriction. Some greater reluctance was felt by the oil producers of Texas and Oklahoma, but in 1931 they were overborne by the Governors of these states, who compulsorily closed and picketed wells, on the ground that the states could not afford to lose natural resources in oil for less than one dollar per barrel. These are exceptions. Generally it is only large-scale producers, so organised as to form agreements easily, who will consent to or be able to enforce restriction. Large-scale producers rather than family farmers will best appreciate restriction as a means of reducing prime cost, which storage does not, and they will better realise that storage is expensive. Also, if permanent overproduction is in prospect, large producers will be the readiest to contemplate and arrange restriction at least, if not amputation of capacity, especially if their own capacity is marginal. Restriction is nearly always *pro rata*, but the extinction of surplus capacity, however it comes about, may be expected to go furthest in the marginal regions. When overproduction is desperate, governments, as well, may find no alternative but to co-operate by enforcing restriction on a multitude of small producers. As a rule governments find tariffs a line of much less resistance, and sugar is the only clear example of present-day international restriction.

It is clear generally that valorisation in some form is not

an unreasonable method of combating overproduction, or any other circumstances in which supply and demand have temporarily diverged. The case for such treatment is strengthened by the frequent unwillingness or inability of ordinary speculators to carry the whole of the surplus crop, or any part of it, over a period so long as, say, four years. Generally speaking, orderly centrally governed marketing according to a planned policy is preferable to disintegrate *laissez-faire.* But here in agriculture, as everywhere, creep in the dangers of monopoly and inertia in the face of obvious long-standing maladjustment. The sugar interests, as far as is known, have decided to do no more than curtail acreage for the time being ; tea and tin aim no higher. Apparently all the producers are to work below capacity until stocks are cleared. Perhaps in the meantime some of the higher-cost producers will get bored by the quota and sell up.

The courses of possible development within the restriction area may be most diverse. The ruling factor is the level to which stocks have already attained. So long as large stocks are present, the likelihood of prices rising to any great extent is small, and the restriction should not be undermined by the entrance of new capacity.

On the other hand, if surplus stocks were not the reason for restriction, then the aim of the scheme is usually to effect a *pro rata* curtailment of production in general in the interests of the high-cost capacity. The method will probably be the fixation of a pivotal price requisite for the covering of high cost or, more usually, of intermediate cost. Either pivotal price may be its own undoing unless restriction is enforced against expansion in the low-cost group. Past valorisation schemes have suffered also from the development of capacity outside the restriction area. Chilean nitrate, U.S. copper, Cuban sugar, and Ceylon plus Malayan rubber, are cases in point. The earlier aim of each of these restriction or analogous schemes was comparatively modest—to clear stocks, regularise marketing and protect the high cost. Later on, in the cases of copper, nitrate and rubber, attempts at monopolistic exploitation supervened, and nemesis was not far behind. It does not follow, however, that some more judicious pivotal price could not have been established, which would have warded off overproduction in the restriction area without expanding the unrestricted. A repetition of the greedy price-fixing policy which was in fact pursued is not in prospect for the commodities which have lately taken to restriction. Nearly all of them are faced with glutted markets and surplus stocks, and exploitation of the consumer is out of the question. Unless an unprecedented degree of restriction is enforced, too high a pivotal price, or its equivalent, will prolong the period of restriction beyond endurance. Accordingly, in the instances of sugar, tea and tin, to take notable examples of present-day restriction, time is fighting against the institution of exploitive monopoly.

The pivotal price is a familiar piece of regulative mechanism, whose working Mr. Rowe has closely examined in relation to rubber, but the more recent restriction schemes appear to be using the volume of stocks as a pivot. This method diminishes whatever danger of greed otherwise existed, though it is impossible to dismiss the fear that a pivotal price will be annexed to the scheme, as happened in rubber, so soon as the problem of stocks has declined to manageable dimensions.

Unless an injudicious pivotal price is incorporated in a restriction scheme, its general effect, with relevance to the fundamentals of adjustment, is to preserve the status quo. So soon as surplus stocks are worked off, and restriction nominally ceases, the problem is presented once more of coping with chronic oversupply, if such was latent throughout the restriction period. The restriction itself has been a bromide. In medical practice it is convenient to soothe the system in the hope that natural recuperative forces will seize their chance. In the world of agricultural oversupply, the opportunity is presented to high-cost capacity of re-equipping, and to the whole industry of instituting co-operative self-help. In mild cases of oversupply such measures may be sufficient to restore the industry and most of the firms to equilibrium. Even if the period of standstill is not used for readjustment, it has this further merit : If attempts were made at the height of the slump to weed out surplus capacity, it is almost certain that any measures which seemed adequate then would, by the time trade had recovered, have become too drastic.   A restriction scheme, by postponing reorganisation until trade in general has reached normality, isolates the long-period elements of the problem to be faced.   If it be argued that a history of restriction, during which time the most pressing evils of oversupply had been abated, would make subsequent pruning seem unnecessary, the reply is that restriction and other efforts at conscious control are more likely than not to reconcile producers to stern action.   The history of many rationalised industries shows that a prelude of controlled competition—for instance, oligopoly—was necessary to insinuate the idea that any competition, in the circumstances, was a mere barbarity.   Even the story of Brazil shows that partial control paved the way to so heroic a course as the statutory prohibition of new planting.   In the liquidation of oversupply, as everywhere, the last known encroachment on *laissez-faire* becomes the standard for judging successive proposals. A successful restriction scheme implants the idea of centralised regulation as a norm, from which the suppression of certain capacity is not out of reach.   Some writers have felt sceptical about this line of argument, but, at all events, it has not yet been shown that any other course of action, or even inaction, was more likely to end in conscious reorganisation.   Rather it is probable, in the absence of valorisation, that the slump, following on secular overproduction, would have plunged some raw-produce industries into sheer debacle, and left the others plunging in quicksands where the most tenacious struggler does not always survive.

Curtailment of Capacity.—Whatever be our hopes for the future of currently restricted industries, nothing deliberate has yet been done, either in these industries or any others, to eliminate redundant capacity.   In most instances, equilibrium, at the end of vistas of oversupply, is not yet within sight, nor has the low cost capacity won its battle against the high. Hence it is not entirely barren to suggest one or two courses of possible policy.

Presumably, it is not impossible for single governments, like Brazil, or consortia of governments, to extinguish surplus capacity by fiat. But in practice, democracy likes its pills gilded. Mr. Rowe has made a suggestion that the governments of exporting countries should collect a special export tax and use the proceeds for buying out surplus producers. It is an advantage of the proposal that export taxes are not new. Despite the indignation of the United States, most raw-material countries use them as a staple source of revenue. Brazil, now having raised the tax, is using the surplus yield to buy and destroy coffee. But in Mr. Rowe's words, Brazil would be better advised to use the tax on coffee to confer bounties on firewood. The existing stocks would take care of themselves, or take care of themselves better, if so many million trees were permanently put out of production. Since the export tax has the appearance of being paid by the producer, the dangers of abuse of monopoly are not very great.

On the other hand, it is a pity to recognise the nuisance values created by high-cost producers. It is hard to ask anyone to make a contribution to the support of vested interest. Also, to the extent that the tax is paid by the producer, and curtails capacity in general, that favours the continuance of high-cost capacity until its nuisance value is greater.

Accordingly, some measure even more Gilbertian than that of the state buying out its citizens seems preferably indicated. The governments should fix a maximum price, substantially below prospective market price, and, to enforce it, become a monopoly buyer. The maximum price would be a clear sign to the marginal producers that they have nothing to hope for or expect. They will not be paid, nor will the maximum price be raised until they have gone. The receipts (market price less maximum price) could be used to remit taxation or institute technical reorganisation. We may confidently expect, nevertheless, that though the most efficient means will necessarily be the most Draconian, nothing drastic will in fact be done. Instead, the tea industry will continue advertising that beverage in India, and the wheat interests will continue baiting the Russian bear.

PART II
THE RESPONSIBILITY OF AGRICULTURE
FOR TRADE CYCLES

CHAPTER VII

SOME THEORIES OF THE TRADE CYCLE

Methodology.—This chapter is not intended to be an exhaustive critique of trade cycle theories. It merely notes some difficulties that have been encountered in the application of a few leading theories to the sort of facts discussed in these pages. We will begin with a consideration of the respectable theories, and work up to the meteorological theories. The latter use the organisation and instability of agriculture as a link in the chain supposed to connect pure physical phenomena with general economic fluctuation. Study of the meteorological theories will lead on to a consideration of alternative views on the part played by agriculture. It will be seen that agricultural and meteorological theories are separable, and that the former do not imply the latter. But first of all it is worth noticing that almost all trade cycle theories fall into one of four classes :

(*a*) In the first case the trade cycle is supposed to be self-generative in the sense that the economic system is inherently unstable and, apart from secular change, unable to maintain equilibrium. Any movement in one direction, either in the direction of slump or boom, continues until some limiting factor is reached. The action of the limiting factor or factors leads to a recoil, which in turn carries trade toward the limits on the opposite side. The momentum of change is relatively independent of, or could arise without the intervention of, any disturbance outside the system.

(*b*) The presumption of inherent instability is retained, but it is not supposed that reaction from the limits of oscillation is necessarily forcible enough to drive trade to the opposite extreme. The instability would work itself out in a series of oscillations of diminishing dimension. At times, however, the course of diminution would be interrupted by special events, such as inventions, wars, currency changes, and so forth, which would enlarge the amplitude of fluctuation and defer indefinitely the attainment of equilibrium. In the United States the fluctuations of 1920–3, 1923–6, and 1926–8, were successively milder. Possibly this might be interpreted as above, or possibly in relation to some larger movement occupying the period 1920–8. In the former case, it would not be difficult to find reasons why the amplitude of instability, from 1928 onwards, violently increased, and finally exceeded that of 1920–3.

(c) To some extent the third case merges with the second. In the section just considered the energising force of instability was spasmodic or accidental : here we conceive of some regular irruption of forces initially generated more or less outside the economic system, but impinging on it at critical moments. For instance, a regular fluctuation in harvests might impart instability to trade at large by inhibiting equilibrium at large. At any moment when the course of trade was hesitative it would be susceptible to the effect of the regular harvest variation, and be launched on a course of variation in sympathy.

(d) In the last case, the external or semi-external periodic disturbance, of which climatic variation may be taken as the type, is supposed to energise throughout and to govern the fluctuation in general trade. Hence it follows that the timing of the trade cycle and its length are functions of the external cause. This view implies either that the behaviour of the industrial organisation is extremely tractable to the external rhythm, or that the external rhythm agrees well with the intrinsic variability of the system. In a subvariety of this scheme, the external rhythm is allowed to be relatively ineffective for a time, but regains command over periods which are small multiples of the (say) physical cycle. For instance, Professor H. S. Jevons is prepared to count two or three harvest cycles to every one cycle in general trade, and supposes the latent force of the earlier cycles to be cumulative.

These four main schemes have been arranged in a sequence

running from pure internal to pure external causation. The extreme positions on either side tend to be mono-theoretical and mechanistic. We shall now examine some such positions associated with the hypothesis of self-generation, and then work towards the equally rigorous views of the specialists on weather.

Monetary Theories.—Most of the monetary theories of the trade cycle assume that the course of credit provision is inherently unstable. The engine of this instability is the semi-automatic behaviour of the banking system, which relaxes or contracts credit alternately after commitments are already meagre or unduly extended. The banks allow the credit machine to get out of control before they apply the brake, and it almost ceases motion before they resort to the accelerator. Two of the strongest writers who employ these beliefs are Messrs. Hawtrey and Robertson. The former looks to the behaviour of the banks as almost an ultimate initiating cause : the latter sees it as a proximate force, through which the fundamental disequilibria work.

Mr. Hawtrey's familiar position [1] seems to consist in a view about the variability of dealers' stocks in relation to the cost of carrying them. When banks have unemployed funds, they lower the rate of interest, and this tempts dealers to enlarge their orders, and so set in motion a boom.

The banks have now to finance both a larger volume of trade and any rise in the cost of production (e.g. in wage rates) that may have occurred. Beyond a point their capacity to finance this inflated turnover is exhausted, and, indeed, they take alarm at the growth in their liabilities. Hence a resort to contraction. If the momentum of trade expansion is strong a severe contraction becomes necessary to cope with it, and therefore, when the impetus of the boom is overcome, trade plunges into the depths. Recovery ensues when interest rates have become low enough, and the terms of lending attractive enough, to arrest and over-bear the momentum of decline.

Some of this, when suitably presented, seems self-evident.

[1] *Currency and Credit ; Trade and Credit.*

When the cost of holding stocks is interpreted to mean marginal cost, and when the rate of interest is viewed as a deterrent as well as a cost, it becomes reasonable to suppose that stocks will tend to vary with the rate of interest, unless subject to stronger discordant influences, perhaps such as that of varying consumers' purchasing power. But what in fact is the correspondence between changes in stocks and changes in the quantity of trade ? Mr. Hawtrey appears to claim that dealers' orders will stimulate trade so much that the rise in consumer incomes will draw off more stocks than ordered, and conversely. Hence stocks would be low during the boom and high during the slump.[1] Statistical test is difficult to apply. The evidence of such compilations as those of the London and Cambridge service—of the stocks of mainly raw commodities—is doubtful so far as a rise in visible stocks merely means that dealers are unwilling to buy while the supply is inelastic. A priori reasoning would suggest that the maximum of (dealers' non-speculative) stocks was attained just after the peak of the boom, and the minimum just before the trough.[2] In the first case stocks would accumulate because new output could not be readjusted to relapsing demand. In the second place stocks would fall during the slump because, as far as is known, falling prices make it risky to hold stocks. The minimum would be attained just before the slump because once the minimum is attained, prices must necessarily rise—dealers must either buy more or sell less. Mr. Hawtrey's position would seem to imply quite a different course of events, particularly during the slump, for in his scheme dealers are unable to evacuate stocks as rapidly as the public is curtailing purchases. This is probably true for stocks as a whole, when we include stocks that dealers are unwilling to hold, but these stocks are residuals, and the result of the condition of trade. Again, that changes in trade are not caused even indirectly by movements in the rate of interest

[1] Mr. Hawtrey seems to mean here, most usefully, dealers' stocks carried for the purposes of their business, and not residual stocks carried speculatively. Variations in the two kinds of stocks need not be in the same direction.

[2] Cf. Kuznets, *Cyclical Fluctuations.*

is indicated, though by no means conclusively, by the fact that interest rates tend to lag by twelve months.[1]

The instability of credit also plays a part in the views of Mr. Robertson.[2] This instability is, in a sense, a function of a cycle in working capital, but also as almost a pure monetary factor, it governs the turning points of trade.

During the course of a boom it becomes necessary to build up working capital. This involves short lacking by the general public (to release resources), and so far as fixed capital is also created in a substantial quantity—not wholly by lacking on the part of investors—the public must also be forced into long lacking. The means by which the lacking is imposed on the public is a rise in prices, and this

---

[1] See Pigou, *Industrial Fluctuations*, p. 33.

[2] Mr. Robertson has not systematised his complete position, and it will not be right to regard his theories of recurrent industrial disequilibrium as parts of a theory of the trade cycle. From *A Study of Industrial Fluctuation*, from *Banking Policy and the Price Level*, and from certain chapters in *Economic Essays and Addresses*, it appears that he would implicate as principal fundamental cause of the trade cycle, the " lumpiness " of industrial growth as opposed to the continuous growth of population. From time to time there is serious overproduction, not perhaps of things in general, but chiefly of manufactured mass-produced goods, due to the maturity of past investment projects which could not have been undertaken on a smaller scale ; and when the market is thus glutted, a depression ensues, until the growth in population, or some internal adjustment, has liquidated the oversupply. Any particular oversupply, for example of agricultural produce, which impinges on an inelastic demand (as sudden or large agricultural oversupply is held to do), will produce general disequilibrium and depression ; but the chief evil in practice is the outpouring of the products of fixed capital. At the same time there terminates the employment of the factors of production formerly engaged on the construction of that fixed capital, and, indeed, of non-industrial capital also.

That part of this compendium of ideas which concerns the instability of fixed investment has affiliations to the views (to be later examined) of Professor Schumpeter and Mr. Keynes, particularly, in the first affiliation, to the theory of post-innovation disequilibrium, and in the second, to the cyclical course of investment. There are also some reminiscences of *Les Crises Périodiques* in the notion of overproduction, and this is separately examined in a later section. But so far as Mr. Robertson is concerned with the overproduction of a number of specific commodities, and not with generalised overproduction, he occupies different ground from Aftalion. The difficulties in the way of building a trade cycle theory around this point are in the idea of an irresistible emergence of overproduction at a more or less determinate moment. The supply and demand would need to be inelastic for each " overproduced " commodity, and overproduction of each would have to occur more or less at the same time. Perhaps monetary factors provide a link between the commodities— at least, there is the possibility of such a link, which is examined in the text.

rise is achieved by an expansion of credit put at the disposal of capital creators. As the rise in prices proceeds the value (and the real cost) of the capital to be created rises, and thus prices rise still more. Eventually the banking system, in self-protection, has to campaign against the boom. It appears that when the somersault is thus tilted, its movement is continued, first by the cessation of capital creation, and then by the dissipation of capital.

Evidently the critical moment in this course of affairs is that at which the banking system reacts from credit expansion to credit contraction. To overturn trade in the manner suggested it would seem as if the reaction of the banks must be both sudden and energetic. A mild and gradual application of restriction should do no more than inhibit the boom without reversing it. A violent reaction will mean that the boom has been impossible to control until there have been established terms of lending so harsh as positively to diminish the volume of loans once the boom sentiment has been quenched.

In questioning these interpretations of fact it is not necessary to challenge the view that oscillations of working capital do actually occur. These on any showing should involve oscillations of prices and trade. But are the causes of the oscillation to be found in the unstable behaviour of the banks ? Some authorities believe that the banking system will acquiesce in cyclical movements of trade of not unprecedented dimension, even if they do war against hyperactivity in the Stock markets ; and on some readings of monetary history the Central Banks apply their policies of restriction with caution and gradualness. Even if the banking system did seek vigorously to limit the boom, it does not follow that the control it wished to exert could be made very effective. Control of the quantity of money issued can be evaded in some part by changes in the velocity of turnover, which increases when trade is good ; and the short-term rate of interest taken as a burden is less oppressive in such circumstances, even in the few cases where it is a substantial cost. As a deterrent the short-term is seldom effective, it seems : it is not stable enough to warrant being used as a gauge of economic projects except those which liquidate themselves very rapidly.

These comments are not intended to deny that monetary contraction can be used to precipitate a slump, or that certain types of deflationary finance are capable of intensifying a depression. But monetary theorists of the trade cycle have more to prove : they must show that the behaviour of the banks is effective in procuring changes in the state of trade which would not otherwise have occurred. They should show that the banks have a control of industry and use it not merely to arrest an expansion of trade, but also to promote either a decline or such a condition as is liable to pass into a decline, and an uncontrollable one at that. The most favourable conditions for a deliberately procured relapse to pass into an unintended debacle are those in which the Central Bank has had to apply to industry punitive interest rates really designed to explode a financial boom. In 1929 this was the American situation, but it is not the standard case of a crisis, and trade was failing some time before the Wall Street collapse.

Errors and Anticipations.—The theory of error appears still to occupy the central position of Professor Pigou. " Errors of optimism, when discovered, generate errors of pessimism, and vice versa." The rationale of this theory is well known. The source of errors of optimism is the tendency of entrepreneurs to suppose that they may neglect, or the fact that they do neglect, the parallel dispositions of others directed to benefit from any given openings in trade. The opportunities for these errors are given by the fact that modern industry is activated by anticipations, and errors are not exposed until time has elapsed for anticipation to mature in realisation. This is the time taken for production and delivery. The error spreads not only because a host of entrepreneurs is confronted by much the same situation, but because industries are interlocked in psychological interdependence and are largely the source of one another's trade credit. For these reasons errors cumulate rather than cancel. For the time being, during the production period, the errors go undiscovered and lead to an expansion of activity. Since entrepreneurs extrapolate from past experience, even if it be misleading, they find reasons for further expansion, and the boom cumulates. The hyperactivity is aggravated by the behaviour of the company promoters who exploit the public's psychological states, and by the practice of dealers multiplying their orders to avoid disappointment on non-fulfilment (which in turn leads to later cancellations and so intensifies the slump).

At length the errors are unmasked and it is found that the real outlet for commodities falls short of the volume of production. Confidence is overturned and at once converted to pessimism, since neutral feelings cannot succeed emotional tension. The reaction is further intensified by unsuccessful gambling when the market first fails, by bankruptcies, and by the calling in of credit.

In due course the error of pessimism is discovered. Also stocks will have been depleted, and during the period of depressed trade technical innovations will have been made, such as will spur on activity. Trade then revives, and proceeds in due course to regions of optimistic error, only to be followed by inevitable decline.

It is not clear, however, how the exposure of pessimistic error leads on to optimism, and evidently the process is not the converse of the transformation of inflated optimism to suspicion and scepticism. For, as Professor Pigou admits, the initial stages of the upward phase of the cycle represent merely the liquidation of pessimism, and unlike the initial stages of the slump, owe nothing to the panics and " detonations " that accompanied the crisis. The explanation of the slump is convincing on the argument of revulsion from the boom, because at the peak of the boom traders have found themselves faced with losses or vast risks : it is not so common at the other end of the scale, in the vicinity of the trough, to experience profits and certainties on any great scale, except perhaps in association with the exploitation of new methods invented during the slump.

A second difficulty occurs in the matter of the gestation period of the commodities produced in error. At times

Professor Pigou appears to be concerned with the gestation period of instrumental goods, at times with goods in general (compare *Industrial Fluctuations*, Chapters VII (1) and XXIII (2)). It would seem at first sight that if errors are common to all industries, it is the gestation period of all commodities which is relevant in determining the space of time during which errors might be generated, and thus the period of the confidence cycle. It will be argued in Chapter IX that a period of two or three years seems to fit the production period of goods in general, that is of all commodities in some sense weighted by their aggregate value, and some such period seems to be commonly accepted. It does not follow, however, that the confidence period is only two or three years long, for two gestation periods might be needed, one for the exposure of optimism and one for pessimism. But a confidence cycle of six years is not the ordinary trade cycle. This objection is diminished, however, to the extent that supply is inelastic and overproduction must wait on the construction of new plant.

From the fact that the gestation period of all goods is not the same, two further, alternative, objections arise. First, when the mean gestation period has arrived and exposed an error, it will pay the producers of non-matured goods to take the opportunity to cancel outstanding commitments. Or, alternatively, if they persisted in their error, it would tend to cancel the opposite error of those who had had their mistakes exposed and had then revolted to the other extreme. This would diminish net error ; and the former alternative would limit the cumulation of error.

A final difficulty occurs so far as error, if sufficiently widely made, becomes not error, but fact. If everyone decides to expand, then to some extent each entrepreneur has warrant for his optimism in the behaviour of others. Professor Pigou seeks to minimise this objection by an argument based on diminishing marginal real reciprocal demand of which the upshot implies that each entrepreneur (or group of factors) will find himself confronted with rising real costs and diminished utility of income if he responds to the general buoyancy of trade. If this argument is relevant to the short cyclical period, it holds not only against the proposition that generalised errors are not errors, but also against the proposition that errors involving extended activity might be large in scale.

These three objections apart, Professor Pigou has made plain that oscillations of confidence are intimately associated with the course of the trade cycle, and his position in this respect has been absorbed into the make-weight of most other theories.

Theories of Recurrent Overproduction.—In some sense all theories of the trade cycle are theories of successive over- and underproduction, but two or three schools find in the volume of production the clue to the mystery of self-generation. Sometimes it is finished consumption goods which have been overproduced, sometimes working capital, and not infrequently, fixed capital. In some theories it is total overproduction of consumers' goods which is immediately at fault, and in others a disequilibrium between consumers' goods and producers', notably fixed instrumental goods. Theories of the last sort have some affinity to theories concerned with maladjustments of savings and investment. The resemblance is usually but superficial since in most schemes (except perhaps those of Spiethoff and Hull) savings and investment are regarded as two aspects of the same thing, or supposed to be necessarily equal in value.

The position of Professor Aftalion appears to be this : When after a depression prices rise, manufacturers enlarge their equipment. When the equipment is made the supply of consumers' goods is enlarged. The marginal utility of these goods is less than before and the total volume of them cannot be sold at the same prices as before. The redundancy leads on to crisis and depression. This is liquidated by the gradual growth of consumers' wants. The period of the cycle is determined by the production period of instrumental goods.

Two latent assumptions are worth noticing : (*a*) that the existing equipment is insufficient to take care of a boom, and (*b*) that under- and overproduction do not alter the consumers' demand schedule, but only bring into play different points on it. (It is true that larger incomes accompanied the manufacture of instrumental goods, but apparently the same does not apply to the use of these instruments in the manufacture of consumables.[1])

The same sort of view appears to be held by Mr. P. W. Martin, who writes :

> . . . from time to time industry must increase its liquid capital. This means that part of the consumers' buying power, which is needed to pay for goods if equilibrium between the flow of buying power and the flow of prices is to be maintained, goes instead to induce the production of more goods for sale.[2]

This is the same story in terms of " liquid capital."

Professor Lederer finds an aggravation in the maladjustments that occur between changes in the rewards of the factors of production. During the boom " the prices which make up the incomes of the propertied, the salaried, and the wage-earning classes lag behind the prices of commodities. Hence the buying power of these classes is reduced, or, at least, fails to keep pace with the expansion of output." [3] These incomes are also costs, and since they lag, profits mount up and lead on to capital development and further overproduction.

Disequilibria between incomes are also a feature in the theory of Mr. Hobson. Since wages are too small a proportion of the national income, capitalists and others are in a position to accumulate a surplus over their needs. These they invest in the production of more goods. Periodically congestion ensues.

A deficiency of consumer incomes is likewise at the kernel of the theories of Messrs. Foster and Catchings, and their school. Equilibrium depends on a balance between incomes and output. This is destroyed in the first place by the savings made by corporations and individuals, and in the second place, by the use of these savings to procure a larger output.

---

[1] I gather this from Professor Mitchell's summary, *Business Cycles*, p. 30. Mitchell's summaries of the various theories extant are invaluable material for a critical review.

[2] *The Limited Market*, pp. 53–4.

[3] Quoted from Mitchell, op. cit., p. 36.

In all these theories it is imperfectly perceived that changes in the volume of production, even when carried to excess, involve parallel changes in business outlay, and therefore appropriate changes in consumers' incomes, which are the disbursement of industry in another aspect. In general terms, the incomes of the community are always equal to the costs of production, and if these incomes are spent, no difficulty arises.[1] It is not to be denied, however, that disequilibria between particular classes of earnings or between particular forms of production are not similarly innocuous. But it is a feature of the theories considered that these disequilibria are mutually destructive. The disequilibria between earnings lead to savings, it appears, and the disequilibria between forms of output take the shape of increased investment. The first causes the value of available output to exceed money demand, and the second, vice versa.

Theories of Savings and Investment.—It is perhaps unnecessary since the publication of the *Treatise on Money* to devote much attention to the theories of Spiethoff and Hull, even if they have discerned the importance of changes in savings and investment and not excluded the possibility of a disequilibrium between them. The more substantial work on this subject is due to Mr. Keynes, and though he has not written primarily to elucidate the trade cycle, his theories apply to it.[2] Movements from equilibrium follow the courses suggested by these indications of variability :

(*a*) The Inherent Instability of Fixed Investment.—The best investment propositions are used up first, eventually leaving only those which cannot earn the current rate of interest. When investment thus ceases, losses ensue, a slump develops, and other things equal, continues until arrears of investment are patent. This happens when former fixed capital has worn out, when secular development

---

[1] This proposition is evidently not true in all circumstances and does not apply to windfall incomes. Nevertheless, it will not be greatly strained by being used to rebut the notion that productive activity as such can lead to disequilibria between output and incomes, in the sense that profits are altered.

[2] Most of what I have to say is to be found in the *Treatise on Money*, and except for minor points I have not made use of its author's unpublished amplifications.

can no longer be interrupted, and when replacements postponed during the slump can no longer be postponed. The instability of investment is intensified by movements of confidence, and by those variations in the earning power of investments which the profit and loss cycle has caused. The period of the investment cycle is not the period of gestation or duration of industrial instrumental goods, since these account for hardly more than a third of the total of investment.

(b) The Course of Savings.[1]—At the critical moments of the cycle changes in the volume of savings add to disequilibrium. When the boom is at its height the expenditure of profits (due to optimism and the rise of current prices and of paper values) diminishes aggregate savings. This situation is reversed when prices and values collapse and pessimism sets in.

(c) The Spread of Losses.—For any given aggregate of profit or loss the impact upon output varies according to the distribution of profit or loss among firms and industries. Were the distribution equal, the effect of falling prices upon output would be given by the aggregate elasticity of supply. If prices fall comparatively little, output should not contract much, since round and about the point of optimum capacity supply is likely to be rather inelastic—the marginal prime cost curve is steep. Only when the fall in prices is severe does the more or less horizontal part of the curve come into play. But when the total loss, for instance, is unevenly dispersed—as will necessarily be the case—some producers will be driven into these regions, and will contract output

---

[1] Savings are here defined as the excess of normal (transfer or attractive) income over expenditure. The excess of actual income over expenditure is useless quantity, since (as simple analysis will show) this is always equal to the value of investment, and is governed by investment activity, irrespective of the decisions of individuals to economise. Also, individual economy would not affect savings, in the latter sense, if actual income fell by the same amount as expenditure.

There is of course nothing sacred in this definition of savings. It is to be justified by the suggestiveness of results based on it and their internal consistency, and by its agreement with actual usage. If it does depart from such usage by covering only the difference between normal income and expenditure, this is a smaller failing than the two failings already noticed in the rival definition, because it does not set up an immediate contradiction.

substantially. This concentrates the loss on a smaller volume of remaining output. Contraction spreads until at length, in the remaining firms, the postponable fixed charges will only just cover the loss. The margin of contraction is such that unit loss just balances postponable unit fixed charges. In the course of contraction a substantial volume of disinvestment in working capital will take place—orders will be restricted and stocks disposed of—and this will increase the total loss, generating secondary waves of induced contraction.

In these relationships of output and profit or loss, the results of boom and slump are not symmetrical (by reason of inconstant inelasticity of short-period supply), but nevertheless the fact that losses spread when output is contracted, even if the converse case were not important, will add to the amplitude of cyclical movement.

(*d*) Fluctuation in Working Capital.—The amplitude is also increased to the extent of movements in the volume of stocks and goods in process, and of their correlative extensions as above. When a disequilibrium between savings and investment, due to a change in fixed investment, has materialised in a changed level of prices, the amount of working capital carried is altered in sympathy. When prices are falling dealers evacuate stocks and manufacturers diminish the rate of input of resources into the productive machine. Such developments add to the decline, and conversely for rising prices. These changes in the working capital of those who continue in business are additive to the effects on working capital of variations in the scale of business as noticed under (*c*).

The fluctuations of working capital tend to express themselves as a minor cycle. On the one hand prices rise so soon as working capital touches a minimum, since its former decline has been depressing prices ; and on the other hand, prices fall so soon as a production period is over and new output emerges. These price movements tend so to affect anticipations as to generate in turn further fluctuations in the volume of working capital. This mutual relationship between prices and working capital which tends to perpetuate the cycle may nevertheless be disturbed by external occurrences.

These working capital cycles are superposable upon the fixed investment cycles. There is, however, a tendency for the movements due to each to synchronise at the turning points of the major cycle, since neither cycle is independent of such states of confidence and anticipations as may be generated by the other. Accordingly the major cyclical movements are aggravated by the minor, and both are further extended by cognate variations in savings and output—under (b) and (c).

The lower limits of the movements depend upon the following :

> (i) the remedial action of the Governments or the banking system ;
> (ii) the drafts made upon savings for keeping up incomes, either publicly on behalf of the unemployed, or privately by distressed individuals ;
> (iii) from (c) above, the point beyond which output cannot contract ;
> (iv) from (a) above, the point at which fixed capital wears out and replacement cannot be postponed ;
> (v) the minima of stocks of finished and semi-finished goods—when these are reached prices rise.

The upper limits depend upon :

> (vi) the repressive behaviour of the banking system ;
> (vii) the• maximum of fixed investment that can be arranged at the time—after this has been attained prices start falling ;
> (viii) the production period : when the creation of working capital has been undertaken, its emergence in finished form causes prices to kick back. Similarly when stocks, having been accumulated, reach their maximum, prices fall ;
> (ix) the maximum of output of those factors of production used in a critical capacity ;
> (x) the rise in the rate of interest due to demands made upon liquid money resources.

These are the principal limits to the cyclical swing. Within these limits is accomplished something like a standard cycle, though actual cycles will be distorted by non-repetitive events both as to their course and their amplitude. The normal limits are such that when reached they cause recoil, and hence the cycle is perpetually self-renewing.[1]

If we examine these limits in detail, to find which of them repel as well as inhibit the movement of trade, only six seem to fulfil both criteria to a significant extent, of which two, representing the behaviour of the banking system, are doubtful. The remaining four represent respectively the upper and lower limits of fixed and working capital, and, as has been shown, they are turning-points.

So far as trade cycles are each different and obey no rigid periodic law, we should not expect to find these turning-points determinate nor definitive. Thus it will be consistent with the facts that the limits of trade are not fixed in degree or time. But the latitude that can be allowed under this head is not unlimited, or the notion of a turning-point would be lost. The turning-points which Mr. Keynes' scheme seems to establish are not beyond criticism on these grounds.

First we will consider the re-emergence of fixed investment at the end of a slump. Evidently the extent to which fixed investment can be contracted or postponed is not rigid. Contraction does not usually go so far that the remaining capital equipment becomes inadequate to serve indispensable needs, and so require supplementation at any given moment. For these reasons there is no specific time at which fixed investment re-emerges, and no specific urgency prompts it.

Secondly, the maximum of investment that will be undertaken is a quantity depending not alone on the rate of interest and the true earning power of the projects, but also upon the state of confidence and the current receipts from similar enterprise. Thus the position at which the upper limit comes into play is variable.

---

[1] Up to here I have been summarising and regrouping material from the *Treatise*. It will easily be realised from recollection of the *Treatise* what opportunities for misinterpretation this procedure offers.

Nor is the working capital cycle necessarily continuous in the sense that rise and fall follow each other without intermission. The facts seem to suggest that intervening periods of hesitation are not uncommon. When stocks have been in the vicinity of their minimum trade has been seen to drag on without apparent change for as long as a year. Such seems to have been the condition of American business in late 1921 and early 1922. Again, at the conclusion of a production period, further hesitancy may precede disinvestment, until it is seen that the boom is over and that the price fall is not just a temporary check. The events in the United States in 1923 appear to have been of this nature.[1]

The common feature in these four cases—maxima and minima of fixed investment and of working capital—is the dependence of the maxima and minima on confidence and anticipation. It may be, as in Professor Pigou's scheme, that changes in anticipations are capable of virgin birth, and need not be begotten by objective events. But it is also possible that those subjective states which determine the position of the turning-points are themselves the product of such real causes as innovations, harvest conditions, and so on, whether these causes be regularly recurrent or not. If so, the trade cycle is affected at its critical moments by forces not obeying the same or any periodicity. In the course of proceeding to investigate these possibilities more closely, we shall now notice Professor Schumpeter's view of innovations as the mainspring of the cycle.

Inventions and Innovations.—Professor Schumpeter points out [2] that economic growth is almost bound to proceed in waves. It is conditioned by the discovery and application of innovations,[3] which are discontinuous and often of large

---

[1] I believe that evidence in support of these observations is given by the Business Indexes of the American Telephone and Telegraph Company, of Dr. Persons, and of Dr. Snyder (both the general index and the distribution to consumer index). There is evidence of similar business hesitancy at earlier dates, and particularly before the beginning of a slump.

[2] In *Economica*, May, 1928 ; and see also Professor Mitchell's summary of the versions in German.

[3] These are not only technical innovations, but include such developments as the conquest of new markets.

scope, and which take time to digest. In the first place these innovations are made by the exceptionally able, but they are copied and even improved upon by the rest of the business community. As a consequence of the activity represented in the application of new methods, prices rise and optimism spreads cumulatively. In these circumstances, former innovations that entrepreneurs have held up their sleeves get the chance to be tried out. Hence the combined flow of innovation will be considerable, and until checked, will gather momentum.

The check comes as " large supplies flpoding the market, high costs of materials and labour, shifting of demand to new products, supersession of old sources of production . . ." [1] and other evidences of inter-industrial disequilibrium. This muddle has to be liquidated. Some firms retire, others revise the extravagant commitments which the innovations led them to make, and in general, new plans and programmes are laid down which are better adapted to the long-period consequences of the innovations and their repercussions. This is a period of subnormal activity in which industry is feeling its way and in which lenders are not unnaturally cautious. Innovations themselves cease. Eventually the long-period adaptations are made and stability is restored. Then the industrial climate is again favourable for a further crop of innovations.

This is the sort of theory which can only be adequately tested by facts. We shall require to know to what extent innovations are in practice monopolised by means of patents and secrecy, and to what extent a boom discourages innovations by making trade profitable by the old methods. (Conversely, it is said that a slump forces entrepreneurs to overhaul their technique.) We shall require to know whether net confidence is increased by innovations which at the time do no more than aggrandise one entrepreneur at the expense of others. Do those of them that economise the factors of production increase business outlay ? Do they consume much capital and so increase purchasing power ? Finally one would ask, how is the comparative

---

[1] Mitchell, *Business Cycles*, p. 21.

regularity of the trade cycle compatible with the spasmodic element in invention and discovery ?

These questions, even if they had to be answered in a sense unfavourable to Professor Schumpeter, represent scepticism only of the periodicity of innovations and their immediate consequences. It is generally admitted that inventions profoundly alter the economic framework on which the trade cycle swings, and could not fail to impress themselves on the cyclical course of trade. They are undoubtedly responsible in large measure for the differences among successive cycles which all observers have found. If the trade cycle had a tendency to diminish in dimension as time went on, no doubt the occurrence of a profound innovation would re-magnify the amplitude and possibly govern the character of at least one immediately succeeding cycle. This possibility should be of some importance if the innovation were such as to require a large increase in investment, as was the case in the railway booms. But even Professor Schumpeter (as far as I know) has not explained the railway slumps purely in terms of disequilibrium and congestion, except as a reaction from over-investment, which, after all, occurs even when the expanded investment has been in familiar forms. Thus we shall not be unreasonable in suggesting that innovations of not more than normal importance merely determine the character of the investment for which the circumstances were in any case ripe. And although one innovation may breed others, we must suppose that none of them will be applied until prices have begun to rise, which, in turn, is less likely to be the result of the assimilation of past innovations than of recovery in the staple categories of investment.

It would seem at first sight that Professor Schumpeter would get considerable support for his position in the disequilibrium which has ensued on the innovations of the past five years, especially in agriculture. We noticed in Chapter VI that the overproduction of agricultural staples has at least greatly aggravated the slump. It is hard nevertheless to believe that apart from these innovations, and simultaneous innovations in manufacture, that no relapse in trade would have occurred. Prior to 1929 investment was inflated by prodigious lendings to undeveloped countries, notably in South America, which were on the whole used to finance public works and railway construction. These must in any case have come to a rapid end, especially as so many were unsound, and then, how could savings find an outlet, or gold fail to become worse distributed ? Up till 1928–9, while investment was increasing, the extraordinary intensity of innovation, which had already effected substantial changes in relative prices, was easily absorbed into the general activity of trade and did not crystallise out as disequilibrium. The latter had to wait for the sudden chill of the slump.

So far, all the theories examined have on the whole implied a self-generative cycle. Some of their authors hold an eclectic diversity of views, and Professor Schumpeter's theory in particular links up with the notion of a diminishing cycle at times regenerated by inventions. Most of the other theories that have attracted any attention are at the other extreme, and postulate a cycle governed from outside the industrial system. Attempts to bridge the gap will be made later. Meanwhile we will briefly notice a theory which occupies an intermediate position so far as it straddles over the physical and the economic.

Disequilibrium between Organic and Inorganic Goods.— Professor Sombart has propounded a theory that during a boom the production of organic commodities, made up either out of animal or vegetable raw materials, would get out of gear with the production of inorganic commodities, such as the metals. The supply of the former is limited by physical and biological factors : the supply of the latter can be expanded according to the state of business within the limits of the capital equipment. Thus, should inorganic goods be oversupplied, in consequence of the momentum of a boom, and be demanded inelastically, there should be a tendency for activity to decrease all round so soon as the new position was squarely faced. But the importance of this consideration is diminished by the ease, on Professor Sombart's showing, with which the production of inorganic goods can be readjusted.

The 3½-Year Meteorological Cycle.—Professor H. S. Jevons[1] has a theory, supported by some statistical evidence, of a 3½ years' cycle in barometric pressure which leads in due course to a cycle in trade. The links in this chain are rainfall and harvests.

The causal connections are as follows : Changes in the sun's heat are reflected on the earth as changes in average barometric pressure. There are two types of pressure cycle, inversely correlated, of which those recorded respectively at Bombay and at Cordoba in the Argentine are representative. The pressure cycles, or at least those phases of them appropriate to the critical period of crops, April to October, lead to variations in rainfall and therefore in harvests. The Cordoba cycle is correlated with the cycle in American crops ($r = - \cdot 437 \pm \cdot 101$). Abundant crops lead to trade activity for several reasons. First of all, the purchasing power of the agricultural community is enhanced. The railways place orders for additional rolling stock. The earnings of distributors are increased. Manufacturers enjoy lower prices for raw materials. Confidence is generated. Thus trade in general enters upon expansion. A three and a half years' cycle is discoverable in many economic records, particularly in the American, and the impulses liberated in two or more of these cycles cumulate until a major cycle either of seven or of ten or eleven years is generated. This cumulation of forces takes place because both the industrial system and the emotion of the business community take more than 3½ years to revolve. Also, the length of the major cycle depends on " the degree of abundance of the crops in the years when they are abundant."

Now it is generally agreed that most similar crops tend to vary in their abundance together, and hence in checking up Professor Jevons' theory we may not rely for disproof on the possibility of large inter-crop compensations. Perhaps also, though here Professor Jevons offers no substantial proof, inter-local compensations are similarly negligible, and this despite the inverse correlation of the barometric pressures of the Western and Eastern Hemispheres. The

[1] *The Causes of Unemployment.*

consequences of contradictory inter-regional variations are possibly diminished by the predominance in the world's markets of the crops of the West. Again, since there are in fact significant variations from year to year in the world production even of widespread single crops such as wheat, we must further suppose that the areas in which low rainfall is a limiting factor more than balance those in which the difficulty is excess. This predominance would make rainfall the limiting factor on the whole so far as other limitations may be taken as constant. Finally, in view of the correlations which Professor Jevons has established between barometric pressure and crops, we need not dispute whether rainfall is causally correlated with pressure, so long as they vary in some sort of harmony.

Granted that crops as a whole respond to weather, how does trade respond to fluctuations in the crops ? Professor Jevons has attempted to show a correspondence between United States agricultural output (in volumes) and the production of pig iron, the latter being taken as an index of trade. There is some evidence of correspondence at the extremes, so far as the eye can judge from curves, and very abundant harvests do seem to be followed by spurts in the production of pig iron. Nevertheless, the correlation between the two series taken as a whole, and not only at the turning-points, is but slender ($r = - \cdot 105$—probable error $\cdot 091$).[1] But Professor Jevons claims that pig iron lags behind agricultural output—by two years up to 1888, and by one year between 1888 and 1895, but that thenceforward the two movements are almost simultaneous. When adjustments are made in this respect, and when the years 1915–19 are excluded from count, the correlation becomes positive and slightly greater ($r = \cdot 195$—probable error $\cdot 071$). Such a small measure of congruence seems hardly sufficient to establish the probability of a causal connection between harvest variations and pig iron, at least in the United States,

---

[1] The data which Professor Jevons himself compiled do not lend themselves to correlation analysis, and I have had recourse to the series constructed by Professor Day, with trend removed by him—*Review of Economic Statistics*, 1921, pp. 259 and 297—as quoted by Professor Pigou, op. cit. The correlations refer to the years 1879–1919.

when the harvest variations are judged from aggregate output. This result does not however exclude the intermittent correspondence nor the correspondence which we found at the extremes. The principal reason for the small measure of correlation is probably the nearness of the elasticity of demand for the agricultural produce of the United States to unity. Some other statistical evidence has established a presumption of roughly unit-elasticity of demand (namely the almost zero correlation which has been found between agricultural output and farm receipts [1]), and the feeble effect which harvests appear to have on pig iron, except in special cases, would seem to confirm it. An explanation of the occasional correlation between agricultural output and pig-iron production may be found in the following : Suppose trade to fluctuate in a $3\frac{1}{2}$-year cycle—this alternately raises and lowers the demand curve for agricultural produce—some eighteen or twenty-four months later changes in output, stimulated by these changes in price, will have occurred—these will appear to precede subsequent movements in trade also by eighteen or twenty-four months —and might be imagined to be the causes. The shortening of the apparent lag between the output of agriculture and pig iron might then be explained on the ground that the gestation period in agriculture became longer as the methods of cultivation became more elaborate. In advancing this explanation, one would not exclude the direct relationship between crops and pig iron that might occur in the United States if very large crops in that country, coinciding with short crops elsewhere, were especially encouraging to trade.

It must be admitted that the agricultural output—pig-iron correlation of ·195 given above is not in agreement with the correlation which Professor Moore has found between agricultural yield per acre and pig-iron output— $r = \cdot719$ where pig iron lags either one or two years. One would have expected a closer agreement between these coefficients since changes in yield and aggregate output (when trend is concordantly removed from each) closely correspond. But in the output–pig-iron correlations twelve

[1] *Review of Economic Statistics*, February, 1920.

crops were used, and in the yield–pig-iron correlations, nine crops, weighted differently, and with trend removed by a different method. Here are part explanations of the apparent inconsistency : (*a*) different dates—Professor Day gives 1879–1920 and Professor Moore takes 1871–1908 ; (*b*) different number and weighting of the crops ; and (*c*) the fact that crude output and yield diverged between 1873 and 1895 because falling prices were depressing the yield while expanding population was increasing the acreage. This last consideration raises pointedly the question of method in trend removal. Professor Moore judged that yield would do duty for total output (when correlating with price) from an equivalence of result obtained with first differences. But in correlating yields with pig iron he uses instead undifferentiated data corrected by the removal of a linear trend. But from the curves tracing the undifferentiated yield and pig-iron series it seems that trend was curvilinear. Both series dipped into the trough of 1880–96 and then rose.

Professor Moore's method in fact was to smooth his data by arranging them as three-year moving averages, and then take out a linear trend which left 17 out of 37 pairs of observations below the mean in the middle (1880–96), and 10 pairs above the mean at the extremes of the series. The first operation, smoothing, might have been *prima facie* justifiable had the deviations smoothed out, due largely to the weather, been outside the inquiry. But the inquiry was essentially directed to the relations of weather and trade. As it happened the method of smoothing tended strongly toward establishing a positive correlation. So did the use of a linear trend, and the coefficient of correlation which this treatment has established is probably inflated. In so far as widely different coefficients can be obtained according to the method of trend removal, and the way in which the raw data are otherwise corrected, as by smoothing, it is legitimate to question even a high coefficient when these preliminary operations are not immediately explicable. Furthermore, Professor Moore not only obtains a coefficient of ·7 when pig iron lags one or two years, but three others all positively greater than ·55 for other lags, zero, three and four years. This curious situation suggests that if there is any cyclical connection between crop yield and pig-iron production, it is not reasonably sharp and immediate, but diffuse and vague. In all, we shall be ill-advised to accept the yield pig-iron coefficient at the value given : and it happens that the output–pig-iron correlation, based on Professor Day's figures and method of trend removal, offers very little support to the case of Professor Jevons.

We should not expect to find that abundant crops increased trade activity so far as they operated through increased farm incomes, since there are almost certainly no grounds for supposing the demand for agricultural produce in the United States to be elastic. For the world as a whole the elasticity is probably less than unity. The item for increased outlay upon rolling stock, which Professor Jevons mentioned more than once as a contributory cause of the boom, is clearly of no great importance in itself, and we need not suppose that the earnings of distributors of raw produce will be greatly increased, since those who gain by handling a larger volume of crops will be substantially offset by those who lose through charging a fixed proportion of their buying price. The confidence which is supposed to follow abundant harvests, or be created by the prospect of them, could hardly survive the fact of lower agricultural prices sufficient to balance them and keep farm incomes relatively stable. The strongest of Professor Jevons' arguments connecting harvests with trade is probably this— that abundant harvests reduce the cost of raw material and provide manufacturers with profits. This type of argument has been well formulated by Professor Mitchell,[1] as may be summarised :

The cost of materials exceeds wages in every one of the leading branches of manufacture, and in a majority of cases is over twice as large. Indeed on the average it makes practically two-thirds of the total outlay. If wares for re-sale be substituted for materials, this proportion must run far higher in wholesale stores, while in retail shops it cannot be much lower than in factories on the average and may well be considerably higher . . . etc., etc. . . . The relative fluctuations in the prices of

[1] *Business Cycles*, 1st edn., pp. 481–2.

those commodities which are bought and of those which are sold are therefore of great, and in many cases of decisive, importance in determining profits. Now . . . statistical evidence points to the conclusion that what must be taken as buying prices creep up on selling prices during a period of prosperity. . . . While a difficulty of this character seems to be encountered in most branches of business it is likely to become particularly acute in those manufacturing industries which use animal and farm products as their leading raw materials . . . for we have found that these classes of products are more erratic in their price fluctuations than are the products of mines and forests. . . . The census indicates that more than three-fourths of all the " materials purchased in the raw state " by American factories in 1900 belonged to this class which is peculiarly unstable in price.

Professor Moore has added that the proportion of raw materials contributed by the farms is over 80 per cent.

These passages are somewhat misleading when used (not by Professor Mitchell) to establish a connection between harvests and trade. In the first place, the violent fluctuations in the prices of agricultural raw materials noticeable in primary markets will be greatly softened by the time the goods reach manufacturers after several doses of handling and transport, and very often, of semi-manufacture.[1] Nor are the fluctuations always in the same direction as among a number of commodities—some compensations should occur. Secondly, the proportion of agricultural produce in total raw materials at source (given as 80 per cent.) is probably less at factory, since agricultural products (e.g. cotton yarn), although they incur large preliminary charges between farm and factory, nevertheless on the whole require less working up than mineral products (e.g. steel sections), which thus incur even greater charges, bringing their proportionate value at factory to more than 20 per cent. Thirdly, the prices of raw materials as such, contrasted with agricultural produce as a whole, vary mainly in response

[1] Agricultural raw materials can only amount to 80 per cent. of two-thirds—or anything like it—of the costs of industry on the supposition that the same physical materials are handled many times and processed more than once, since the net value product of agriculture has only once or twice since 1909 exceeded 20 per cent. of the total national value product.

to the manufacturers' own demand. The variations in price springing from spontaneous variations in output are probably small, since the supply of raw materials consists in a large measure of animal products. Animal products are less subject to changes in output such as might result from climatic influences than the staple crops are. For the United States agriculture as a whole, animal products have become a larger source of income than crops (1909, 44 per cent. ; 1928, 51 per cent.), and this fact also diminishes the force of arguments connecting crops and trade via farm incomes. Fourthly, such gains on materials as manufacturers obtain from abundant harvests are gains on profits only in the proportion of materials to total outlay, given as two-thirds.

To sum up all these considerations, we may conclude that the importance of a fall in the prices of agricultural raw materials due to increased supply is small in the matter of inducing extra activity among the users of them. This view is further confirmed by the weight of marketing and processing costs which we notice in Appendix IV. It also finds support in the probability that the value of agricultural raw materials used in United States manufacture (including hand trades) cannot have been—for 1909 at least—more than one-quarter of value added, or rather less than one-fifth of total outlay after allowing for non-agricultural raw material.[1] It must not be concluded, however, that there is no transitive nexus between harvests and trade operated through cheaper raw materials, for such a nexus is probably needed to explain such occasional positive correlations between American crops and trade as have been established.

The Eight-Year Meteorological Cycle.—Some of these objections urged against the statistical conclusions and theoretical analysis of Professor Jevons also apply to the theories and expositions of Professor H. L. Moore, who, in particular, places some reliance on the cost of raw material argument. Professor Moore has found an eight-year rainfall

---

[1] I have pieced this calculation together from sundry sources, which do not combine very well except to give a general view of the relative magnitudes.

cycle corresponding to the movements of the planet Venus—with which we are not concerned—and this rainfall cycle is evident both in the American annual average precipitation and in the precipitation during critical periods of growth. It generates a regular cycle in all economic affairs. No evidence is offered of correlations with barometric pressure, and no significant periodicity appears to correspond with periods of $3\frac{1}{2}$ years—though this does not seriously disturb the pressure-crop correlations of Professor Jevons, which may be taken to have operated not only through gross rainfall, but also through temperature, sunlight, and daily distribution of rain. Professor Moore's complete position is to be found in two works [1] separated by nine years, of which the earlier employed mainly correlation analysis and the later mainly periodogram analysis. The two methods have not in every case yielded concordant results.

In the first exposition, we begin with the use of Fourier analysis to establish an eight-year cycle in the rainfall of the Ohio Valley. This is moderately well correlated with rainfall in Illinois, and establishes a presumption that the rainfall of the whole country varies in much the same way. There are correlations ranging from $r = \cdot290$ for oats to $r = \cdot666$ for potatoes between the yield of crops and rainfall in the critical period. When the four crops (oats, corn, hay and potatoes) are combined there is a correlation of $\cdot584$ with the rainfall of the combined critical periods. As already noticed, the yields of these crops closely correspond with output—that is for the United States as a whole.

We now find high inverse correlations between the total production of the four crops separately with the prices of them, ranging from $- \cdot715$ for hay to $- \cdot856$ for potatoes. The demand is found to be inelastic (that is, by a method involving the use of scatter observations) for oats and potatoes ($\cdot84$ and $\cdot66$), but very near unit elasticity for corn and hay ($\cdot92$ and $1\cdot06$). The changes in yield of these crops for the United States as a whole is highly correlated with changes for Illinois (ranging from $\cdot745$ for hay to $\cdot855$ for

[1] *Economic Cycles, Their Law and Cause*, and *Generating Economic Cycles*.

corn). Thus we have proceeded from the crops of Illinois to the four crops as a whole, and now we extend from four crops to nine (whose combined weighted yields are correlated, $r = \cdot 960$). (The weighting of the first four crops was not the same, however, or anything like the same, when considered by themselves as when subsequently combined with the other five.) The movements in the yield of the nine crops is correlated with movements in pig iron, one or two years later ($r = \cdot 719$ and $\cdot 718$). There are further correlations between crop yields and prices (Bureau of Labour and other indexes). Thus crops may be considered to be correlated with trade in general, as trade conditions are well represented both by pig iron and wholesale prices.

It will be seen that Professor Moore proceeds stage by stage detecting correlations; using high measures of correlations as evidences of cause and effect in some cases; and treating quantities sufficiently well correlated in series as equivalent or substitutable. If the alienation factors in each of the measures of correlation were due only to observational error, this method would be free of reproach. But if the alienations are due to imperfect synchronisation or agreement in movement, there is the possibility that the alienations should in some sense be taken as cumulative. So far as it is fair to assume that any of the given series obeys an independent law to which the others are not subject, the alienations should be taken to cumulate rather than cancel. Since one cannot use the assumption that all the phenomena are controlled by the weather to check the method, it follows that the only other hypothesis upon which the alienations may be taken to cancel is that they are due only to the intrusion of random factors, themselves in no way correlated. The hypothesis may seem violent.

We have already considered some reasons for questioning the degree of correlation obtained between crop yields and pig iron. Another difficulty occurs in accepting the assumption that rainfall in the critical period obeys the same periodic law as annual rainfall; and a third in accepting a periodicity in Illinois crops (and thus also in United States crops) when the Illinois rainfall is correlated only by ·600 with Ohio rainfall, which latter is the only phenomenon shown directly to obey the eight-year law. Further, since the elasticities of demand are shown, when the four crops are taken together, to be not far removed from unity, one is forced to wonder what is the sequence of causes underlying whatever measure of correlation really exists. Rather than question whether true elasticities were established, we may advance a tentative explanation of the correlations as follows :

Suppose that there is a general cycle of about eight years to which all the phenomena conform in response to appropriate fluctuations in prices. Then we may further suppose, since trade cycles are not symmetrical about the norm, that each trough precedes each boom by five or six years, say sixty-six months. When prices, including agricultural prices, are at their minimum, they lead to contractions in agricultural output, operated in part by means of curtailing outlay on maintaining the yield. These contractions are realised in the output of some eighteen months later, since some such period is the gestation period of cereal crops if we include in it the lag between past harvests and next sowings. Accordingly, some forty-eight months before the ensuing peak, yields are at their maximum. Now if the crops—and indeed other commodities—run in a forty-two months' cycle, as appears to be the case in the United States, twenty-one months later again, that is, twenty-seven months before the coming peak, yields are at their maximum. If pig iron precedes general trade by three months, we have accounted for a correlation with a lag of twenty-four months between yields and pig iron. The production of pig iron was itself running in three- or four-year cycles, and hence has synchronised, except for a lag, with crops throughout. Needless to say this passage does not purport to describe a trade cycle, but merely to show, in an abstract outline, how some part of Professor Moore's correlations is consistent with trade cycle theories other than his own.

But we must remember that some of his results obtained by correlation analysis are supported by periodogram analysis. This latter method rests upon a theorem that if there is some cycle (truly periodic and of significant amplitude) of any period within a relevant range, it will be disclosed by the analysis. A significant cycle is deemed to be one whose amplitude squared exceeds the mean of the squared amplitudes corresponding to all the trial periods in the given range as they appear in the periodogram, and the significance increases as the excess over the mean grows. It is evident that the presumption of significance is confirmed if only one cycle fulfils the given conditions.

Along these lines Professor Moore derives an evidently significant cycle of eight years in the rainfall of Ohio, with a semi-harmonic at four years. For the United States as a whole (over a shorter period—thirty-nine years) there is again a good cycle at eight years, with secondary cycles at six and seven years. Next we are given a periodogram of the combined yield of six crops (responsible in 1919 for 70 per cent. of the value of American farm produce) as studied in deviations from trend. This periodogram again shows a significant cycle at eight years—but also another of nearly equal amplitude at seven years. Deviations from trend of coal and iron combined also yielded a cycle at eight years, but even more significant cycles at eleven and twelve years. When the crops and the mineral products were combined so as to form an index of deviations in raw materials as a whole, there was still a significant cycle at eight years, and an only less significant one at seven years. It does not appear, however, that the six crops—corn, wheat, cotton, hay, oats and potatoes—when combined, are important as raw materials, though they may have been so as farm produce. All these combinations of deviations in crops and minerals, both within and between these categories, were made, as in the earlier study, by summing the respective yearly deviations from trend. In the context of variations in the cost of raw materials one would suppose that some weighting by value would have increased the relevance.

In all these cycles the maxima occurred together at 1882, 1890, 1898, 1906, and 1914. The same cycles were then found in the Sauerbeck wholesale price index (taken apparently as an index of the prices of manufactures) and in the representative crops of the United Kingdom and France.

Some of these results must naturally follow from the treatment by Fourier analysis of the data as combined. But when cycles of eight years co-exist with others of six, seven, eleven or twelve years, the movements due to each are governed also by the period of some other. The cycles combine in the sense that they are alternately tending to cancel and amplify each other. Hence it does not follow from the presence of an eight-year cycle (if there are also other periods) that significant maxima in the series are actually registered every eight years. This would not matter if the secondary period in each series was of the same length, for then both periods in one series might be the cause of corresponding periods in another. But since the secondary periods are not all equal as among the weather, the crop yield, the coal and iron, and the raw materials series, the supposition that the latent eight-year cycle in an earlier series will lead to eight-year cycles in later series becomes treacherous. There will not be marked actual eight-year movements in any, such as are needed to generate eight-year movements in another.

Accordingly, if there have been maxima at 1882, 1890, etc., in the yield cycle, this is perhaps due not only—or at all—to the weather, but to further economic factors which too run in cycles of approximately eight years. Or, to extend this point, we may claim to find in the actuality of the eight-year cycle not only a confirmation of Professor Moore's periods, but an explanation of them.[1] That is, we agree that eight-year cycles do occur for economic reasons, and their occurrence explains why eight-year movements turn up in Professor Moore's mutually unrelated series.

But the observable eight-year cycle is not regular. One wonders what is a permissible irregularity for a cycle supposed to be astronomical. Professor Moore's maxima have diverged from the recorded maxima by as much as two years. Perhaps he would insist that these divergences were

[1] Though not of course of the weather cycle.

merely perturbations about the fundamental cycle displayed so clearly in rainfall, crops, pig iron and coal, and Sauerbeck. One must decide at discretion whether these perturbations are not more interesting than their rhythmical accompaniment.

Conclusions.—It will be clear that all the theories reviewed have facets of relevance and adequacy that could only be obliterated, if at all, by elaborate and probably sterile analysis. If so, each must be deemed to have contributed something to the sort of composite explanation that will probably be found best to describe the facts. A large number of cyclical factors or cycle-generating factors may very well operate simultaneously. As Professor Pigou has pointed out,[1] these would not be simply additive : as each factor was successively removed the observable effects of the remainder would probably increase, because as it is, some of the factors share their effects. Furthermore, some of the factors, each by itself capable of generating a cycle, might in practice be consequences of one another. Thus at the turning points of an investment cycle associated with inventions we may find perturbations of confidence working through money and credit and leading to something which may be reasonably called temporary over- or underproduction, almost certainly in further conjunction with disequilibria among incomes and forms of output. It would be a matter of some difficulty to isolate the original and ultimate cause, should there be one. If one factor is responsible for the amplitude of and main movement of trade in a cycle, and another for the turning movements at the limits of variation, the priority of the two, in order of just notoriety, is disputable.

Perhaps we may now say that the fixed investment cycle and the working capital cycle, though their capacity to perpetuate themselves is in doubt, may reasonably be regarded as usable explanations of the movement of trade within the limits, especially if considered in conjunction with their inevitable repercussions. But at the same time it is still necessary to understand in some detail what is

---

[1] *Industrial Fluctuations*, p. 209.

occurring at the limits, possibly timing the cycle, and almost certainly turning it. It might almost be judged unlikely that the factors operating at the critical moments were the same as those responsible for the control of intra-limit movements, and if so, we are entitled to look away from the organisation of industry in a search for such factors. The claim of inventions and wars to be regarded in this light has been considered and in part conceded : we now go on to study some less spasmodic occurrences, connected with agriculture, which should operate in much the same way.

CHAPTER VIII

FLUCTUATIONS IN AGRICULTURAL ACTIVITY

The Three Years' Cycle.—We have noticed that a cycle of trade occupying round about three or four years is a regular event in the United States. Professor Mitchell has found [1] twin modes in the duration of the cycle in combined English-speaking countries at three and four years; and the American indexes of Dr. Persons, Dr. Snyder, and the Associated Telephone and Telegraph Company, show mean durations respectively ranging from forty-one to forty-four months.

This short cycle is not nearly so marked in other countries, and in Great Britain, for instance, is not immediately apparent in the usual indexes. Perhaps the trade of Great Britain is subject to influences emanating from abroad which do not synchronise. In some other countries of Europe the indexes are hardly delicate to display prominently enough variations in trade other than the large eight-year cycle. Whether in these countries there is a latent short cycle or not is probably better discovered by analysis than observation. The raw material for the latter, the statistical sources, are, except in Germany, not very reliable. At least we may say that the grounds for accepting a short minor movement in European trade are not ruled out by the fact that the available indexes do not display this movement unmistakably. If this is not due to inferior statistical practice, the explanation is perhaps to be found in the economic sluggishness of the Old World.[2] Again, as in the case of Great Britain, if various European countries engaged in reciprocal trade attain maxima at different dates

---

[1] *Business Cycles*, p. 404. There is no great concentration of actual observations on these modes.
[2] And see footnote on p. 233.

for political, psychological, or institutional reasons, and if these different maxima are not assimilated into a common maximum by the solvents of free trade and a common money, they will each be restrained and diminished by influences emanating from beyond the frontier. We may safely suppose that the conclusions suggested by an examination of short cycles in the United States will also be relevant for Europe.

It has sometimes been supposed that cyclical movements occupying such short periods as three years can be explained merely by reference to theorems in probability. There would be no necessity for the assumption that there is some real periodicity, even if the period is irregular. Such an argument will proceed as follows : If the average price over a period is known or determinate, then the greater the number of years of (say) sub-average price, the greater each successive year becomes the likelihood that the next year's price will be above the average. In a six-year period in which prices have been below normal for three years, there is a certain probability that the next three years will be above normal. Still more so for the succession of ups and downs in shorter periods. In a three-year period, good prices for two years definitely argue bad prices in the third.

These conclusions follow from the conceptions either of an average price discoverable from the prices which have actually ruled, or of an average price which is fixed by the arrangements entered into by the factors of production. In the first case the average is only discoverable *a posteriori*, and is therefore worthless as an indication of the normal about which fluctuations are random. In the second case, where the normal price is supposed to be determinate as a long-period equilibrium price, the objections to the three-year cycle as a real cycle fall away so far as for three years at least, prices can markedly diverge from normal without modifying long-term expectations. And if the long-period normal price is thus irrelevant, the long-period normal volume of trade, if such exists, is evidently even more so, unless, rather questionably, it is taken to represent the maximum employment of all the factors. These observations apply less strongly, however, to the idea of a middle-period norm of price (long-period normal less profits). But here again, the notion of a normal price which must be established within three or four years is erroneous. If, to begin with, prices are above normal, it does not follow that they must then fall below, for the surplus over the normal will be taken for profits without greatly expanding production. Or if, to begin with, prices earlier are low, they have not in fact to rise unless they have failed to cover prime cost and so damped down production. The reason here is that the fixed outgoings, which a middle-period price must cover, can in a large part be postponed almost indefinitely, and in part again, be avoided by retrenchments.

Probably the only sense in which sub-average prices, in any way defined, are likely to be followed by super-average, is that in which some deduction may be made from past experience and applied to current events. This notion of sequence is only empirical. We are still left to find causes for the cyclical movements, and the tendency of the system to return ultimately to equilibrium will not suffice. In other words, we are not merely concerned with perturbations of trade that are automatically cancelled, but with a real cycle that obeys definite laws.

It is convenient to study short-period movements in trade under the heading of a three-years' cycle. This term—three-years' cycle—is not used to suggest that three years is the mean duration of the cycles or the modal duration. It is merely a brief name for a rhythmical movement usually occupying between two and four years. Hence the notion of a three-years' cycle is not incompatible with that of a longer cycle averaging eight years or actually in many cases occupying just eight years. As it happens, most of the major movements in trade, which on the whole have been accomplished in a period between six and eleven years, have contained or been superimposed on either three short minor movements or two longer ones. Equipped with our definition of a minor movement—that is the three-years' cycle—we go on to study three-year cycles in agriculture. We shall examine, to start with, some arguments against the adequacy of variations in the weather as substantial explanation for derived cycles in agriculture.

Cycles in the Weather.—Although the theories of Professors Jevons and Moore have attracted no extensive support, it is still not uncommon to find fluctuations in rainfall regarded as the origins of substantial fluctuations in harvests.   The correlations between physical phenomena and harvests obtained by both Professors Jevons and Moore would seem to confirm such views, but as it happens, these authorities are not mutually corroborative.   Professor Jevons finds a 3½-years' cycle in barometric pressure : but Professor Moore finds next to no periodicity in rainfall (for the United States as a whole) at either three or four years.   There is no need to quote these pieces of evidence against each other in the sense that both are to be taken as unreliable, particularly so far as rainfall is not uniquely correlated with barometric pressure—wherein no conflict arises.   Nevertheless, the evidence of each authority must be examined in the light of physical causes other than pressure and rainfall.

Against the rainfall theory we must stress the potency of such governing factors as temperature, sunshine, hail, hurricanes, floods, severe dry spells, the occurrence or absence of frosts, and the distribution of rainfall within the critical period of growth.   It is too much to believe, even if the aggregate rainfall over the critical period is a limiting factor in the same sense for most crops in most places, that its potency outweighs that of the other physical conditions sufficiently to warrant their neglect.   Again, we can hardly believe, though a number of meteorological stations in a region may agree closely in their rainfall records, that all farms in that region are benefited or afflicted by rainfall conditions at all equally.   It follows from the liability of farming to diminishing returns in terms of climatic advantage that an uneven dispersion of these advantages will have a smaller favourable effect on output than an even dispersion, and conversely.   Similar unevenness of dispersion characterises the physical conditions other than aggregate rainfall, and in these cases subnormal advantage from such conditions on some farms is not unlikely to be counterbalanced by super-normal elsewhere. It seems, therefore, apart perhaps from the very widespread movements of rainfall so far as they affect most crops in the same way, that climatic events cause variations in yield in some places, or for some crops, contrary to those pertaining to other places or other crops. Consequently the effect of aggregate rainfall upon the harvests of a large area, whether or not it be associated with the action of other physical conditions, is much limited to acute floods or droughts.

The barometric theory is more inclusive than the rainfall theory in that variations in pressure are associated with changes in temperature and so forth, as well as with changes in precipitation. But changes in pressure are not necessarily correlated with advantages to the crops. In Great Britain a low barometer in summer is associated not only with rain but with the absence of sun, and according to the circumstances, either may be a limiting factor. In general, it is the distribution of barometric pressure over a large area that determines climatic variation rather than absolute pressure in any one place. Accordingly we are forced to suppose either that the correlation between pressure and harvests is fortuitous, or that each obeys some periodic law causing cycles three years in average duration. If there is any causal nexus proceeding from variations in pressure it cannot be of sufficient scope or power to account adequately for the variations in the output of crops. The same observation applies to rainfall. One cannot rule out rainfall altogether, but merely question it on grounds of " adequacy and relevance."

Compensations in Agricultural Variation.—In the circumstances we must fall back on non-climatic explanations of agricultural variation. These are explanations in terms of variations in activity, within the limits of the elasticity of supply. They are relevant not only to crops but to animal products. We saw that animal products have accounted during the present century for 40–50 per cent. of the United States farm output by value. For Great Britain, at the present, about 70 per cent. of output is animal. Some proportion of this magnitude is also indicated for Europe in view of the intensive dairying which many countries have developed, in conjunction with pig and poultry raising. In the Southern Hemisphere, the grain production of Australia and Argentina is well balanced by their flocks and herds. What the relative proportions of animal and vegetable production for the world as a whole may be is unknown, but if we use agricultural theories of the trade cycle we should employ an analysis that takes into account both types of produce at least equally.

It is necessary before any argument based on agricultural variability can proceed, to show both that the variations are large and that particular variations in the output of certain crops or certain regions are not among themselves compensatory. As it happens, the aptest material for this purpose is the statistics of crops.

Inter-crop Compensations.—(i) The importance of these compensations can be studied by comparing the fluctuations of four separate crops (corn, hay, oats and potatoes) with the fluctuations of the four combined. These are crops for which yield and output are highly correlated, so that fluctuations in yield will suffice for our purpose. The crops are of Illinois for 1870–1910.[1] The method is as follows : We construct first an index of fluctuation in yield for each of the crops separately, consisting of deviations from the mean divided by standard deviations.[2] These indexes are then algebraically added, and the sums divided by four, to give an index of fluctuation in the crops combined. We can now compare the fluctuation in each of the series with the fluctuations in the combined series by comparing the mean deviations in the indexes (sign disregarded). The results are :

Mean Departures :

Corn . . . . . ·83		Oats . . . . . ·87
Hay . . . . . ·71		Potatoes . . . . ·77
	Combined . . . ·59	

(ii) This method can be extended to six crops (wheat and

[1] I have used Professor Moore's data with most of the calculations already performed (*Economic Cycles*, p. 60).

[2] To divide by the standard deviations avoids weighting the crops in proportion to their variability.

cotton added) and from Illinois to the United States, and shifted to the years 1892–1918.[1]   The following is the result :

Mean Departures :

Corn	·92		Oats	·79
Hay	·83		Potatoes	·81
Wheat	·84		Cotton	·74

Combined   .   .   .   ·45

(iii) It may also be noticed that Professor Moore has found a coefficient of correlation of ·960 between the four crops (corn, oats, hay and potatoes) and nine crops.   This is circumstantial evidence for the belief that the extra crops did not compensate for the fluctuations in the original four, except so far as indicated above.

(iv) Mr. Robertson has found the following synchronisations among crops : [2]

(a) United States, 1885–1911.—Wheat and corn moved together 15 times out of 27 and attained common maxima 3 times ; wheat and cotton moved together 11 times and attained common maxima 5 times ; cotton and corn moved together 17 times and reached common maxima 5 times.

(b) In India rice and wheat during twenty years reached their minima together, and their maxima usually diverged by one year.

(c) In Germany wheat and rye attained their respective maxima and minima as shown in table on page 172.

It is added that no such congruence of maxima and minima is to be found in the crops of the Argentine.

Inter-local Compensations.—(i) From the examples given in (i) and (ii) above it will be found, in the cases of corn, oats, hay and potatoes, that fluctuations in the United States crops as a whole were no less violent than in those of Illinois.

(ii) The world wheat crop and the United States wheat crops, in the years 1890–1913, were correlated, $r = ·603$ (probable error, ·091),[3] as regards yearly changes.

[1] Data from Moore, *Generating Economic Cycles*, p. 37.
[2] From *Industrial Fluctuations*.
[3] United States wheat crop index taken from Moore as above—world index from Stanford University, *Wheat Studies*, Vol. VIII, No. 1.

TABLE 15.—MAXIMA AND MINIMA IN GERMAN WHEAT AND RYE PRODUCTION, 1878–1910

Maxima	Wheat	1878	—	—	—	1882	—	—	1887	—	1890	—	1892	—
Maxima	Rye	1878	—	—	—	1882	—	—	1887	—	1890	—	—	1893
Minima	Wheat	—	1879	—	1881	—	1883	—	—	1889	—	1891	—	—
Minima	Rye	—	—	1880	—	—	—	1884	—	1889	—	1891	—	—

Maxima	Wheat	—	1896	—	1899	—	1902	1904	—	1906	1908	—	1910
Maxima	Rye	—	1896	—	1899	—	—	1904	—	—	—	1909	—
Minima	Wheat	1895	—	1897	—	1901	—	—	1905	—	—	—	—
Minima	Rye	1895	—	1897	—	1901	—	—	1905	—	—	—	—

(iii) We may recollect that Professor Moore has found, from his study of apparent periodicities, a high degree of congruence between fluctuations in the crops of the United States, England and France.

(iv) It is desirable to compare variations in the general agricultural output of countries far removed ; and if any correlation were evident, it would seem that world crops varied with previously registered international prices. Unfortunately, no reliable statistical material is available for a sufficient number of years. Comparison of American and Australian data, the latter probably imperfect, yielded a coefficient of correlation of ·3, with about the same probable error, and no conclusion can be drawn. Accordingly we must resort to indirect methods of comparison, in which fluctuations in output are deduced from fluctuations in price. The method is to compare the magnitude of year-to-year changes in the prices of selected American crops with similar quantities observed in the world market. Shifts in demand enter into the determination of both sets of prices, but there is no reason to suppose that the American demand for staple agricultural produce was less variable than the world demand—if it was more variable our results will be fortified. The selected American crops, corn, hay, oats and potatoes, are among the least elastically demanded of crops, and prices will vary more than the average. They hardly enter into the world price index which we shall use, and the American output is not in the ordinary course internationally traded. Hence we are dealing with independent markets. For world prices, as quoted in London, Liverpool, and other British wholesale markets, we shall use the food and raw material constituents of Sauerbeck's index, weighting raw materials by their proportion (five to one) in the American price series. The period studied is 1890–1914. We compare the mean deviations from the mean of link relatives—that is, we are comparing successive price changes. In the American crop price index, compiled at farm and so arranged, the mean deviation was 11·2 per cent., and in Sauerbeck, at London, etc., 4·7 per cent. This last underestimates the variability of world crop prices at farm by at least one-third, and we may conclude that world crop prices at place of origin had a fluctuation equal to at least two-thirds of that of the given American crop prices. This suggests, if the American demand has not been less variable than world demand, that American and world outputs will have varied similarly. It is not yet proved that movements in the American and world series, year by year, were simultaneous and corresponding, but this correspondence is sufficiently shown by the correlation ($r = \cdot 53$) between Sauerbeck and the four American crop prices.

Inter-temporal Compensations.—The inter-crop and inter-local compensations within any one country are eliminated in the statistics for agricultural output as a whole. But we have to make a further allowance, when considering the effect of crop variability on general trade, for the carrying over of stocks. This raises several points.

(i) The facilities for storage, when considered with respect to risk and inducement as well as space and cost, are limited, and some crops cannot be carried at all. It is as well, therefore, to notice whether good harvests are rapidly followed by bad, so that carrying propositions can be performed cheaply and quickly liquidated. As it happens, while the standard deviation in the output of twelve crops [1] in the United States in 1880–1919 was 6·7, the standard deviation in the same series considered as three years' moving averages was 3·7 ; and, accordingly, it seems as if the demands made upon storage facilities are quite considerable, apart from fluctuations in consumption.

(ii) Since normal stocks of staple commodities are probably quite small (possibly only two or three months' supply [2]), there is no reason to expect when crops are short any relief which is the counterpart of storing an excess.

(iii) The cost of carrying is such that only a part of price fluctuation is avoided by even the most comprehensive programmes of storage. In some examples considered in

---

[1] From Professor Day's index, *Review of Economic Statistics*, 1921.
[2] *Vide* Keynes, *Treatise*, Chap. XXIX. Only a small portion of these normal stocks will be available to redress deficiencies in current supply.

Chapter IV the fluctuation in price due to oversupply was cut down by one one-half by complete storage as compared to selling the crops for what they would fetch.[1] It will be seen from the manner in which these estimates were made that only a considerable divergence of actual carrying costs from the examples taken would disturb the substantial reliability of this result. Accordingly, we shall allow that intertemporal compensations smooth out the supply of crops, but not that they exercise the effect on prices apparently appropriate to the proportion of stocks to current supply.

(iv) Storage undertakings often exercise a supplementary effect on prices additional to that which arises out of the requirement that the undertakers shall eventually recoup themselves out of a recovery of prices from early low levels. The stocks are treated as potential supply. This is best regarded as a temporary collapse in demand due to the possibility of postponing orders, and prices accordingly are driven down. This matter did not lend itself to generalised algebraical treatment since the repercussions on demand of visible stocks depend very largely on how far they are visible. On the one hand, in the case of staple agricultural produce, the opportunities for postponing demand are not great ; but, on the other hand, surplus stocks are usually known and reported upon.

---

[1] The only example quoted which displayed just that degree of alleviation was that in which the combined elasticities of supply and demand were equal to one, and in which there was an oversupply of 40 per cent. If the combined elasticities are less than one, the alleviation is greater, but this advantage, as may be seen by reference to page 69, will be reduced again if smaller stocks than 40 per cent. are in question. (This observation, that the relative alleviation is small as the stocks are small, does not of course reflect on the measure of absolute price fall appropriate to any given amount of oversupply.) It may be safely taken that excess stocks amounting to 10 or 20 per cent., in conjunction with combined elasticities equal to one, would cause prices to fall by 8 or 12 per cent. with storage, as against 10 or 20 per cent. without. These are roughly the quantities with which we are now concerned, except that the elasticity of supply hardly enters into the direct effect of oversupply on price. It is assumed for the purpose of making the estimates given that carrying costs are in the neighbourhood of 15 per cent. per annum for two- or three-year storage propositions of the magnitudes indicated. Judged by current experience (1932), 15 per cent. is too small, but I am inclined to make an allowance for the view that, for short movements in trade, speculators in commodities look for recoupment not only in the restoration of prices to normal but to more than normal.

The Direct Relations of Agricultural Variation to Trade.—
The direct relations may be taken to work themselves out
through variations in the purchasing power of agricultural
producers and their associates, consequent on variations in
output. The importance of these relations depends primarily on the quantitative variability of output, on the elasticity
of demand, and on the proportion of farm and associated
income to income at large.

(i) Variability of Output.—From Professor Day's calculations of the production of twelve crops in the United States
we can discover the magnitude of variation by comparing
a number of minima in the series with subsequent maxima
one or two years later. The average amplitude (between
maximum and minimum) was 16 per cent. of normal in
respect of seven pairs of observations. The correlative
amplitudes for the world at large will no doubt be smaller,
possibly 10 per cent.

(ii) The Elasticity of Demand.—Professor Pigou has come
to the conclusion that the pre-war elasticity of demand for
American farm produce was greater than unity, but only
slightly greater.[1] We may agree that an estimate of
elasticity fairly near unity is suggested by the statistical
sources,[2] but not that the elasticity is greater than one.
This latter conclusion is established neither by the references
made by Professor Pigou [3] nor by evidence considered in
these pages ; [4] and from considerations of the inelastic
nature of consumers' demand for staple agricultural produce,
in conjunction with the costs of processing and marketing,
from wholesale markets onward, an estimate of elasticity of

[1] *Industrial Fluctuations*, p. 62.
[2] Professor Persons' report that the correlation between output and
receipts in the United States in 1879–1913 was only $r = - \cdot 04$. *Review
of Economic Statistics*, 1920. Also the agricultural output—pig-iron
production correlations found in the last chapter. But see note 1, page
177.
[3] *Industrial Fluctuations*, p. 62. Professor Pigou seems to have drawn
rather generous conclusions from Jevons' case for a correspondence
between agricultural output and the production of pig iron, but he does
not specifically rely on any one or two sources, and states merely, " On
pre-war evidence as a whole I conclude that the elasticity of demand for
agricultural produce in general is greater than unity, but that it only
exceeds unity by little " (p. 62).
[4] Appendix III, etc.

something rather less than unity is suggested.[1]   Let us take
·8 as a plausible estimate for the U.S.   World elasticity is
even less.   In the twenty or thirty years preceding the
1914–18 war, trade was freer than to-day, and the crops of
the United States, particularly staple export crops like the
cereals, encountered fairly keen competition.   This suggests
that the elasticity of demand in the world market for the
twelve crops was not more than about ·6.   If this seems
too low, let us remember that the twelve crops taken by
Professor Persons underweight raw materials, for which
demand tends to be rigid unless the finishing to be done is
but slight.   Furthermore, when we leave the United States
for world markets, the costs of transport and distribution
become larger, as distances increase and barriers of language
and commercial custom become more numerous.

Now if we take the typical amplitude of world agricultural
fluctuation as 10 per cent., and the elasticity of demand as
·6, we may deduce that prices will fluctuate by about
17 per cent., and receipts by about 8 per cent.   But the
supposition as to elasticity is too simplified—we cannot
usefully assume constant elasticity despite fluctuations in
output of 10 per cent.   There seems better reason to suppose
that the elasticity of demand is less when markets are
glutted than when supply is short, for though the tastes
and customs established in regard to staple produce may
tend to stabilise consumption, incomes are not elastic, and

[1] It is true that Professor Persons' correlation between farm output
and receipts ($r = -·04$) must stand, but I believe that the indication
of almost unit elasticity which this apparently gives, is misleading, for
three reasons :

(a) The occurrence in 1892, and at other times, of a rather unusual
event in the synchronisation of great European crop failures with American
bumper harvests.   This would raise the apparent elasticity.   I have no
evidence that any converse occurrences were ever so striking.

(b) If the elasticity of demand is less for greater volumes supplied than
for smaller, there is no association between the mean of supply and the
mean of price, such as the evaluation of linear coefficients of correlation
must assume.   This means that a disagreement between supply and
receipts would tend to arise, and it is this which is used as evidence of
unit elasticity.

(c) The tendency to disagreement is further extended by the practice
of storing surplus supplies.

Apart from these three influences, I should have expected a small
negative correlation.

cannot contribute much to the support of high prices when crops are small. If the demand schedule become less elastic as supply increases, this augments the variability of prices and hence of farm incomes. Seventeen and 8 per cent. perhaps become 20 and 12 per cent. That 20 per cent. is a reasonable variation in agricultural prices is suggested by Sauerbeck's index, in which agricultural prices are very liberally weighted. And if the London price of food and raw material went through cyclical fluctuations of 15 and 20 per cent., it seems as if the farm prices of agricultural produce must have varied by 20 or 25 per cent.

The impact of these variations on trade, in that context of direct effects with which we are concerned, depends in the first place on the proportion of farm income to income in general. Professor Pigou has used Dr. King's estimate that in 1910 agriculture accounted for 22 per cent. of the net value product of the United States. The net value product of agriculture consists in the gross receipts of the industry minus outgoings to other industries. Professor Pigou multiplied by 22 per cent. the fluctuations in farm incomes which he had found, to arrive at an indication of the variation in the income of the United States for which agriculture might be held responsible. This procedure seems to use a supposition that the direct effects of fluctuation ceased at the farmer's fence—all else being deemed " repercussions."

It is evident, nevertheless, whether we consider the matter under the head of repercussions or extended direct effects, that not the producers alone are affected by changes in crop prices. The elasticities of demand with which we are now concerned, and which have been roughly estimated, are elasticities at wholesale prices.[1] Accordingly, the proportion of the national value product to which the fluctuation in crop receipts (at wholesale) is relevant, is that not only of farmers but of primary distributors. Under this

---

[1] Professor Persons, in working out the correlations noticed above, seems to have used farm prices, but I have shown reasons for questioning the evidence of elasticity which those correlations appear to give. Wholesale prices more easily permit international comparisons, and allow arguments from the American elasticity to world elasticity.

latter denomination we must include the railway companies, the governments in respect of farm taxes, auctioneers, bankers, etc., etc. If the charges levied directly or indirectly by some of these persons upon the crops do not vary (directly) with wholesale prices, the earnings of the remainder are thereby caused to fluctuate the more. Since most crops incur primary distributive charges equal to at least one-third of wholesale price (that is, one-half of farm price), we shall raise the proportion of the net value product assigned to the farming community by one-half to get the net value product of farming plus primary distribution. The proportionate net value product so assignable, averaged in the United States from 1909 to 1928, was 21 per cent. approx. In most other countries of the world, except, of course, Great Britain and Belgium, the proportion will be much higher, and reach in some countries perhaps 70 per cent.[1]

But whether 20 per cent. or 70 per cent., or nothing at all, is of no great consequence, apart from repercussions, if what consumers save on agricultural produce is devoted to the purchase of other commodities. There would then be no decline in total income (no matter what the farm proportion was), though of course the national incomes of some particular countries would suffer. Again, it is true that the diversion of purchasing power from farm produce to other commodities might alter the volume of output and employment, but for our purposes the activity of trade is not well measured by these standards so far as changes in output and employment do not connote gains or losses in aggregate profit. If the presence or absence of profit (that is, an excess or shortfall of net receipts over so-called "normal profit") is the substance of good or bad trade, then a mere diversion of purchasing power does not alter trade unless there are coincident changes in saving or investment—for instance, a change in outlay on working capital. There is no reason to expect a large gain or loss on working capital so far as the building up of non-agricultural working capital

---

[1] In estimating the proportions for the United States I have had recourse to Dr. King's *National Income and its Purchasing Power*, p. 98.

is accompanied by the contraction of agricultural, and con-versely. In practice, changes in agricultural prosperity appear to affect trade much more potently than through any changes in net working capital ; and since changes in working capital are largely the product of changes in senti-ment, they are probably overruled by more general forces than the mere diversion of purchasing power from farm produce. The principal of the potent repercussions, if it may be so called, consists in the savings which are made by the consuming public when their agricultural produce bill is smaller, and conversely. In Chapter III we con-sidered British and American data which seemed to show that savings among the working classes, who consume the greatest part of the produce in question, increase when agricultural prices are low, despite coincident growth in unemployment. These savings, which withdraw purchasing power from the market, cause equivalent losses. Losses, in the ordinary course, drive down output, and pyramid themselves.

In Mr. Keynes' analysis, as summarised in the preceding chapter, the end point in the spread of losses was reached as follows : Losses will in any case lead to a contraction of output, but if the loss is unevenly dispersed among in-dustries, the contraction is greater, and the given amount of loss is concentrated on a smaller volume of production. At the same time the contraction either leads to, or is accomplished by, disinvestment in working capital. This increases the total loss, and sets going secondary waves of spreading loss. Finally, a position is reached in which the final total of loss is not greater than the postponable fixed charges (including " normal profit ") of those firms that remain in being ; and the contraction of output ceases when unit loss is just equal to postponable unit charges at the margin. Unfortunately, one has very little idea what is the margin appropriate to the magnitude of any given initiating disturbance.

Professor Pigou has also developed a scheme of analysis intended to examine the extent to which an agricultural disturbance would spread. The analysis is conducted in terms of real costs, incentives and rewards, but does not exclude the psychological perturbations which any disturbance will usually generate. The principal difference from Mr. Keynes' analysis, apart from the almost barter assumptions which Professor Pigou uses, is this : according to the theories of the *Treatise on Money* and their corollaries, the immediate loss may be judged to fall entirely on the farming community, and the repercussions of this loss will spread from agricultural areas outward. (The agriculturists have suffered losses in the fall of prices and these are not offset by the profits of non-agriculturists due to the diversion of some part of consumers' purchasing power.) But in Professor Pigou's scheme we examine the behaviour of the non-agricultural world as presented with a given change in cost or reward in the form of lower or higher prices of agricultural produce.

The first case to consider is where trade between the agricultural community and the non-agricultural (considered as homogeneous) may grow progressively if stimulated in the first place by rising prices for agricultural produce. Community A spends more money on B : B returns the compliment, and so on, probably in a diminishing series. This possibility has a connection with repercussions via savings. Professor Pigou has concluded, on the ground that A's expenditure on B really takes the form of an offer of A's goods, that the transactions are over, and do not grow, when the goods have changed hands and the money returned to its original holders. If A cannot enlarge his expenditure on B except he recoup himself from sales to B—or if he can only offer more to B in goods—this conclusion is correct. It is also correct when A borrows for the purpose and must soon repay. But if A draws on his own savings it does not follow that he will replenish them from the proceeds of sales to B. The available evidence shows that the public (represented in A) has no normal or desirable level of savings in view and that savings vary considerably over the cyclical period. Within the limits of this variability, changes in trade between A and B can grow progressively.

In the next case, A is regarded as a series of industries

organised in vertical and lateral series, and may be described as *a*, *a*1, *a*2 . . . , *b*, *b*1, *b*2 . . . , etc. Of this non-homogeneity the vertical constituents may be neglected : they are no more than an extended case of the employer-employee relation, in which, in individual industries, an internal gain of one party is procured at the expense of the other. There is thus no tendency for activity to extend on account of vertical subdivision, and the firm or person at the head of the column will stand for the whole. But the lateral constituent of heterogeneity is a different matter. If a given extra volume of purchasing power, liberated, say, in respect of an increase in elastically demanded output, circulates around the community, and if each member is engaged in making products which another member will buy with the extra purchasing power when it comes into his hands, the activity of each member will be extended. It is conceivable that £100 so put into circulation might cause each member, in an extreme case, to expand his output by £100.[1]

Having posited this extreme case, Professor Pigou immediately limits it by invoking the law of diminishing utility. If, after a period of transition, the utility of all goods has diminished equally—that is, of the extra elastically demanded goods and of the new output provoked by the repercussion—and if the former comparative marginal utilities have become re-established, the repercussion ceases. In such a case, no inter-industrial transfer takes place, and no

---

[1] It will be observed that these cases, originally devised by Professor Pigou in a form appropriate to non-money analysis, are here presented and considered in money terms. This raises possibilities of misinterpreting Professor Pigou, but there would be an even greater danger if I attempted unfamiliar forms of exposition. Furthermore, so far as I have been able to comprehend the assumptions of non-money analysis, I am inclined to mistrust them. The principal objections to " real " analysis are these : (i) in the cyclical period at least, activity seems to be unresponsive to changes in real income as such, for there exists no objective criterion of real income as there is of trade profit ; (ii) a change in trade profit will only convey an equal change in real income when the price of income goods is stationary. Such circumstances as alter trade profit nearly always alter price levels as well ; (iii) in adjusting his output to a change in " offers of goods " the entrepreneur simultaneously alters the efficiency of production, so that net profit is not an even function of the value of " offers " ; (iv) it is at least equally convenient to regard trade activity as a function of the position and shapes of supply and demand curves, and of changes in such, without recourse to matters not directly within the entrepreneural survey.

encouraging stimuli continue to be transmitted from industry to industry. This absence of transfer resolves industry into a homogeneous group which makes one conclusive adjustment to the initial disturbance. It is not possible to know how far marginal utilities do diminish equally, and during the period when industries were adapting themselves to the original disturbance, there would have been some extra expansion on the part of those to whom the utility of goods supplied by others had least fallen.

Among the marginal utilities which diminish in the circumstances given above is that of income—commodities taken collectively. This diminishing utility of income is taken to be a limiting factor in the expansion of trade. At the same time, in money terms, the utility of money diminishes, and prices rise. This reinforces the diminishing utility of income as a limiting factor among those whose growing incomes are being offset by rising prices—that is, so far as growing real rewards are necessary to call forth greater activity.

But the rise in prices is better regarded as symptom of a limitation than as a cause. Following an initial expansion of purchasing power, rising prices are evidences of some inelasticity of supply. The less elastic is the supply of commodities in general, the less is the favourable repercussion of trade. If the elasticity of supply were zero, and the amount of activity in the community were fixed, aggregate real income would be unalterable. The question of incentives and rewards would not arise, except so far as lack of incentive is responsible for the inelasticity.

Now if the elasticity of supply is greater than zero, we obtain a mode of measuring the repercussions in estimating the actual elasticity. For any given increase in purchasing power finding its way into the public's demand schedules, the increase in output is determinate for given conditions of supply, if only we suppose the entrepreneur to seek to maximise his profit without regard to his real income and the effort involved in producing. A scheme of repercussions based on supply curves has been elaborated by Mr. Kahn,[1]

[1] " Home Investment and Unemployment," *Economic Journal*, June, 1931.

and it is available for our purpose. Returning to the sort of problem which agricultural oversupply presents, we shall apply this scheme to the case where the public has effected a saving—having withdrawn from expenditure money otherwise spent—on agricultural produce.

Now the producers formerly patronised by these consumers are involved in a loss (granted that formerly they were just paying their way and making "normal" profit) and consequently they must reduce expenditure—on goods, labour or anything else—or diminish their savings (perhaps be forced into negative saving). If expenditure is reduced this transmits the loss to some other party—in the case of goods, to the suppliers thereof, and thence in turn to the suppliers (of any sort) of those suppliers—or in the case of labour, to the persons or the government responsible for maintaining unemployed labour. While this contraction is going on, tax receipts fall, and the government is faced with a deficit (or smaller surplus). Ultimately the original saving is nullified in these principal ways : (a) diminished new saving by entrepreneurs suffering losses, or inroads upon old savings ; (b) outlay ultimately on capital account for the maintenance of unemployed factors ; and (c) deficits, but minus (d) the increased further saving of the public since prices generally have fallen. Conversely, if agricultural prices had risen, and the public had diminished its savings to meet the extra cost, this extra outlay would eventually have found its way—after completing circulation it must end in someone's pockets—to new savings by profit takers, savings on maintaining unemployed factors, principally labour, and to budget surpluses—minus the diminished savings of the public confronted with rising prices in general.

This analysis traces out the consequences of an increase or decrease in savings. They are bound to lead to spreading waves of contraction or expansion until at last the change in savings has been cancelled. The degree of contraction or expansion depends on the readiness with which this cancellation is effected, and on the supply curves of the industries affected by decline or growth in demand during the course of contraction or expansion.

The method of measurement is first to assume that supply is perfectly elastic, and then determine quantitatively the conditions (Mr. Kahn's " alleviations " and " aggravations ") favouring or disfavouring the cancellation. Then adjustment is made for incomplete elasticity of supply. It is not possible for us to make these calculations directly relevant to world agricultural oversupply, but we may judge whether or not the world repercussions (relative to the original disturbance) will be greater than Mr. Kahn has found to attend an increase of investment in Great Britain in the conditions of 1930. Measuring trade activity in terms of employment, and taking the elasticity of supply at four, Mr. Kahn found that the ratio of secondary to primary effects was at least three-quarters. In passing from Mr. Kahn's case to agricultural oversupply, deemed to occur during times otherwise normal, we are first bound to notice that the elasticity of supply will be less than four. But though the difference to the measure of repercussion as between zero and infinite elasticity of supply is vast, the difference as between elasticities both but little greater than unity is comparatively small. It does not seem as if, at the outside, Mr. Kahn's estimate should be reduced, for normal times, to less than two-thirds. Then we have to observe that Great Britain is an open system, and one of the most important " alleviations," tending to limit repercussion, was the increase in imports attendant on home investment activity. To remove this item brings us from two-thirds to something certainly greater than one—we shall suppose 1·3.[1] Then thirdly, we must notice that the ratio of repercussion is low in Great Britain because the ratio of unemployment pay to a normal wage is higher there than in the world as a whole. This makes even 1·3 too small, and suggests at least 1·7, at a conservative estimate. It seems most improbable that the ratio is less than 1·7, and if we recollect that the ratio would be infinity for the world as a whole if only the unemployed " lived on air " and if losses were " recouped " by economies on consumption, the removal of

---

[1] To follow the working here it is necessary to refer to Mr. Kahn's article. As far as possible I have used his quantitative estimates.

these not very violent conditions should leave in a proportion of repercussion of at least 1·7, or even 2.[1]

Now in order to attempt a numerical example, addressed to the problem of agricultural oversupply, let us suppose that the primary disturbance to trade, caused in this fashion, and however measured, generates a further fluctuation double in magnitude. The task is then to find what magnitude of trade relapse should ensue from a given fall in agricultural prices. This problem is complicated by the fact that the primary activity—of the farmers—is actually (or has recently been) greater than normal, and according to the method of working the total disturbance to trade should be a multiple of the same sign, which is absurd. But the extra activity of the agriculturists, if their produce is demanded inelastically, was unprofitable, and may be represented, analytically, as negative activity. It seems that the word activity can be safely left undefined provided that the same definition is taken to apply both to primary and secondary activity. Since the changes which take place in the outlay of human effort and in paid employment in agriculture are extremely small for any given change in the prosperity of farmers, activity is certainly best not defined in terms of either effort or employment. If employment were the criterion, primary and secondary activity could not be added together, or considered in the same sense. There seems to be no physical measure of activity that would apply to farming and non-farming alike. But if we measure activity by yield rather than by effort, the difficulties disappear. A quantum of activity, so considered, can be supposed to produce a definite appropriate amount of repercussion when activity is transmitted from one industry to another. Since most theorists have encountered difficulty in formulating measures of trade activity, although the idea of activity is clear, our apologies for some vagueness need not be effusive.

---

[1] The assumptions of a closed system, absence of unemployment relief, and of a practice among loss takers of economising up to the total of their losses, remove all the alleviations that were diminishing the repercussion.

Now let us call the income of the world £x, and assume one-half to be spent on agricultural produce—both food and raw materials, taken at wholesale values. We further assume that if the price falls, one-half of the difference in prices is saved. This fraction is too great to represent the saving of consumers alone, but we must remember that distributors absorb some part of the gain to the non-agricultural world arising out of a fall in farm prices, and the savings performed in this field are likely to be considerable—mainly as corporate or business savings, held in part against an anticipated or apprehended reversal of the price movement.

Now if we take a typical fluctuation in agricultural prices to be 20 per cent., we see that the saving performed amounts to 5 per cent. x. The assumed direct contraction of trade—taking an expansion of inelastically demanded output as negative—on the assumption that the money value of commodities produced per unit "activity" is constant throughout, is measured by 5 per cent. y, where y measures world activity. Now applying the ratio of secondary to primary activity, we find that the total relapse in trade following on a 20 per cent. fall in agricultural prices is 15 per cent.

It would be silly to insist on this last quantity for its own sake, considering the guesswork estimates on which it is based. But unless a substantial part of the error involved in making successive estimates has cumulated, it is fair to say that a fall in agricultural prices is at least adequate to account for a substantial recession of trade. A recession of 10–20 per cent. in dimension would usually be reckoned a cyclical slump on the ordinary principles of trade measurement. The connecting link between agriculture and trade has been taken to be savings alone, apart from the obvious repercussions of a change in savings.

Now when we relate Mr. Kahn's scheme of repercussion —which the analysis above has loosely followed—to the schemes of Professor Pigou and Mr. Keynes, we find that whereas Professor Pigou's account is a description of substantially the same sort of phenomena as we have tried to measure, Mr. Keynes', on the other hand, contains items that have not been allowed for. There are two principal such items, whose inclusion in the scheme widens the limits of fluctuation.

First of all the unequal incidence of any given disturbance upon different industries. If some industries, which suffer most severely in the case where savings increase, cease production, the given loss is cumulated on other industries, and leads to further contraction. In the analysis given above, industry was taken as homogeneous, and each separate firm was supposed to contract its output by an amount appropriate to the shortfall in demand without giving up production entirely. Secondly, we have not made allowance for the decline in working capital that is likely to accompany the repercussions of savings when they occur at a time when stocks were at normal. So far as the fall in prices does cause a liquidation of working capital, the effect of excess saving is reinforced by a contraction of investment. The degree of feasible contraction of working capital is at least equal to the greatest increase in savings imaginable. In an extreme case the contraction of trade by 15 per cent. due to savings alone might easily amount to 30 per cent. if the initial 15 per cent. were taken as the signal for pessimism. It is not claimed, however, that amplitudes of 30 per cent. are likely to be reached through variations in savings and working capital alone. Fixed investment also comes into the picture.

The Special Significance of Savings on Agricultural Produce. —Now so far the analysis of repercussion which we chose to apply to savings caused by a fall in agricultural prices might very well have applied to a hundred other types of disturbance. The cheapening of any inelastically demanded commodity due to technical improvement, a deflationary policy imposed by the banks, an orgy of economy in public expenditure, or the revaluation of some currency at a fancy figure, might all liberate essentially similar repercussions. Before we proceed, it is as well to give reasons for thinking that variations in agricultural prices are a frequent or specially significant type of disturbance. Some of these reasons we have already examined at length, so that a very summary repetition will suffice : the last three are new, and will be investigated promptly.

(a) Agriculture is a very large group of industries which tend to behave uniformly. An increase or decrease of agricultural output is a matter of more importance than an increase or decrease in the output of any other group of commodities, except investment goods.

(b) Cognately, a very large proportion of world income is spent on agricultural produce, and brought under the influence of agricultural variation.

(c) Though variations in agricultural output are small relatively to the output of manufactured or other elastically supplied commodities, the variations are nevertheless appreciable. They have furthermore, owing to the comparative length of the production period, the character of proceeding independently of prices for a while, cumulating during that time, and at length making a striking impact on the market. Since the supply, though comparatively elastic over a complete gestation period, is extremely inelastic until the conclusion of such a period (or its counterpart in contraction), the excess output cannot be immediately cancelled by short supply, nor a deficiency redressed by a burst of special activity. For a year, at least, the market remains glutted or starved. Owing to the inelasticity of demand, such variations as do occur exercise a profound influence on prices, and give abundant opportunity for saving.

(d) The weight of fixed marketing costs in agriculture intensifies the fluctuation of agricultural prices at farm, and creates the illusion of a large fluctuation in demand or in world conditions of supply to which the farmer must make such adjustments as he can. In some countries only the preliminary stages of marketing are carried out within the country, and the influence of large external marketing costs causes violent fluctuation of the national income. Large-scale perturbations of confidence are created, and the farmer finds some support for the character of his own expectations, based on immediately preceding prices, in the mood of the whole country. As already noticed, the most imperfectly competitive character of the market system permits the absorption of some part of a fall in agricultural prices into the distributors' profits, and thence into savings, and conversely for a rise in prices.

(e) The farmers' incentives to alter the scale of production in response to price changes are reinforced by coincident changes in land values. These create recurrent and alternating impressions of loss and gain, which in turn modify the scale of the farmer's expenditure, and increase or diminish the security which he can offer against advances of credit.

(f) Farming requires a vast capital outlay, since, in general, capital is only turned over once a year, and the production period is rather long. Cyclical variations in agricultural output tend to be accompanied therefore by large variations in the amount of outstanding credit. These can be regarded either as variations in investment or in the supply of money.

(g) In agricultural countries the scale of fixed investment tends from time to time to be regulated by the prosperity of the country, as determined by agricultural receipts.

Cyclical Changes in Land Values.—This is not a matter of overwhelming importance for the world as a whole, but it is specially interesting in relation to cycles in the United States, where owner farming is the general rule.

The size of variation can be seen from the following table (see next page). Column A sets out the entire current receipts on American farms, less working costs, rent and interest, in millions of dollars, and Column B the year-to-year differences in those receipts. Column B is to be compared with Column C, which shows (in millions of dollars) the farmer's land value gains : [1]

We do not need to resort to elaborate statistical measures to see that the farmer stands to gain or lose more each year on a change in property values than on a change in current receipts. This is of some importance if the farmer feels rich or poor according to the value of his land, and if

[1] From Dr. King's *National Income and its Purchasing Power*, Tables XCIV and XCVIII. Not the whole of property gains accrue to farmers, since some of the farms are rented.

TABLE 16.—FARM RECEIPTS AND LAND VALUES IN U.S.A.,
1909–1927

	A.	B.	C.
1909	3,714	—	—
1910	3,904	190	464
1911	3,413	— 491	175
1912	3,905	492	681
1913	3,699	— 206	1,697
1914	3,647	— 52	922
1915	4,015	368	1,127
1916	5,030	1,015	3,875
1917	7,275	2,245	3,133
1918	9,002	1,727	3,624
1919	9,546	544	5,802
1920	8,234	— 1,312	4,436
1921	4,486	— 3,748	— 1,938
1922	5,148	662	— 9,824
1923	5,848	700	— 3,279
1924	6,096	248	— 898
1925	6,801	705	— 1,097
1926	5,912	— 889	— 943
1927	6,158	234	— 1,780

some part of the increment (or decrement) of his wealth is expended (or saved). It is true that a prudent farmer will not treat capital and income alike, but, nevertheless, it is generally agreed that changes in land values are taken into account when making a decision to expand or contract the scale of production. It seems to make no practical difference that if the nominal values were corrected each year for changes in the value of money, the gains and losses on this item would be much reduced, and in some years a nominal gain would have disguised a " real " loss.

Of the consequences of these fluctuations in land values, the most important seems to arise from the habit of treating gains and losses as an encouragement to or warning against expansion—a habit especially found among farmers who look for their principal rewards in farming not in current income but capital appreciation. Secondly, the changes in land values constitute changes in the value of collateral against mortgage credit. Thirdly, when farmers feel rich they are more likely to spend than save, but so far as an increase in expenditure requires new money, the actual importance of the disposition to save will depend very largely on the rate of turnover of farms, and the realisation of higher values in actual cash.

The changes in land values appear either to coincide with appropriate changes in receipts or succeed them by one year. In either case the farming community is likely to be spending more at about the time when the world at large is enjoying some prosperity, and this sort of behaviour adds to the prosperity. The stimuli to expansion, both psychological and via the increased value of pledged securities, are also liberated in time to coincide with the stimuli presented by improved current receipts.

It is arguable that some part of the farmer's gain from enhanced land values is somebody else's loss, especially when the land actually changes hands, but this alleges too much. In respect of incentives, the bidding up of land values is a symptom of buoyancy and the earnest of an intention to enlarge production or undertake new production. In respect of the money which changes hands, it is not the sudden saving of one year that pays for a farm, but a draft on past savings, either the buyer's own or those kept at the disposal of the banks.

Working Capital in Agriculture.—In Great Britain the amount of working capital required on a mixed farm is equal to the value of about fourteen months' output.[1] If this proportion holds generally, the amount of working capital sunk in agriculture is colossal and the year-to-year variations constitute one of the most important fluctuations in total investment.

For a great many reasons it is rash to place any reliance in published statistics of agricultural credit—which is of course the source of a large part of farm working capital —principally for the reason that official statistics cover only a corner of the field. Credit granted by mortgagees may be used to pay off the banks, and credit granted by banks may be used to pay off the merchants, so that the statistics

---

[1] Dampier Whetham, op. cit., and see Chap. V.

of only one form of credit may be misleading. However, for what they are worth, we present below figures of new credit releases by American agencies during 1918–31. Opposite them, for comparison, is a table of gross agricultural receipts in the United States [1]:

TABLE 17.—FARM CREDIT ISSUES IN U.S.A. 1918–31, AND GROSS FARM INCOME

(*millions of dollars*)

Year.	Federal Land Banks.	Joint Stock Land Banks.	Forty Insurance Companies.	Member Banks.	Federal Intermediate Credit Banks to		Farm Income.
					Co-operatives.	Other Finance Agencies.	
1918 .	126	8	—	—	—	—	15,101
1919 .	138	52	—	—	—	—	16,935
1920 .	56	18	—	—	—	—	13,566
1921 .	83	7	—	—	—	—	8,927
1922 .	206	124	—	—	—	—	9,944
1923 .	161	174	—	—	—	—	11,041
1924 .	128	53	117	—	10	10	11,337
1925 .	78	100	101	—	10	7	11,968
1926 .	72	86	65	—	— 1	14	11,480
1927 .	78	35	30	— 11	— 21	4	11,616
1928 .	38	— 62	— 12	— 34	2	1	11,741
1929 .	3	— 20	— 15	— 56	10	5	11,911
1930 .	— 10	— 32	— 37	— 1	38	16	9,347
1931 .	— 24	— 23	— 23	— 11	— 19	9	6,920

Since fluctuations in farm receipts can be taken to represent fluctuations in farm prosperity, it appears that issues of credit also vary with farm prosperity. If we may assume that in the world as a whole agricultural prosperity usually coincides with general prosperity, it then follows from the association between farm prosperity and credit releases that shortly after prosperity has materialised it is further extended by a growth in farm working capital.

In the more rigorous interpretation of the statistics above, it must be remembered that labour was being supplanted rapidly by machinery during the latter part of the decade. The demand for intermediate credit, predominantly repre-

[1] Data from *Year Book of Agriculture.*

sented above, was diminished as against fixed capital. This is evidently responsible for the falling trend in credit releases, which slightly obscures the cyclical picture.

Fixed Investment in Agricultural Countries.—We come now to what is probably the most important single connection between agriculture and trade—a connection via the investment activity of the developing (and debtor) countries, whose credit and incentive to develop vary with their agricultural receipts.

The fixed investment which goes on in these countries is a considerable proportion of the total, and is the most variable section of the total, as witness the following table of long-term issues [1]:

TABLE 18.—LONG-TERM CAPITAL ISSUES, 1927–31

	Millions of Dollars.				
	1927.	1928.	1929.	1930.	1931.
United States :					
Domestic	6,230	6,795	9,425	6,014	2,855
Foreign	1,561	1,320	759	1,009	254
Proportion of foreign .	20·0	16·3	7·4	14·4	8·2
United Kingdom :					
Domestic	857	1,066	776	620	207
Foreign	675	698	459	534	224
Proportion of foreign .	44·1	39·5	37·2	46·1	52·0
Netherlands :					
Domestic and colonial	61	131	96	123	77
Foreign	145	107	45	103	16
Proportion of foreign .	70·4	45·0	32·1	45·6	16·9
Switzerland :					
Domestic	79	57	131	61	125
Foreign	38	18	21	60	19
Proportion of foreign .	32·7	23·5	13·9	49·6	18·5

[1] League of Nations' *Balances of Payments in 1930.*

By no means the whole of the issues on foreign account was destined for agricultural countries. Nor were the domestic issues completely free from agricultural influences —in the United States the capital raised in several states must feel the effect of agricultural prosperity and adversity. By how far these two considerations cancel out, and the extent to which new issues are representative of capital transfers as a whole, it is impossible to judge. However, if we reckon that at least 30 per cent. of the world's new capital is devoted to projects whose earning power depends on agricultural prosperity at one or two removes, and that this proportion is about twice as variable as new capital as a whole, we shall hardly be guilty of overestimates.

Now what are the reasons for which the raising of capital, or more directly, the undertaking of investment projects, will tend to vary with agricultural receipts. Let us consider a dozen reasons, without undertaking to place them in order of importance, or pretending that all of them operate simultaneously everywhere.

(a) Public Investment : roads, railways, docks, elevators, public buildings, etc.—

(i) Agricultural prosperity breeds optimism, and not even Finance Ministers are impervious to sentiment.

(ii) An expectation of greater tax receipts is created, and part of the extra receipts (principally on export and import taxes) is already tending to create a budget surplus. This creates a prospect that the debt service on the investment will be easily met.

(iii) The revenue yielding public enterprises are increasing their earnings and seem as if they will repay expansion and improvement.

(iv) The extra activity of trade makes the public services seem deficient. For instance, the railway rolling stock in new countries is seldom more than barely sufficient even at times of average activity.

(v) When capital begins to come into the country from abroad, largely in commodities, it pays customs duties and further inflates the public revenues.

(vi) Realised surpluses are applied to debt redemption and improve a Government's credit among lenders.

(vii) The gain in the country's economic position as a whole makes lenders better prepared to consider further subscriptions. Borrowers submit their propositions with more confidence, and all the trade and revenue statistics bear them out. The existing debt service appears assured. In some countries, an improvement in the rate of exchange, in those countries' favour, is taken as a promising evidence.

(b) Private investment :
(i) It becomes more profitable and promising for foreigners to invest in the country's land and natural resources, and new money comes in. Confidence among lenders abroad is increased in respect of most types of enterprise, however speculative ; and as a matter of fact, there have recently been many scandals of recklessness (American investments in Colombia, etc.).

(ii) Similarly, the citizens of the agricultural country find it reasonable to increase their plant, build new houses and offices, or engage in every type of new project.

(iii) The banks are in a position to pursue a more liberal credit policy, and in this they are aided by the replenishment of London or New York balances, due both to the country's increased raw exports, and to the beginning of new capital imports.

And so we could continue, arriving at some of the nicest points.

In support of these descriptive observations on the relationship of investment to agricultural prosperity we now offer statistical verification in the shape of eight diagrams showing movements between 1921 and 1930. The diagrams are shown on pages 199–206, and consist of the following :

Diagram III.—Canada, 1922–30 : construction contracts and value of field crops in prairie provinces.[1]

Diagram IV.—Australia, 1923–9 : value of agricultural exports and net increase in public indebtedness. The latter series, owing to its enormous year-to-year varia-

[1] From material supplied me by Mr. A. F. Plumptre.

bility, has been cast into the form of moving two-year averages.[1]

Diagram V.—Argentina, 1921–9 : raw produce exports and gross long term capital imports.[2]

Diagram VI.—India, 1923–30 : export receipts from nine crops (accounting for 64 per cent. of total value) and gross capital imports.[3]

Diagram VII.—New Zealand, 1923–9 : all exports and gross capital imports.[4]

Diagram VIII.—South Africa, 1922–9 : agricultural exports and net capital imports on long term.[5]

Diagram IX.—Twelve of the United States, 1920–9.[6] These are twelve of the sixteen states whose agricultural income amounts to more than one-quarter of the total. The investment series is of the aggregate value of building permits issued in twenty-seven cities of the twelve states. The agricultural series is of gross receipts from seventy-five leading crops, weighted as among the states by the sizes of the populations of the cities they contain. It was not possible, owing to the nature of the statistical resources, to approach the matter more directly, but it may be noticed that the building permit index used closely agrees with the Dodge construction series for eleven of the twelve states considered.

Diagram X aggregates the separate observations for 1923–9, and extrapolates, from more partial data, for 1921 and 1922. The method of aggregation was to compile a weighted average of percentage year-to-year movements in the constituent data of the various countries. The weights taken were—Canada 11, Australia 7, New Zealand 2, South Africa 2, Argentina 10, India 6, and the American agricultural states 22.

[1] From League of Nations' Reports on Balances of Payments.
[2] Ibid. In this and all diagrams where investment is represented in capital issues, I cannot be sure of the exact dates to which the investment observations really belong. Some countries, on balance, may anticipate public works and borrow in advance, while others finance the works on short term and then fund later. Hence we should not expect a strict year-to-year agreement between investment and crop receipts, but merely a picture of similar movement.
[3] From League of Nations' Reports on Balances of Payments.
[4] Ibid.   [5] Ibid.   [6] Raw data from U.S. Statistical Abstracts.

It is needless to say, no doubt, that the seven countries selected for the comparison of investment and agricultural prosperity were the seven for which the least inadequate data were available, and not the seven which exhibited the closest correspondence. In fact, some of the seven studied show only an intermittent or general correspondence, and no close association of investment and farm receipts throughout the whole range of years. However, the picture of correlation, taking the seven countries together, is reasonably vivid, and in the cases of Canada, Australia, and the United States, even striking.

Not the least interesting feature, moreover, was the correspondence in several countries which appears to have obtained during minor cyclical movements within the larger cycle of 1921–30. Unless extraneous events are operating, investment seems to respond almost uniquely to the rise and fall of all but negligible changes in the fortunes of agriculture. That minor movements did not appear so clearly in the combined countries is probably due to some of them reaching maxima or minima a year later than others. Still, even in the combined index peaks at 1923–4 and 1928 are clear, as well as the general correspondence. Even if the combined curves had both been decidedly flat, the possibility of individual cycles for the constituent countries would not have disappeared. The existence of an open market for most agricultural produce, and the fact that changes in output in all countries are inspired by a common price experience in the immediate past, should mean that movements in all countries go in the same direction together. A divergence of end dates should be the only reason for apparently uncertain movements in the combined supply.

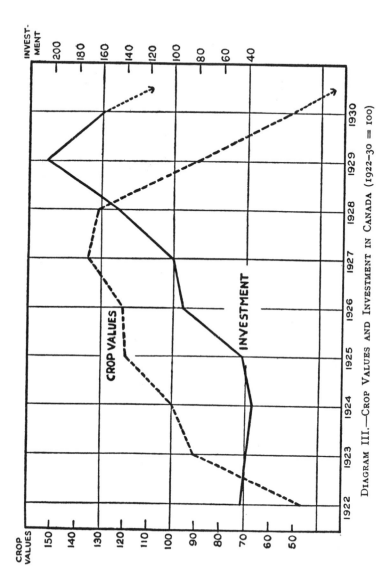

DIAGRAM III.—CROP VALUES AND INVESTMENT IN CANADA (1922–30 = 100)

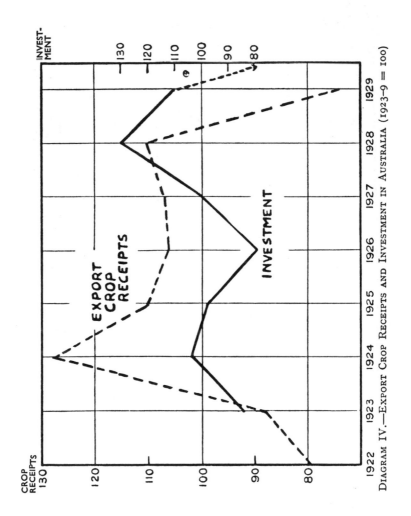

DIAGRAM IV.—EXPORT CROP RECEIPTS AND INVESTMENT IN AUSTRALIA (1923–9 = 100)

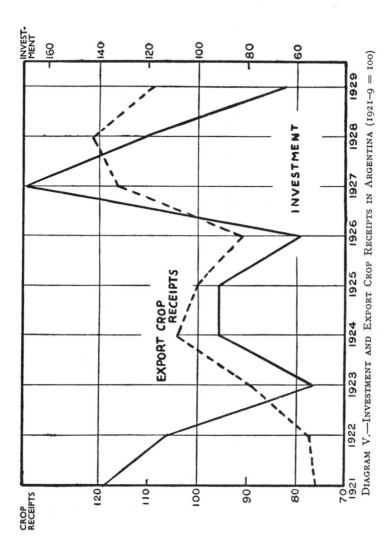

DIAGRAM V.—INVESTMENT AND EXPORT CROP RECEIPTS IN ARGENTINA (1921–9 = 100)

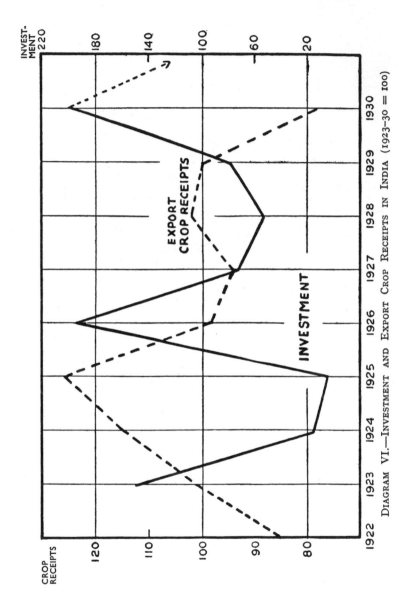

DIAGRAM VI.—INVESTMENT AND EXPORT CROP RECEIPTS IN INDIA (1923–30 = 100)

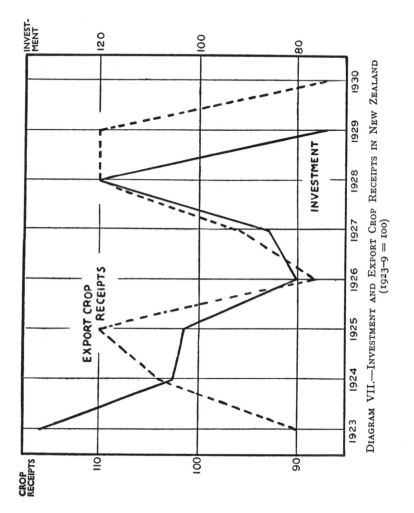

DIAGRAM VII.—INVESTMENT AND EXPORT CROP RECEIPTS IN NEW ZEALAND
(1923–9 = 100)

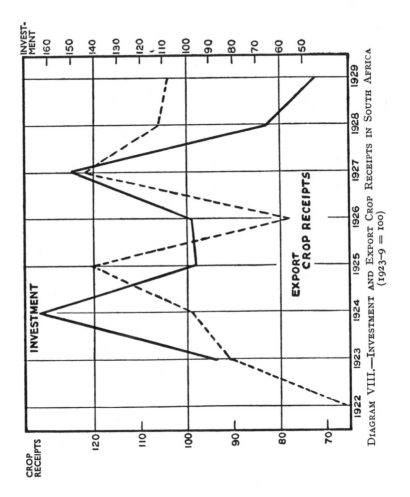

DIAGRAM VIII.—INVESTMENT AND EXPORT CROP RECEIPTS IN SOUTH AFRICA (1923–9 = 100)

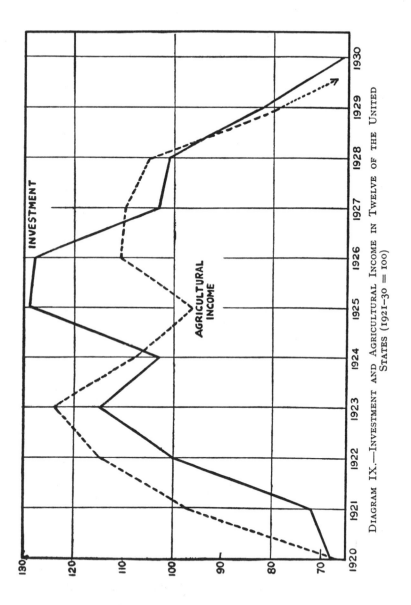

DIAGRAM IX.—INVESTMENT AND AGRICULTURAL INCOME IN TWELVE OF THE UNITED STATES (1921-30 = 100)

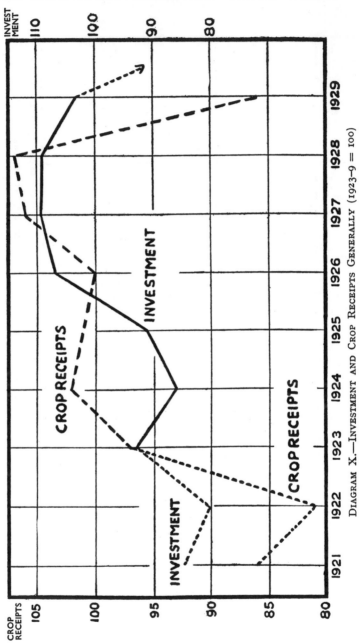

DIAGRAM X.—INVESTMENT AND CROP RECEIPTS GENERALLY (1923–9 = 100)

CHAPTER IX

THE CYCLE OF THE PRODUCTION PERIOD

Recapitulation.—So far we may claim to have established that fluctuations occur in the output of agriculture ; that they are capable of causing pronounced fluctuations in general trade ; and that the principal links between the two are to be found in the behaviour of savings and of investment in agricultural countries. It remains to consider whether the initial fluctuations are periodic or cyclical in the sense that trade is cyclical. If so, what is the length of the cyclical period, and how do these fluctuations combine with fluctuations due to events external to the agricultural system? So far we have not proved more than that agricultural fluctuations are significant in the etiology of trade disturbances, and that they predispose to such disturbances when trade is otherwise quiescent. Before proceeding further it will be desirable to summarise the position arrived at so far, both recalling the argument and adding a few interpretations to foreshadow what follows.

(i) Individual crops and the agricultural production of particular regions are subject to pronounced fluctuations in supply which run in periods in the neighbourhood of three years. The crops of regions near apart, and crops biologically akin, tend to vary in the same way because they experience the same weather or react similarly to the weather ; but, more important, agricultural output varies under the stimulus of preceding prices, and similar market experience tends to link together most of the crops over very considerable areas. Tendencies for the separate prices to diverge as time elapses are further controlled and limited by the infliction of similar price fluctuations on the crops by periodical fluctuations in demand—which themselves may or may not have been caused by previous fluctuations in supply.

(ii) The scale of amplitude in effective agricultural fluctuation is diminished slightly by the possibility of storing commodities, but this relief is easily exaggerated. Indeed, the practice of storage may indirectly contribute to subsequent fluctuations.

(iii) The typical amplitude of fluctuation in supply is 10 per cent., of prices, 20 per cent., and of agricultural receipts, 12 per cent. This is an average of major and minor fluctuations, respectively tending to occupy eight and three years. The proportion of the national income affected in the United States is about 20 per cent., and grows larger as the country is more specialised to agriculture.

(iv) The first important impact of fluctuations in supply upon the market is accomplished by variations in the savings of consumers and middlemen, and therefore is felt within a year of the establishment of a changed level of agricultural prices.

(v) Shortly afterwards, the changed prosperity of the farmers is reflected in the budgetary position of the various governments of the agricultural countries, and in the mood of the inhabitants of these countries. Such consequential changes in turn lead to violent and extensive variations in investment. These latter variations are already well under way within a year of the impact of excessive supplies upon the market, and are generally in time to reinforce the effects on trade provided by alterations in the scale of saving.

(vi) Among those who vary their savings are the farmers themselves, who are enriched or impoverished according to the prices of their produce. In the case of farmers particularly, there is evidence for belief that the standard of living is considerably revised in the same direction as the change in receipts. This may be seen clearly in the United States by comparing variability in mail-order business, particularly patronised by farmers, with corresponding series less directly under agricultural influence.[1]

---

[1] From Kuznets, *Cyclical Fluctuations*, pp. 37, 41, 102, 114.

TABLE 19.—STANDARD DEVIATIONS, 1919–25, OF SALES BY VALUES IN THE U.S.

Business.	Standard Deviation.
Mail-order houses	16·4
Department stores	6·3
Grocery store chains	10·6
Dry goods	11·5
Five- and ten-cent stores	5·1
Shoe stores	9·6
Drug stores	4·4

The effect upon the farmer's expenditure of violent fluctuations in the capital value of his property is of importance also.

(vii) A change in the prosperity of the farmer, accompanied as it usually is by a change in property values and the value of the security he can offer against loans, makes it both easier and seem more worth while to borrow for the purpose of expanding his activity. This is tantamount to an increase in investment. Since vast quantities of capital are consumed in farming, a further element of variation is imparted to investment, at a date approximately one year after the establishment of farm prosperity.

(viii) All the influences upon trade so far noticed are only complete after the initial impact has given birth to a chain of repercussions, and when the repercussion is at length exhausted. (That is, when the last repercussion is negligible, and not necessarily after the lapse of an appreciable time.) Any given number of initial stimuli working themselves out through these repercussions will travel a common path. Thus the stimuli will be assimilated to one another in their effects on trade. The type of assimilation is likely not to be a simple averaging—either where the stimuli are concordant or at any moment discordant—because any one dominant stimulus may well be potent enough to establish a definitive condition of confidence. Or likewise, a policy as to the working down or building up of working capital. Succeeding stimuli find the appropriate responses already made. Or, again, where the stimuli are discordant, a net stimulus of either favourable or unfavourable nature may well be strong enough to evoke a complete response. The assimilation of the stimuli, as indicated, and the existence of a common path of repercussion, also tend to make the whole of industry behave in much the same way at the same time. It need not wander through a protracted and vacillating course of response if the various stimuli are not simultaneously at their maximum.

Direct Correlations between Agriculture and Trade.—In order to discover whether the reactions of agriculture on trade which we have described and analytically demonstrated actually occur, one would naturally seek to discover statistically whether agricultural variation has in fact been followed by adequate and appropriate variation in trade. Unfortunately this is impossible. The following description of the difficulties encountered applies mainly to the method of correlation analysis, but it seems also to apply to such analogous methods as the comparison of the movements in series between reference dates. The difficulties are the same whether the comparison is made between agricultural and trade series in one or more countries.

Theory suggests that large harvests will be correlated with low prices and poor trade one or two years later. But in any one country surplus harvests can be sold at the world price (or a deficiency can be redressed by imports). Taking these two factors together, both positive and negative correlations are concealed in the data and appear to cancel. No one country is large enough in the world market to be independent of the course either of agricultural prices or of trade activity, and the effects of harvests on trade cannot be studied in isolation. Nor are these inconclusive results given by the statistics of separate countries likely to be seriously modified if we aggregate the agricultural and trade data of a number of countries for successive years.

Time series based on collocations of heterogeneous matter can rarely be made to yield a large measure of correlation, and in the sort of series we have in mind, the general tendency to low correlation will be extended in several ways. First, the elasticity of demand for agricultural produce enters into the relations of agricultural output and trade, and this elasticity will almost certainly vary with the size of the harvests. Secondly, agricultural output data will not be very helpful unless adjusted in respect to the presence of surplus stocks. Thirdly, the relations between world agricultural output and world trade will depend on the particular countries in which each year's excess or shortfall primarily occurs. A fluctuation is usually less important to world trade if it occurs in Poland than if in Canada.

In the circumstances it has proved impossible to obtain a coefficient of correlation greater than − ·2 between agricultural output and general trade, even in the United States. The reasons are much the same as made the elasticity of demand for American raw produce seem to be unity.

The Production Period in Agriculture.—Now we come to the reasons for believing the fluctuation in agricultural output to be cyclical, over a period of about three years. Let us first recall the responsiveness of output to preceding prices, extending the investigation from separate crops, as in Chapter II, to twelve crops taken together. The results may be set out as follows : [1]

TABLE 20.—CORRELATIONS BETWEEN OUTPUT AND PRICE OF TWELVE AMERICAN CROPS, 1880–1920

"Lag."		$r =$
(a) Crops and prices simultaneously	.	·82
(b) Crops one year after prices .	. .	·47
(c) Crops two years after prices .	.	·20
(d) Crops three years after prices .	. .	·08
(e) Crops 12–24 months after prices	. .	·27
(i.e. crops compared with average prices of the two preceding years).		

Since even the utmost elasticity of supply would not be represented by a coefficient greater than one, it appears that correlations in the neighbourhood of ·2 or ·4 are sufficient to establish a probability of reasonable elasticity of supply. (It must be remembered, however, that the weather probably played a part in determining coefficients (b) and (c). The weather tends to vary from year to year, so that after (say) bad weather has established good prices

[1] It is not necessary that any of the coefficients be, in themselves, "significant." They are used only for comparing one with another.

(cf. coefficient (*a*)) good crops follow the next year, and possibly indifferent crops the second year after. Also, the soil is alternately rested and strained. Both correlations (*b*) and (*c*) should probably be nearer zero.) The coefficients seem to suggest that crops vary with the average of the two preceding years' prices, tending particularly to respond to the price of the second of these two years. This seems to be consistent with a view that the production period in agriculture lies between one and two years, and we shall soon notice a few technical considerations which appear to confirm this supposition.

There seems no reason to doubt that these adjustments of output to previous prices, which in turn lead to a reversal of the price movement, occur endlessly in cyclical form. The actual existence of a periodicity, especially an irregular periodicity—if the contradiction may be allowed—is hardly possible to demonstrate positively. Even periodograph analysis based on the Fourier theorem is liable to give inconclusive results. This method, as we shall see, is not really appropriate to crop fluctuation, and failing it, the statistics of output can only be interpreted by eye. But visual interpretation of the statistics for any one country is also beset with difficulty, for oscillations of output, due to the weather, are apt to be so pronounced as to obscure all else. In particular, the American crop statistics display frequent weather oscillations at two-year intervals. If these are purely random, we should not expect to find synchronous oscillations in non-American series, and in the world aggregate oscillations of this type should cancel out. In other words, if we have a number of series displaying apparent periods of two, three and four years, but not synchronous periods, the average period is likely to be close to three years. The lack of congruity between variations of the crops of various regions which we have in mind in this context does not, of course, disturb the general tendency for inter-local crop compensations to be destroyed by similar price experience at much the same time. All that we have implied is that, as between various regions, the crops do not always reach their maximum in exactly the same year.

Similarly, we must disregard the negative evidence of Professor Moore's periodograms, though the amplitude of cyclical movement in the crops of the United States which he found to correspond to the period of three years is greater than corresponds to four and five years. In a periodogram when the phenomena are measured by years, an amplitude is built up by a succession of cycles all corresponding to the period (in years) in question. Now if a short cycle indifferently occupies two, three or four years, in the experience of any one country, the amplitude corresponding to each of these periods will appear small. In particular, the real amplitude is dispersed between three and four years, because more often than not the short cycle occupies between three and four years, and is easily capable of appearing to occupy either three or four years, and cannot be represented at its true period. (As for the large eight-year amplitude, this was built up out of the dimension of the longer movements as well as their tendency to occur at just eight years—the dimension of the short cycle is rather less.)

So if we may be allowed to retain the hypothesis of a three-year movement, frequently occurring at three years, as well as averaging three years, and since output is sufficiently well correlated with preceding prices, we may take it that movements in each of prices and production are due to appropriate preceding movements in the other. This is only in accordance with the observed tendency to make over-adjustment and promote instability that almost all economic phenomena display.

The principal reason for a three or three and a half years' period in agriculture, rather than a shorter or longer, is that the production period and the " liquidation " period taken together occupy just about that time. The production period is naturally a reflection of the technical conditions obtaining in agriculture which determine the time taken to procure an enlarged crop.

It is possible to indicate the lower limit of this period with some certainty. We know from the technical studies of Mr. Dampier Whetham that in England mixed farming requires fourteen months' working capital—or to frame the point more relevantly to the present context—the working costs of mixed farming in England are incurred on the average fourteen months before harvest. The corresponding time for animal farming is seven months.[1] It is suggested, therefore, that the average time, under English conditions, is about twelve months, and since English farming is mostly "high," the corresponding time abroad is probably a little less.

These periods, of course, are minima. In order that the weighted average of costs should be incurred twelve months before sale, some of the costs must be incurred even earlier. What is the importance of these earlier costs in regulating the time taken to increase production ? It depends on the contribution they make to the final value of the crop. In part this contribution can be judged from the magnitude of the cost : in part it is a function of technical necessity. Taking the first consideration first, we shall find that the earlier costs (costs incurred before the weighted mean date) amount, in the three instances worked out by Mr. Dampier Whetham, when these costs themselves are weighted by reference to relative dates and amounts, to the following proportion of the whole :

			Per cent.
Barley following roots carried off field	.	.	76
Barley following roots fed on field .	.	.	78
Milk—rearing stock and dairying	.	.	51

As far as is known, the work done on these three farms in England is the only attempt ever made to weigh the relative importance of costs in respect to time. While it is necessary to present the results of this work in order to get an idea of the magnitudes of relative costs, it cannot be pretended that English experience is at all representative for farming in general. This observation applies particularly to grain farming. In the two instances given above (of barley) the costs reflected high farming carried out by elaborate rotation, so that the earlier costs were extraordinarily high. Nevertheless, we can see that the earlier

[1] Because the heavier costs, for fattening, occur late in the animal's history.

costs—incurred in general more than ten months before harvest—are not negligible in the determination of the production period. In the cases shown above, the productive effort represented by the costs was applied intensively, and had this effort not made a substantial contribution to final value, it would not have reached the recorded magnitude.

But on the other hand, the method of rotating barley with wheat and roots is a mere refinement, convenient in arranging production on a given scale, but not entirely essential if a rise in the price of barley made an expansion of this crop seem worth while. Without rotation, the weighted lag (in the clearance of costs) is nearer six months than twelve, and 60 per cent. of the costs (properly weighted) are earlier than six months before harvest. So in arguing from rotation to one-crop cultivation, we must make allowance for a decline in the lag by about eight months, and a further decline in the proportion of early costs from 70–80 per cent. to 60 per cent. This allowance diminishes the importance of the early costs and probably puts the composite production period into the immediate vicinity of one year. And even when rotation is practised, it hardly pays to forego the benefits of a rise in price by maintaining the rotation although it occupies three years. An extra dose of fertiliser would take the place of a cleaning crop. Similarly, in the case of milk production, while it is true that new stock takes three years to breed, an increase in milk yield can usually be procured by enriching the feed.

In presenting a picture of crop farming as a whole, it is fairly safe to ignore a substantial part of the early costs incurred on prior crops, and place the earliest individual cost at fourteen months (in the case of a rotated crop preceding by roots, on ploughing) or at nine or ten months without rotation. Animal production, similarly, is best represented as occupying two years.

If the earliest important cost in arable farming is at fourteen months, this may mean that the farmer, ploughing (say) in August, sets the scale of production before knowing the coming autumn price. Then he cannot seriously correct this scale until the next August, or later, and the actual change in his output does not materialise until the following year—the third year. In this instance, the complete gestation period is in the neighbourhood of two years. But in one-crop cultivation, the ploughing is usually performed after the establishment of the new autumn price, so that the size of the crop may be substantially modified the very next year. Probably the bulk of arable crops have a production period of just one year when cultivated without rotation (or not invariably with rotation), and of two years with rotation ; and animal farming, again, takes two years. Farming as a whole seems to be subject to a production period of one to two years, possibly averaging out at about eighteen months.

The liquidation period is even more a matter of conjecture. It depends on the type of contraction resorted to. If in response to a fall in the prices of commodities the farmer merely ploughs a smaller acreage, and cuts down his fertiliser bill, this can usually be managed within one year. It is true that many fertilisers are not exhausted in one year (farmyard manure retains half its value after one crop, and potashes and phosphates a quarter or a third), but the nitrates, which are the commonest fertiliser, are almost exhausted by one crop, and the economy on fertiliser produces an immediate effect. Delays of longer than a year are more common when the contraction takes the form of laying down ploughland to grass—which requires about twenty-one months. On the other hand, if the prime economy is on labour, hands can usually be dismissed after the last harvesting and before the next sowing. If animal farming is affected, and the farmer decides to cut down stall feeding and turn to the stock to grazing, this takes about a year—in England—owing to the succession of the seasons.

The exact liquidation periods on any particular farm, to say nothing of agriculture as a whole, have not yet been investigated, even as partially as the production period has been. Yet one can safely say that most of the types of contraction that come most easily to the recollection occupy

between one and two years.   One would expect, a priori,
that the liquidation period would be about equal to the
production period, for presumably, if a crop takes eighteen
months to grow, the scale of that crop is fixed for eighteen
months, and cannot be corrected until eighteen months
after a change in price.   If this is correct, and both production and liquidation periods can be represented (supposi-
titiously) on frequency curves showing large values between
twelve and twenty-four months, then the complete cyclical
period occupies twenty-four to forty-eight months, centring
on three years.

It is not claimed, of course, that three years is an invariable
period.   The dimension of the cyclical movement varies
from cycle to cycle, and it is only reasonable to suppose that
different amplitudes of variation take different lengths of
time to accomplish.   Whether the relation is direct or
inverse one cannot confidently conjecture.   Technically, the
smaller the adjustment the quicker can it be made—psycho-
logically, the greater the variability of prices, the greater is
the inducement to make every effort to adjust production
however large the necessary adjustment may be.   It is not
beyond possibility that these two factors tend to cancel,
and keep the complete adjustment period fairly steady at
three years whatever be the dimension of movement.   Nevertheless, one cannot altogether exclude the emotional element
in farm policy, even if it be counterbalanced by the technical.
Farmers may or may not pay respectful attention to price
changes according to their readings of past price experience
—they will vary their behaviour according to whether they
expect the price change to be permanent or not.   Generally
they wait a while, if technical considerations permit, before
attempting a substantial adjustment to output, until price
indications are clearer.   This element of hesitation is responsible for a slight discontinuity of the cycle in the
vicinity of troughs and peaks of supply.   In the history of
the United States, agricultural production has occasionally
remained at rather inert levels of deficiency or excess for
as long as three years, despite significant price changes in
the interval.   Circumstances of this sort are not invariably

recurrent, but since they do occur, they prolong the cycle, extending its period to more than three years on the average, but not much more.

These theoretical conclusions which we have reached as to the length of the agricultural production period cycle can be tested by reference to Professor Day's index, quoted on page 15. If we cast it into the form of two-year moving averages, so as to damp down pure weather oscillations, we obtain twenty-two readings, from peak to peak and from trough to trough, which average 3·4 years. It is not possible to increase the number of observations by also reading from normal to normal, since the series also displays a longer cycle (of about eight years), which stands as a trend to the short cycle—a trend which it is dangerous to remove.

The frequency distribution of the twenty-two readings is shown in Diagram XI.

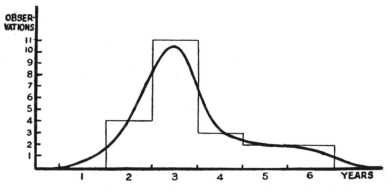

DIAGRAM XI.—FREQUENCY DISTRIBUTION OF CYCLES IN U.S. CROP
PRODUCTION (1879–1920)

While it cannot be claimed on the strength of this distribution alone, that the three-years cycle in agriculture is very regular, we are nevertheless in a position to bring further evidence in support of the notion of a three-year cycle in agricultural prices. But let us first notice what are the mean and modal values of the observed periods in the price fluctuations. By constructing an index similar to the production index from the raw data,[1] we can obtain twenty-

[1] *Review of Economic Statistics*, February, 1921.

one observations covering the period 1880–1920. The average interval is 3·57 years, and the frequency distribution is shown in Diagram XII.

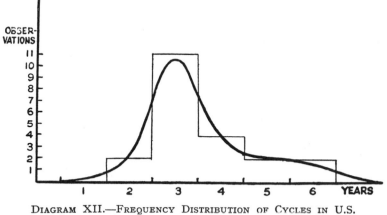

DIAGRAM XII.—Frequency Distribution of Cycles in U.S. Agricultural Prices (1880–1920)

It is proposed now to show that the regularity of the price cycle, such as it is, is the product not only of a fairly regular production cycle, but also of a stocks cycle.

The Stocks Cycle.—The authors of Stanford University *Wheat Studies* (Vol. VIII, No. 1)—*Cycles in Wheat Prices*—appear to hold that the influence of stocks upon prices is the chief determinant of the movement of prices, and give as a reason : ". . . it is only after some three years of low prices following a large crop that carry-overs are sufficiently reduced to make any substantial and sustained price increase likely." The cycle connoted here is the " long cycle," but we can use the clue to consider the relations between stocks and prices over shorter periods, and incidentally determine whether three years is not too long a period for the liquidation of stocks of moderate amount.

We return to the algebraical analysis of Chapter IV. This was directed to the establishment of a set of unique relations between the amount of the stocks and the time taken to dispose of them, provided the cost of carrying were known and also the elasticities of supply and demand.

The method was to pose two simultaneous equations for the solution of r, the period, and t, the cost of carrying, where (i) t, as a matter of fact, varied directly with the period of holding, since the longer the period the more burdensome and risky the enterprise, and (ii) t varied inversely with the period, because the shorter it is, the more must prices fall to accomplish rapid liquidation, and it is out of the reversal of the price fall that the entrepreneur is remunerated. The equations were

$$t = \frac{4w}{r^2(m + n)}$$

$$t = f(r, w)$$

where w is the proportion of excess stocks, r the period and m and n the elasticities. The nature of the functions in the second equation is best shown numerically, and numerical quantities will also be substituted for the expression in the first equation. We shall take w to be 8 per cent. (as a typical volume of stocks to be carried of several commodities simultaneously), and $(m + n)$ to be 1. The estimate of cost is also conjectural, but has been reconciled as far as possible with recorded " contangoes " of Appendix V.

$r =$	First Equation. Per Cent.	Second Equation. Per Cent.
$t = 1$ year . . .	32	10
2 years . . .	8	11
3 ,, . . .	3·6	12

The equilibrium value of r is between one and two years, and can be found to be 1·72 years, or approximately twenty-one months. It is suggested, accordingly, that when stocks amount to not more than 8 per cent. of normal supply, they can be cleared in twenty-one months. During this time prices are low, for only low prices, which depress supply and expand demand, can serve to diminish the stocks. At the end of this period prices are free to rise, and presumably will remain above normal until further excess stocks have accumulated. This, as we have seen, tends to occur slightly more than three years, or perhaps three and a half years, after the original excess has developed. At all events, the first half of this cycle, the period of excess stocks, is regular, and may be expected to impart some regularity to the whole cycle, despite the intrusion of spasmodic factors on the side of climate.

The assumptions used in the foregoing example were (a) competition among stock-carrying entrepreneurs; (b) that prices before and after the stock-holding period are equal; (c) that stocks are accumulated and decumulated at an even and equal rate. Taken in the mass, these assumptions may seem violent, but if we observe the sharply diminishing quantities in the first column of our numerical illustration, we see that almost any alteration made in the assumptions or the numerical estimates, unless they very largely altered the first column, will still leave the equilibrium value of r very near 2.

Let us test the whole theory by reference to a commodity for which statistics of stocks, in some form or other, are available for a long period. With wheat we can go back to 1894, and get a list of world visible stocks, except for the period 1914–19, for which we must resort to interpolations from purely American data. The list, which is not continuous, falls into the following sections : (a) 1894–1913, in millions of quarters, August stocks, from the *Corn Trade Year Book* ;[1] (b) 1909–22, in millions of bushels, visible supply of United States ; (c) as (a) from Special Memoranda of the London and Cambridge Economic Service ; and (d) millions of quarters, March stocks, from *Broomhall's Corn Trade News*. (See Table 21 on next page.)

Now to find what is the typical volume of wheat stocks to be carried we must first make an allowance for those stocks which are not spare but in transit or required to tide over the seasons. These we take as two-thirds of the average August stocks for 1894–1909 together with 1920–6. Then deducting these we can find the average amplitude of the peaks of spare stocks, and relate them to the current supply at peak dates, so obtaining peak stocks as a proportion of current supply. This averages out at 8 per cent., over six observations (1894, 1900, 1904, 1907, 1911, and 1925).

---

[1] Tables quoted by Robertson, *Industrial Fluctuations*.

TABLE 21.—WHEAT STOCKS, 1894–1931

	(a).	(b).	(c).	(d).		(a).	(b).	(c).	(d).
1894	21·7	—	—	—	1913	17·8	90	—	—
1895	19·7	—	—	—	1914	—	76	—	—
1896	15·5	—	—	—	1915	—	55	—	—
1897	9·6	—	—	—	1916	—	163	—	—
1898	8·7	—	—	—	1917	—	148	—	—
1899	16·7	—	—	—	1918	—	28	—	—
1900	18·7	—	—	—	1919	—	54	—	—
1901	16·5	—	—	—	1920	—	151	18·4	—
1902	11·7	—	—	—	1921	—	79	18·0	—
1903	11·0	—	—	—	1922	—	57	16·8	—
1904	21·8	—	—	—	1923	—	—	15·1	—
1905	19·5	—	—	—	1924	—	—	17·3	—
1906	16·5	—	—	—	1925	—	—	20·3	—
1907	19·4	—	—	—	1926	—	—	16·3	—
1908	12·2	—	—	—	1927	—	—	—	46·8
1909	9·9	43	—	—	1928	—	—	—	51·0
1910	13·5	88	—	—	1929	—	—	—	65·8
1911	19·5	92	—	—	1930	—	—	—	78·7
1912	15·7	78	—	—	1931	—	—	—	76·6

We saw above, in the general case, what would be the trial costs for 8 per cent. stocks if the joint elasticities equalled one. In the case of wheat we shall take the elasticities as five-sixths (say one-half to supply plus one-third to demand), and continue the remaining assumptions as to methods, obtaining :

		First Equation. Per Cent.	Second Equation. Per Cent.
$t = 1$ year	. . . .	38	10
2 years	. . . .	9·5	11
3 ,,	. . . .	4·2	12

The equilibrium value which solves both equations is between one and two years, approximately twenty-two months.

Accordingly we should suppose, from the method of carrying costs, that stocks will be above normal for periods of twenty-two months. Actually from our table of stocks, which shows eleven peaks in all, in thirty-eight years, we get a cycle averaging 3·45 years. If the years of supernormal stocks are equal to the years of subnormal—the tables do not establish this point except for 1894–1913—

the average period of surplus stocks is 1·73 years, or twenty-one months. The agreement—within a month or so—between actual and deduced supernormal stock periods in wheat, suggests that the method—although its use must depend on guesswork estimates—can be applied fairly generally. Also it seems adequate enough to substantiate the view that stocks in general are above normal for periods of about twenty months, so that prices complete a cycle in periods of about forty months.

The Industrial Production Period Cycle.—We have next to find, apropos of our propositions that agricultural fluctuation affects general trade through repercussions in which agriculture is further involved, and that agricultural fluctuation occurs at three-year intervals, whether three years is a period agreeable to industry. Is it congenial to the type of fluctuation to which industry is rendered subject by the conditions of its structure ? In other words, can industry easily adapt itself to a three-year cycle, and is a three-year cycle the sort of cycle to which it is most responsive ? These questions involve us in a consideration of the nature of an industrial production period with reference to the building up and dissipation of working capital.

Starting from the bottom of a slump, when stocks in hand and work in progress are both at a low ebb, traders find themselves obliged to enlarge their inventories. When stocks are at their minimum, traders must place orders if they are to do any business at all, and now under the combined influence of a cessation of sales of stocks and of a revival in production, prices begin to rise. While disposals of stocks were continuing, prices were unnaturally low, owing to an enlargement of the supply of commodities without any corresponding creation of purchasing power. Now the supply is decreased, owing to the cessation of liquidation, and purchasing power is created, via bank credits, in the revival of production. When for these reasons prices rise, it becomes worth while for manufacturers to increase the input of material and labour to production, and for traders to increase their stocks lest prices rise further, which they then do. Accordingly a period is ushered in of increasing working capital and rising prices. This progress ends at the conclusion of a production period, when goods in process mature, and finding dealers' inventories full, lead to a fall in prices.[1]

Now if the production period for all goods were the same, the form of the cycle would be a gradual rise (in prices and production) followed by a precipitate decline as the finished goods all emerged. But if the production periods for the different commodities are unequal, the curve tracing the cycle has the form of a shallow convex crescent, which is, of course, the standard case. A cycle of this form seems to accommodate, without requiring much further modification, the practice, which may be of some consequence, of increasing liquid capital—pure spare stocks of finished commodities—during a boom.

Now to measure the production period and obtain an average of the individual production periods of the separate commodities. We use the following proposition : if the rate of increment of value to goods undergoing production and distribution is steady, and if the rate of input of resources into production is also steady, and if, further, the value of working capital is equal to x months' output of finished and distributed goods, then the production period (including the distribution period) is equal to $2x$ months. Or starting from the other end : if the production period is one year, the average value of working capital during the year is one-half the finished value (or six months of it), provided that the value of working capital accumulates evenly during the year and that all stages of production and distribution are evenly occupied. Working capital in this paragraph embraces both goods in process and stocks in the same sense, for the stocks are increasing in value as they near their destination. Finished and distributed goods are taken as those occasioning the use of working capital, and thus exclude services.

Now as a first approximation we shall take working capital to be rather more than one-half of finished goods, for the following reasons : In the United States working capital

[1] See Keynes, *Treatise*, Chap. XX.

was directly evaluated in 1922, and found equal to one-half of the national income (or perhaps somewhat less [1]), which suggests that it would equal more than one-half when services (and the use of consumption capital) were excluded. To find the value of working capital in Great Britain we are forced first to make the assumptions given above as to rates of increment and input, so as to get the value of goods in process, and then we can add the value of stocks undergoing distribution. In 1924 the value added by British industry was approximately £2,150 millions, which gives £1,025 millions as the average value of goods in process. Let us take stocks undergoing distribution at three months' retail turnover, or approximately £775 millions. The total of working capital becomes £1,800 millions. The value of finished goods home-produced is equal to the national income minus services, minus finished imports, and plus exports, or £3,500 millions approximately. The proportion of working capital to finished goods is therefore between 50 and 55 per cent., or equal to six or six and a half months of finished production.

Continuing the assumption as to rates of input and increment, we get a production period of twelve to thirteen months. But these two assumptions add their quota to an absurdity. If the production period is thirteen months, and if, further, most goods have just about the same production period, then prices must complete a revolution every thirteen months, or over a period just a little longer. This contradiction with the facts can be resolved in two ways : either the production period is not thirteen months but longer, or the average production period is not a sharply modal period. The latter way out is the wider and we shall take it first. At a time when some commodities have reached the conclusion of the mean production period, others will have passed it and be tending to depress general prices, while others again will not have reached maturity, so that the production of them buoys up prices. It is not until the later commodities are matured that the support they give is withdrawn, and prices return to the level existing before

[1] Ref. Keynes, *Treatise*, Vol. II, p. 107.

new production began.   Now if the dispersion of individual production periods about the mean is quite random and far-spread, the price oscillation will occupy nearly double the mean period.   If the mean period is x years, some commodities will not be completing their periods until perhaps $5x$ years (e.g. heavy machinery), but nevertheless probability considerations as to dispersions about the mean suggest that almost all commodities will have emerged before $2x$ years.   There is a number of almost instantaneously produced commodities, like fish, to balance heavy machinery ; and so far as we can take the commodities occupying every point on a time distribution of production periods as equal in importance, then because the mean is x years, the last commodity in the distribution must occupy $2x$ years, minus an allowance for the fact that few commodities are so produced as to verge on the instantaneous.   In order to avoid overestimates we shall take the price oscillation period at $\dfrac{5x}{3}$ years.

What then is the value of x ?   The assumptions as to input and increment of value suggested thirteen months. But the assumptions must now be modified.   The supposition as to even increment of value ignores the fact that the higher-priced factors of production get to work later in the production period rather than earlier.   It is at the later stages that we encounter skilled machining, high transport charges (based on a higher value), higher distributive margins (also because values have increased), larger charges for interest (due again to higher values and to longer stock-holding periods for the more specialised finished goods), higher rents (as finished goods tend to be manufactured and held near towns), specialised salesmanship ; and generally, the more work done on a commodity the progressively more does it cost to add an instalment of utility.   It is not possible to put these points in quantitative form, but we may usefully take wheat as an example and consider the increment of value by time from ploughing to eating.   Diagram XIII should give a substantially accurate picture, though the individual items can hardly be vouched for.

In the case of wheat the commodity does not attain to half of its finished value until about three-quarters of its production and distribution period has gone. This may be an extreme case : at the least we should raise our general estimate of thirteen months to sixteen. (We had doubled the proportion, in months, of working capital to finished

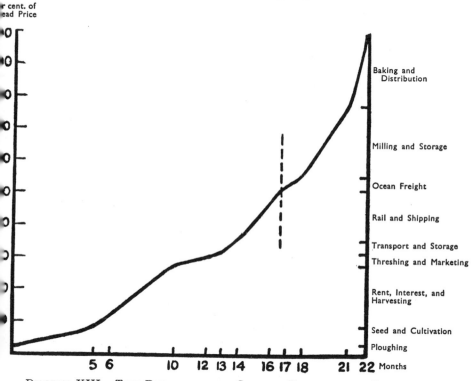

DIAGRAM XIII.—TIME DISTRIBUTION OF COSTS OF PRODUCTION OF BREAD

output, but it now seems that at 6·5 months the value of working capital will be less than one-half of finished output.)

Secondly, the rate of input is probably less rapid at the outset of a new production period, when prices are not yet very attractive, and more active later, since, like all booms, the working capital boom is largely self-feeding, up to the point when available resources are strained. This inequality of intensity of production tends to increase the average length of the production period. During the production period there is a relative excess of nearly raw goods—corresponding to a period of (say) eighteen months—as against the more normal (1924) distribution, corresponding to sixteen months. The larger the proportion of raw goods, the longer it will take before all the goods are completed.

If we may take eighteen months for our value of x, the mean production period, in preference to the value of thirteen months which the proportion of working capital to finished output apparently suggested, the price oscillation period, five-thirds of x, becomes thirty months.

This last period is taken to fit the American conditions best, for the British production period should be rather longer than eighteen months. In the foreign trade area of British production the period must include not only the time taken for manufacture but also the time taken to collect imported raw material and deliver exports. Also the American production period tends to be shorter than the British because standardisation diminishes stocks, and the mass production and distribution of "nationally advertised products" is rather rapid. On the other hand the distances in Britain are less.

Now how does the price oscillation period—from slump to slump—fit into the complete cycle ? Let us notice first that the oscillation is an oscillation about the normal, and that the period contains stages both of supernormal and subnormal prices. Then we must make some allowance for a few months of hesitation at the extremes of prices and production, before reversal sets in, so that a sequence of cycles does not consist solely of a sequence of oscillation periods. The periods of hesitation vary from cycle to cycle for reasons mainly psychological, and impossible to generalise, but since there is some statistical evidence (in trade indexes) both of the absence (at times) of a hesitation period, and of periods lasting more than twelve months, we shall take the mean hesitation period, occurring both at slump and boom, as 6–9 months. It is not essential for the working out of the cycle, or for its responsiveness to external factors, that the hesitation period should be inevitable or at all regular in length.

But the matter is worth mentioning since it fills out the typical production period cycle, carrying it from thirty months to something between thirty-six and forty-two months.

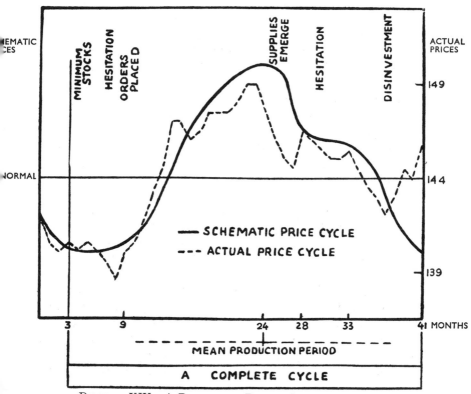

DIAGRAM XIV.—A PRODUCTION PERIOD CYCLE OF PRICES

Diagram XIV is a sketch of the production period cycle, drawn so as to reflect all the various governing factors so far noticed. For purposes of comparison, the actual cycle experienced in the United States during 1921–4 is also drawn.[1] Prices are taken in each case as the index of

[1] This cycle is chosen for the comparative absence of movements in the volume of fixed investment, and because it contained hesitation periods. The cycle of 1924–7 also gives quite a good fit. I have removed neither trend nor seasonal influences.

activity—for the actual cycle they are taken from the Bureau of Labour Statistics index (1913 = 100).

At this point we can claim to have shown the possibility of a production period cycle in industry which can be accomplished in round about thirty months, but which is more likely to take a few months longer. How does it fit in with the sequence of impulses originating with agriculture ? Let us notice first that the minimum duration of the industrial cycle is thirty months, or a period well within the limits of the duration of the typical agricultural cycle. Generally it need not so happen that an industrial cycle overlaps with two agricultural cycles, and gets out of phase with the agricultural cycles. Secondly, the duration of the industrial cycle is elastic. Within the limits of a year it can accommodate itself to the timing of the agricultural cycle. It is likely so to accommodate itself because it contains, or may contain, intervals of uncertainty in which entrepreneurs hesitate whether, at the end of a boom, to prepare for the worst, or at the conclusion of a slump, to begin buying lest prices rise. During this condition of affairs the industrial system is ripe to respond to any external stimulus, such as may be conveyed directly or indirectly by a rise or fall in agricultural prices. We have already seen that the agricultural cycle, by virtue of its repercussions, is competent to generate responsive movements in general trade : now it is worth asserting that the agricultural cycle frequently generates movements within the general cycle, and is likely to govern the timing of the general cycle.

Statistically, the time relations are difficult to disentangle, and the evidence that fluctuation in agricultural prices generally precedes industrial fluctuation is inconclusive. The reason is probably that the industrial cycle in turn works back on agriculture, and makes it uncertain from empirical observation which type of movement—the agricultural or the industrial—occurs the first. Nevertheless, the general tendency of agricultural and industrial cycles to coincide is quite clear. Out of twenty-five observations on agricultural prices and the state of trade in the

United States between 1879 and 1913, there were nine instances of simultaneity, thirteen of disagreement by one year, two of disagreement by two years, and only one of greater disagreement, in the dates at which the two cycles reached corresponding points (peak, trough, or normal). The agricultural price series used was of moving two-year averages.

The Long Cycle.—The next topic is the manner in which the short cycle (of three or four years) is related to the long (average of eight years). Both cycles work themselves out through the same type of final repercussion, in which activity cumulates or progressively declines, and both are likely to engender fluctuations in the volume of working capital. Both cycles are associated with variations in fixed investment—as we saw in Chapter VII, in reference to the theories of Mr. Keynes, the long cycle is primarily a cycle of fixed investment—and the short cycle carries with it fluctuations in the investment activity of agricultural countries—and possibly also secondary fluctuations in the investment activity of other countries. Taking all these points together, and adding the psychological element, we find a large measure of concurrence in the effects and character of the two cycles. This suggests that the two types of cycle are likely at appropriate times to link up, for otherwise they would be tending to work at cross-purposes, neutralising one another, though the long cycle, which is commonly of larger dimension, would still usually produce a small net effect.

It seems to be suggested, therefore, that either the short cycle will be timed by the long, or else vice versa, in the sense that critical moments of uncertainty in either will permit the entry of influences emanating from the other. Because the short cycle is more definitive in its characteristic course and in its timing than the long, it is more probable that the beginnings and ends of long cycles will be fixed according to the beginnings and ends of the short cycles, than the other way on. The course of investment is determined primarily by the number and size of profitable, or apparently profitable, openings for investment, in conjunction with the rate of interest by which the degree of profitableness is gauged. The prospects for remunerative investment vary with the short cycle, which carries with it changes in profits, confidence, and all the rest, and therefore the course of the long cycle is at any moment dependent in its critical aspects on the position reached in the short.

This appears to be the general tendency, so far as mere reasoning can establish it, but nevertheless, it is clear that if fixed investment under the influence of some important invention was progressing very strongly it might override the short cycle and even distort it. Similarly an acute depression reached in the course of the long cycle will be capable—perhaps the year 1932 was an example—of prolonging the depressed phase of the short cycle. The occurrence of anomalies of this sort is indicated by the irregular timing of the cycles as recorded in trade indexes. The anomalies might perhaps be reduced to general principles, but our present purpose is not to discuss the exceptions, but rather to indicate the frequency with which the short cycle appears to have entered into the determination of the period occupied by the long.

Within the long cycles of which records are available both for the United States and Great Britain, there seem to be contained almost always either two or three short cycles. The exact relation is not of course a relation of multiples, and the course of trade is perhaps better described as displaying a sequence of long movements diversified by the presence of shorter waves, either two or three in number. The reason why the number is sometimes two and sometimes three is still unknown, and inquiries addressed to this problem hardly promise a facile solution. Let us take the occurrence of either two or three short movements within the long, apparently at random, as a recorded fact. Now since the short movements occupy round and about three years, the long movements should take either six or nine years. (Actually forty months is more like the average duration of the short cycle, and the periods of six or nine years to which the long cycle should tend are rather longer—$6\frac{1}{2}$ or

9½ years. The latter period contains its short cycles as slightly compressed, especially the last of them (cf. the cycle of 1926–9)).[1]

Let us test our conclusion as to the likelihood of six- and nine-year movements by reference to the trade indexes of Miss Thomas for Britain, and of the Associated Telegraph and Telephone Company for the United States. The long movements in the former are fairly easy to pick out, but there is room for error in disentangling them from the former. For what they are worth we obtain the following frequency distributions of the duration of long cycles : (a) Diagram XV—British cycles, 1855–1914, 26 observations. (b) Diagram XVI—American cycles, 1877–1926, 24 observations. (c) Diagram XVII—British and American cycles, combined but unweighted, 50 observations.

[1] Or, more accurately, the short cycles occurring within a long cycle tend to become successively shorter and slighter—due, I should think, to the dying down of the oscillations set up by the long cycle, whose movements at the turning points are apt to be violent because they concur with similar movements in the short cycle. The oscillations are spontaneous movements which need owe nothing to external events, e.g. agricultural collapse.

Along these lines we get part explanation of the comparative poverty of short-cycle movements in Europe compared to America. In Europe trade movement is sluggish generally ; the production-period cycle has no great dimension ; and only the concurrence of a short and a long cycle at the turning-points of the latter gives the picture of a complete cycle. Movements in the combined cycle set up reflex oscillations, it is true, but purely as oscillations they diminish rapidly. In America, on the other hand, where all trade movement is violent, the short cycle proceeds to almost the same limits as the long cycle or the combined cycle (or is liable to do so), so that all cycles appear as of much the same dimension.

Although fixed investment be quiescent (say on a plateau), there is no reason why American trade should not reach a full cyclical dimension, and the production-period cycle, energised by agricultural fluctuation, reaches the limits. Because all American cycles are of much the same dimension, and because each cycle can be assigned to an external cause, it is best to regard production-period cycles as other than mere oscillations set up by a coincidence of long and short cycle, even though a course of oscillation is in fact accompanying and underlying the sequence of production-period cycles.

In Europe, the successive disturbances which cause production-period cycles are weak, and do not give visible results except in conjunction with an oscillation immediately after a major movement ; in America, on the other hand, the successive disturbances dominate and control the oscillation.

The six- or nine-year movements in trade occur, of course, at six or nine years after the corresponding previous movements, and not every six or nine years for ever.

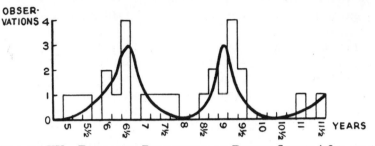

DIAGRAM XV.—FREQUENCY DISTRIBUTION OF BRITISH CYCLES (1855–1914)

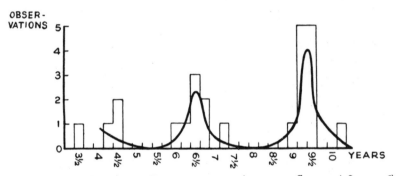

DIAGRAM XVI.—FREQUENCY DISTRIBUTION OF AMERICAN CYCLES (1877–1926)

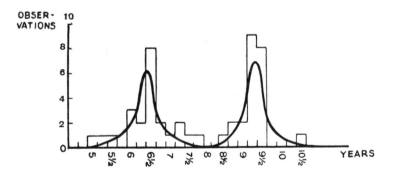

DIAGRAM XVII.—FREQUENCY DISTRIBUTION OF COMBINED BRITISH AND
AMERICAN CYCLES

The explanation of these distributions seems to be the tendency of the long cycle to occupy about eight years, as subject to diversion from this tendency according to the phase of the short cycle.

The tendency to eight-year movements is possibly an expression of the nature of investment goods—houses, railways and public works, in this sense : that during the depressed phase of the long cycle four years of overdue investment work accumulate through four years' deterioration of existing equipment together with the postponement of development. Changes in the rate of savings also enter into the matter, but let us take first the question of arrear investment, and illustrate it with a numerical example. This can be regarded as the first component of the investment cycle, where the instability of savings is the second.

We bring into comparison the growth in demand for investment, as conveyed by the growth of populations, with the actual amount of investment made, during a cycle whose form is denoted by entries in Column I. Column II shows the rate of growth in the demand for capital as a percentage proportion of the value of existing equipment. Column III gives that demand as a percentage proportion of the mean world income of the period, on the supposition that capital generally can be valued at ten years' purchase of income. Column IV gives the investment assumed to be made, and Column V cumulates the differences between Columns III and IV, that is between investment demanded and supplied. The point up to which investment is in arrear is marked.

Column I. Trade Index.			Column II. Growth in Demand for Capital.	Column III. Same as Percentage of Income.	Column IV. Actual Investment as Percentage of Income.	Column V. Cumulated Shortfall.
110	.	.	. 1·25	11·3	11	·3
95	.	.	. 1·27	11·4	10	1·7
90	.	.	. 1·28	11·6	6	7·3
85	.	.	. 1·30	11·7	5	14·0
95	.	.	. 1·31	11·8	13	12·8
115	.	.	. 1·33	12·0	16	8·8
130	.	.	. 1·35	12·1	17	3·9
125	.	.	. 1·36	12·3	16	·2

The existence of arrear or surplus investment compared with the required amount is taken to determine what must be the course of future investment if, over the whole period, actual investment ultimately just satisfies the demand for capital. The estimates of investment made, which average out at 11–12 per cent. of income, are taken as above for the following reasons : first year, investment having already reached its peak, the demand for capital goods is temporarily satiated, and investment now falls off—by the third year, the decline in investment has ushered in a slump which in turn almost paralyses investment—in the fifth year trade begins improving as stocks are now being replenished and opportunity occurs for undertaking arrear investment— shortly afterwards new investment projects begin, and by the seventh year investment is in full swing, culminating in the eighth year.[1]

The second component of the cycle—the cycle in savings —can be illustrated similarly. Columns I and II are the same as in the first table—a trade index and a table of the growth in the demand for capital—Column III gives the savings assumed to be made, and Column IV here repeats Column IV from the first table, giving an account of investment performed ; and finally, Column V gives the cumulated shortfall of investment compared to savings, which is correlated to the trade movements shown in Column I.

Column I. Trade Index.		Column II. Growth in Demand for Capital.	Column III. Actual Savings.	Column IV. Actual Investment.	Column V. Investment Deficiency.
110	. .	11·3	13	11	2
95	. .	11·4	15	10	7
90	. .	11·6	10	6	11
85	. .	11·7	8	5	14
95	. .	11·8	12	13	13
115	. .	12·0	12	16	9
130	. .	12·1	12	17	4
125	. .	12·3	12	16	—

[1] These observations seem to be substantially supported by the statistical measurements of Mr. C. G. Clark (*The British National Income*, 1924–31). But the cycle to which the years 1924–31 refer was a nine- or ten-years' cycle, and this makes comparison with my numerical examples rather difficult.

The savings made, which average out at the same as investment over the period, are taken to vary as above for the following reasons : first year, savings are high during the boom when the public can afford to save—second year, prospects are less certain and optimistic spending is on the decline, so that savings increase slightly—third year, incomes are falling and saving is less feasible—fourth year, some negative saving begins in order to keep up standards of consumption—fifth year, with a revival of trade comes new saving and a reversal of inroads made upon old saving— and during the remaining three years saving continues at a boom level.

In the second table it is shown that savings exceed investment during the first four years, during which trade declines, and then investment gains, and trade revives. The turning-points are the taking up of postponed investment in the fifth year, and the saturation of the demand for capital in the first.

It has been assumed in the examples that the rate of interest has been constant throughout, and we have excluded the advent of any innovation that might consume an unusual amount of capital. Although the relations of the long cycle period to the rates of saving and investment are moderately clear on qualitative lines, the quantities involved are still most uncertain, and we shall not pretend to have arrived at any really demonstrable conclusion. At present there is better ground for hoping that something may be known about the short cycle than the long, and of course it is the short cycle which is the more intimately connected with agriculture as a cause.

Stabilisation.—This section is confined to a few points directly arising out of the foregoing, and is no way an attempt to prescribe a cure for trade cycles. The remedy most frequently urged is to control prices and suppress movements in trade by the exercise of central banking policy, directed immediately to limiting price movements to a narrow compass. Such a policy might be pursued either on a national or an international scale. If the scale is international, the only price index which it is feasible to stabilise is an index composed of the prices of a few commodities entering into international trade for almost every country. This will mean in practice an index of the prices of food and raw materials, weighted heavily in favour of agricultural produce. If fluctuations in this index could be prevented, one would be tackling fluctuations near their source, usually before they impinge on industry. Also, since fluctuations in the prices of agricultural produce are usually violent, a successful stabilisation of agricultural prices will mean that the measures taken will have been more than adequate for prices in general. (This does not mean that reverse fluctuations would occur in non-agricultural prices, but that the measures were successful with a margin to spare.)

It is extremely doubtful, however, whether a stabilisation programme using only monetary weapons could achieve its end. It is notorious, for instance, that prices are extremely difficult to raise when borrowers are pessimistic ; and cheap or abundant money (on short term at least) does not necessarily increase the active circulation unless the monetary manipulations are accompanied by measures which increase private, public, or trade expenditure. Without expenditure, extra money created is apt to find its way into savings or inactive time deposits, or conclude its effects in enhanced values on the capital market. It is true that a rise in security values tends generally to promote investment. But if the slump is at all severe the only rate of interest that will attract borrowers for investment is not likely to be reached by a rise in values by a mere 10 or 20 per cent. It would be necessary to create investment *ad hoc*, or saturate the capital markets with an unbelievable flood of money (that is, via open market operations). Reductions in the short-term rate of interest are perhaps even less effective than the purchase of securities, for given the state of trade, it may well be impossible to reach a rate that is worth borrowing at. In consequence a fall in the rate produces no effect. And, after all, short-term interest is not often a large item in costs, and as deterrent, its influence is weakened by the frequency of changes in the rate.

Monetary contraction is apparently rather easier to secure than expansion, but here again, the velocity of circulation (or the proportion of active to inactive deposits) is somewhat elastic, and the rate of interest as such not particularly effective, except perhaps in precipitating a decline in trade already overdue. It would be stupid to allege that monetary policy, aimed at stabilisation, is wholly ineffective, but we can safely say that its results are uncertain and technically difficult to procure.

A more direct method of stabilisation is to bear directly on expenditure, making adjustments to savings and investment. Contributions to the redemption of public debt are a type of the first, and public works a type of the second —both being in the province of ordinary constituted authority. But any one nation undertaking stabilisation programmes of this type must find itself bearing part of the burden on behalf of its neighbours, via changes in imports, exports, gold reserves, or rates of exchange, so that it would be more equitable as well as efficacious to undertake the stabilisation of investment internationally. But this is a dream : for the present there is even the possibility that delegates entrusted with the control of investment might interpret their mandate as one for economy. In consequence of the number of doubtful dealings that have occurred in the recent investment history of South American countries, and not in them alone, it is beginning to be assumed, in not unauthoritative quarters,[1] that development projects are reckless adventures undertaken by fools at the instigation of knaves. If that is at all true, the control of investment, unless the long-term rate of interest can find a permanently more modest level than that of 1919–32, will tend to extinguish investment.

Even the control of that investment which can be controlled without violence to the principles of private enterprise, is hardly likely to obliterate the trade cycle completely, despite a conjoined control of savings. A large range of

---

[1] See reports of proceedings of the Senatorial investigation into the sale of foreign bonds in the United States. Some instances of disreputable investment are also given by Sir Arthur Salter in *Recovery*.

fixed investment and of savings is out of the reach of authority, and so is investment and disinvestment in working capital, oscillations of which give rise to the cycle of the production period. It may be that these and other ingredients of chronic instability are a fair price to pay for individualism.

APPENDIX I

NOTES ON SAVINGS AND INVESTMENT

SINCE a great deal of the theoretical construction of this book derives from Mr. Keynes' theories of saving and investment, it is advisable to recall the gist of his method.

The following rough summary, though not the pure milk of the doctrine, may be useful to refresh the memory:

Fixed investment in public works, building construction, new plant, etc., is directly and indirectly responsible for about 30 per cent. of the normal activity of such a country as Great Britain, and more elsewhere. This investment activity is extraordinarily variable. The variations are propagated through their effect on profits. For the amount of profit earned in the industrial system is given by the excess of the value of investment (goods made but not marketed) over savings (normal earnings unspent). Investment activity, which augments the aggregate income of the factors of production, that is, of the buying community, tends to raise prices above cost. Savings, which withdraw purchasing power from circulation, depress prices. Profits or losses are the resulting balancing factor.

A curtailment of fixed investment will first diminish profits as a whole. Then, if the loss of purchasing power hits some industries relatively hard, it may knock them out altogether, and end their purchases from the rest, to the latter's injury, as if in a game of ninepins. Moreover, a loss of profits is the signal for the relinquishment of commitments in working capital, or goods in process and stock. The failure to replenish working capital as it matures in finished saleable goods is tantamount to disinvestment. The incomes of the factors of production engaged on making and handling working capital are diminished, but there is no check, rather the reverse, to the stream of commodities placed on the market. This disinvestment is of immense importance since the value of working capital normally carried in such countries as Great Britain or the United States is equal to at least one-half of the national income. Together with the fall in the rate by which addition is made to fixed capital, this disinvestment in working capital may carry down the price level to the minimum set by the bare prime cost of production (of a diminished quantity).

241

Up to a point this disequilibrium is intensified by the behaviour of savings. When industrial profits are high, and when the rise in security values and land values has also created paper profits, saving loses its charm. Then when the slump ensues the moral of insecurity becomes too pointed to ignore, and savings increase. The loss of profits, moreover, has diminished aggregate spending power. So the recession of trade, in these many ways accentuated, proceeds towards the limiting factors.

The principal limiting factors are these : (a) there is a point beyond which investment activity cannot well decline ; (b) disinvestment in working capital ceases when stocks are virtually depleted ; (c) both personal and communal savings must at length be invaded for the purpose of maintaining a minimum standard of life.

Analogously, the principal limits of an investment boom are given as follows : (a) by the maximum of investment that can be arranged at the time ; (b) by the maximum output of factors of production used in a critical capacity ; and (c) by the inexpansibility of credit or a rising rate of interest.

Many readers are accustomed to visualise inflation and deflation, in all their aspects, more readily in terms of the quantity of money than of savings and investment. It is argued in Chapters VIII and IX that changes in money are the consequences rather than cause of changes in trade, but it is not essential to press this point in order to bring the Quantity Theory into fair reconciliation with Mr. Keynes' theories. It should suffice to show that changes in saving and investment normally carry with them changes in the supply of money, either as consequences or simultaneous accompaniments.

First of all, savings, unless utilised forthwith for investment and put into the production of non-available goods, cause a fall in the price level of available goods, chiefly consumables. They will usually also cause a fall in the price level of all output, but with this we are not specially concerned. The working out is given below. Only the leading cases are cited, and among them is a certain amount of overlap.

(a) *Savings.*—(i) Savings slow down expenditure, the circulation of commodities, and the velocity of circulation of money used to finance the production and handling of commodities. (In Fisher's equation a fall in PT produces a fall in V.)

(ii) In one stage of the above it might happen that funds formerly used for purchase are now hoarded. This transfers money from active to inactive deposits, causing a direct diminution of velocity. Such a situation is neither accentuated nor redressed if the hoards are afterwards spent on buying securities (or other assets). For the savings inflicted a loss on producers, obliging them to dispose of securities (or other assets) in order to cover their losses. The price level of securities has remained constant, while the price level of consumables fell.

(iii) It is to be noticed that so long as savings are in excess relative to investment prices must continue to fall. This continuation follows the pattern of widening and diminishing repercussion described in Chapter VIII. So soon as A is short of funds, he is unable to buy from B, nor B from C, and so on. The velocity of circulation progressively diminishes.

(iv) When savings have diminished trade, a smaller amount of business deposits is required to finance production, and bank loans are not renewed.

(v) Savings depress trade, and new projects, which would otherwise have called for issues of money, are held in abeyance.

(vi) There are also cases where savings directly diminish the quantity of money. For instance, savings are vastly used for the purpose of paying off bank loans. A budgetary surplus used to repay ways and means advances is a case in point. Instalments on hire purchase often operate similarly.

(b) *Investment*, on the other hand, usually leads to an increase in the quantity of money in circulation and to a speed up of its velocity.

(i) Most investment projects necessitate direct requisitions of bank money, if not for fixed capital installations, then for working capital. Most projects involving the laying down of fixed capital not only use bank loans in the course of construction (e.g. factory building) but increase the scale of business and the community's requirements for circulating capital. A new machine increases output, and the extra output must be financed during the course of its production. The secondary requirement for working capital may quantitatively exceed the demand for fixed capital.

(ii) Even the laying down of fixed capital often demands issues of new bank money. Whether or not banks themselves subscribe to the new issues, they are often asked to put credit at the disposal of other subscribers. Or they participate in the holding of a larger volume of securities circulating throughout the market, perhaps buying the securities relinquished by those who sold out in order to subscribe to the new investment project. In the United States if the subscriptions are financed by the public out of time deposits, this, by pressing against reserve proportions, may force member banks to rediscount, which tends to inflation. Similarly, in Britain, it might become the policy of the banks to build up the depleted savings deposits by increasing the total of their assets—aiming at stability of deposit accounts than of deposits as a whole.

(iii) If savings deposits are stripped it is only so that they shortly metamorphose into income and business deposits, so directly increasing the efficient circulation of the total supply of money.

(iv) Investment brisks up the whole of trade, and leads to demands for money to finance a higher level of business in all types of ancillary enterprise.

(v) The velocity of circulation of money is likewise increased as the volocity of circulation of commodities speeds up.

(vi) In the special case where output is limited by the maximum productivity of the factors of production, an increase in investment directly leads to a rise in the price level of non-investment goods by curtailing the supply of them.

Generally speaking, savings depress trade, and investment expands it. Within limits both events may spontaneously reverse themselves later. But while they last, they alter the demands made upon the banking system for money, and they alter also the velocity of circulation of money.

Particular cases in saving or investment may not possess easily discernible monetary accompaniments, and particular changes in the supply of money need not be prompted by changes in savings and investment, but it is still reasonable to connote under saving or investment an appropriate associated monetary change that needs no specific identification. To talk in terms of saving and investment is, over a large area of discussion, sufficient by itself.

APPENDIX II

AN ANALYSIS OF FARM COSTS

It is useful in considering the stresses and strains set up in agriculture by a fall in demand to be aware, even but generally, of the distribution of farm costs among various leading categories, especially as assigned to the short or the long period. Agricultural costing is now a well-developed science, but it has a strong technical bias, and unfortunately, there is very little information to be had which bears on the problems of an industry rather than of its separate farms. Our principal quest, leading up to the influence of farm costs on elasticity of supply and resilience to depression, is the proportion of prime costs to capital costs. No statistics of international scope are yet available to elucidate the point, unless labour cost can be taken to stand for prime cost. But since in most branches of farming labour accounts for at least 50 per cent. of prime cost, this substitution can be made without leading to very inaccurate conclusions. In a memorandum of the League of Nations Secretariat (*Labour Costs in Agriculture*) information on labour costs has been compiled for about twenty countries. Generally speaking, the material from the various countries is just comparable enough to make it possible to conclude that labour cost accounts for 30–40 per cent. of total money outlay on mixed farms and 20 per cent. on animal farms. It happens, however, that labour cost is sometimes interpreted to mean "labour income" (the whole non-capital remuneration of the farmer), and sometimes the cost of hired labour together with an allowance for the employer's own labour. The details are as follow:

Australia.—A demonstration farm, 1922–6 :

Labour and management .	.	.	30·2 per cent. of total cost
Rent, taxes, interest	.	.	29·5 ,, ,, ,, ,, ,,
Other costs .	.	.	.	40·3 ,, ,, ,, ,, ,,

Canada.—(a) A demonstration farm, 1925 :

PERCENTAGE OF TOTAL COST FOR MANAGEMENT AND LABOUR

Oats.	Hay.	Corn Silage.	Mangolds.	Potatoes.
14	21	34	56	39

(b) Reporting farms in Ontario :

PERCENTAGE OF HIRED LABOUR IN TOTAL COST

Dairying.	Mixed.	Ranching.
7–25	15–57	15–27

Denmark, 1924-5.—Management and labour are reported to consume 33–40 per cent. of receipts on the average of farms, interest and profits 30 per cent., and rates and taxes 6 per cent.

France, 1912 ; *Germany*, 1914.—Management and labour are estimated at 40 per cent. on mixed farms in France, and at 37 per cent. in Germany.

Great Britain, 1924-5.—On farms in the English Midlands, labour cost 39 per cent. on arable farms, 36 per cent. on mixed farms, 31 per cent. on dairy farms, and 27 per cent. on grass. In East Anglia hired labour cost varied from 22 per cent. on light land (mixed arable, dairy and sheep) to 31 per cent. on medium soil used for mixed arable and dairying. As between various crops the minimum labour cost on farms in the Midlands was 13 per cent. on oats, and the maximum, up to 50 per cent. on root crops. The labour cost on milk worked out at 20–30 per cent.

Ireland.—Hired labour costs are reported at 20–40 per cent. according to type of farm, reaching extreme minima on pasture (11 per cent.) and maxima on flax (41 per cent.).

Holland.—There is a range of labour costs from about 23 per cent. to 45 per cent. according to district.

United States, 1923-6.—Hired labour is stated to cost 13–14 per cent.; interest, rent, and taxes, 27 per cent.; and the exploiter's share is 59 per cent., of which 32·3 per cent. was taken in cash. Of this 32·3 per cent. more than one-quarter would represent interest at 4½ per cent.

Some further calculations on farm costs in the United States have been made by the statisticians of the National Bureau of Economic Research.[1] Thus we find that between 1909 and 1920 15 per cent. of the final value of the crops was spent on such costs (taken together) as implements, fertilisers, transport, insurance and bank interest, which represent the leading payments of agriculture to other industries. Over this period wages and salaries amounted to an average of 13 per cent. of the net proceeds of the industry. In 1909 the money costs of production were divided as follows : labour 20 per cent., fertiliser 3 per cent., feed 9 per cent., seed and threshing 9 per cent., animals purchased 26 per cent., and taxes, repairs and miscellaneous 33 per cent. In these calculations the whole agricultural industry of the United States is averaged.

---

[1] Publications 2 (ii) and 14. I have used mainly the summary tables printed in the former—*Income in the United States.*

TABLE 22.—TIME DISTRIBUTION OF FARM COSTS

		Long. Per Cent.	Middle. Per Cent.	Prime. Per Cent.
Long Period . .	Profits . . .	2		
	Interest on own			
	capital . . .	10		
	Depreciation. .	7		
		19		
Middle period .	Repairs . . .	2	3	
	¾ fertiliser . .	3	4	
	Rent	4	5	
	Own board . .	5	6	
	Interest on hired			
	capital . . .	7	9	
	Rates and taxes	3	4	
	Own wages . .	15	18	
	½ feedstuffs . .	4	5	
	⅓ seed . . .	1	1	
	Miscellaneous .	6	7	
		50	62	
Prime-cost	Hired labour. .	17	20	51
period	⅔ seed. . . .	2	3	8
	½ feedstuffs . .	4	5	13
	¼ fertiliser . .	1	2	5
	Fuel and oil . .	2	2	8
	Miscellaneous .	5	6	15
		31	38	100
		100	100	100

It will be seen that comparisons and corroborations of estimates of labour or other costs are very hard to make owing to overlapping terminologies, and in order to achieve a final analysis some arithmetical labour is necessary, of which the results are summarised above.

The table presented is intended to be a thumbnail sketch of the distribution by time of cost in agriculture. It is based on a bird's-eye view of American mixed farming, as modified by impressions from European sources, and represents the attempt to present something serviceable as a sort of world average.[1]

[1] I have been told these estimates are not altogether inapplicable to England. In preparing them the evidence already summarised has been used, but not exclusively.

Clearly these estimates have no reliability in detail: it will suffice if they are useful to put a quantitative check on theory. Some portions of the prime cost items of seed, fertiliser and feedstuff have been assigned to the middle period, as credit for as much as two years is not infrequently allowed by the merchant. Again, bought seed may be replaced for as much as six years with home produced; and the fertiliser bill is commonly reduced in times of stress by letting the land down. The short-period costs of common parlance may be taken as prime costs together with about a third of middle-period costs.

APPENDIX III

THE ELASTICITY OF DEMAND FOR AGRICULTURAL PRODUCE

THE elasticity of demand is usually defined as the ratio of change in consumption to the change in price, without description of the price. In the case of agricultural produce, where we are liable to find farm price, wholesale price, and retail price per unit in the proportions, 1 : 2 : 3, we shall need to discriminate. This appendix concerns retail price, and the elasticity of demand at other prices is derivative of the elasticity at retail. It is against retail elasticity that changes in supply really impinge, and retail elasticity governs the price displacements that occur during a slump.

The forty commodities with which we are primarily concerned, as listed in Chapter II, include fifteen which are commonly reckoned as raw materials, and hardly any of the remainder are consumed in the state in which they are produced. The leading final products to which they contribute may be summarised as follows :

Bread, confectionery, breakfast foods.
Rice.
Meat and fish.
Butter, milk, eggs, cheese.
Potatoes, green vegetables, fruit.
Sugar.
Woollen, cotton, linen and silk clothing and fabrics.
Boots and shoes.
Beverages (tea, coffee, cocoa and beer).
Tobacco.
Soaps and polishes.
Newspaper and stationery.
Tyres.

We may attempt a few comments on the elasticity of demand ruling in these categories.

Bread is the largest item in the cereal foodstuff group, and the demand therefore is generally deemed inelastic, or even very inelastic.

For meat and fish the demand is generally taken to have

elasticity greater than unity. But a change in price tends not altogether, or mainly, to alter the quantity taken, but the quality. The demand for superior qualities is much more elastic than the demand for the whole supply. Between 1929 and 1931, while the price of prime cuts of beef fell in English provincial districts by about 15 per cent., the fall in inferior cuts was more in the neighbourhood of 25 per cent. The same relations between qualities are to be found also in the dairy produce, fruit and vegetable, and clothing groups, and are most marked in tea and coffee. But from the angle of the producers as a whole, it is the elasticity of demand for the whole output which matters.

The elasticity of demand for meat is extremely difficult to discover, even if only as a ratio of the elasticity of demand for cereal produce. But the comparative stability of meat prices compared with cereals, both through 1916–23, and again in 1927–31, is surely significant. For instance, while the price level of field crops in the United States in 1920 had reached 238 (1911–13 = 100) the price level of livestock reached only 168. Then in the slump they returned respectively to 100 and 106. Even after allowing for differential conditions on the side of supply, the differences between the elasticities must have come into play. But if we reflect that the principal reasons for the price discrepancies were first, that cereal production suffered more damage during the war than livestock; second, that the elasticity of supply of livestock, given sufficient time, is greater than of field crops; and third, that the high prices of crops in 1920 reflected the building up of normal stocks, whereas livestock products are not much carried, then we shall not need to explain the price discrepancies on the ground that the elasticity of demand for meat is much greater than that of vegetable foods. It may perhaps be greater by one-half: the considerations suggested above, in conjunction with the price discrepancies registered, suggest some ratio of elasticities less than two.[1]

The elasticity of demand for dairy produce is probably above unity, but not much: the important items, judged by values, namely milk and cheese, are possibly demanded inelastically, at least in the staple grades.

Most vegetables and some fruit, in season, probably experience inelastic demand. This conclusion is strongly suggested for vegetables, both because inelastically demanded potatoes are a large part of the vegetable bill of the important vegetable-consuming countries, and because there is almost certainly

[1] These estimates refer to the world market. In Great Britain the increased *per capita* consumption of beef during the present century has probably not counterbalanced the decline in mutton, and the demand for meat is rigid or inelastic.

some substitutability between potatoes and green vegetables. The elasticity of demand for potatoes in the United States over the period 1890–1913, at wholesale prices, according to the method of determination invented by Professor Pigou (*Economic Journal*, September, 1930) was between ·3 and ·6 (middle figure ·44). The elasticity at retail was probably about ·7, since most vegetables cost about 30–40 per cent. of the final price to market.

Professor Pigou has estimated the elasticity of demand for sugar in the United States, 1890–1914, at wholesale, to be between ·250 and ·550, middle figure ·4. Not all this sugar was directly consumed, but part was used for manufacture. The retail price in Great Britain tends to be about 15 per cent. greater than the corresponding wholesale price. It is suggested therefore that the elasticity of demand at retail for household sugar is about ·5.

For non-alcoholic beverages the demand seems to be rigid, and since rigidity and inelasticity are usually associated in a common psychological origin, we may use the following evidences as suggestive of inelasticity :

Between 1901 and 1929 the *per capita* consumption of tea in Great Britain increased by 49 per cent., which was not more than the general rise in real incomes. Great Britain in 1929 took 65 per cent. of the world's tea.[1]

Between 1900 and 1930 the *per capita* consumption of coffee in the United States increased by only 4 per cent. The United States takes nearly one-half of the world supply.[2]

It is not to be expected that if the elasticity of demand for tea and coffee is low, that that for cocoa will be much higher. The Empire Marketing Board (ref. *E.M.B.*, No. 27) attributes the increased consumption of raw cocoa to the growth in demand for cocoa products other than liquid cocoa. Since no very substantial fall in price has accompanied this growth over the last ten years, a change in habit seems to be responsible for it. Still, the elasticity of demand for eating chocolate is almost certainly greater than unity, morbid as it may seem.

It is possible to deduce the elasticity of demand for beer in Great Britain by reference to tax statistics. If at any moment the tax is half the price, it will pay to increase it if the elasticity of demand is less than two, or to reduce it if the elasticity is greater than two. From the proportion to the price which the tax bore before the second budget of 1931 and the refusal of the Government to rescind an extra tax imposed therein, we may conclude that the elasticity of demand is not greater than

[1] Ref. Report of Imperial Economic Committee, No. 20.
[2] *Ibid.*, No. 19.

2·0.   In Germany the elasticity is probably less, but in the United States, at present prices, possibly greater.

The substitutability of qualities in the textile group of products is very great, and lends an appearance of great elasticity to the qualities most written about.   For the world as a whole, including India and China, the elasticity of demand for square yards probably is greater than unity.   Yet one cannot expect that the populations of Europe and America would expand the superficial area of their clothing on the mere inducement of a fall in price, though, of course, they would enlarge their wardrobes and discard worn garments sooner.   This last is probably the leading elastic element in the market for textile furnishings also.   However, there is a limiting factor in the glutting of the second-hand markets.

Soaps, polishes, newspapers, and a host of minor products not worth noticing in detail, share the characteristic of being demanded only in small quantities at a time.   A number of them are very cheap in relation to utility.   The demand is probably inelastic.

Tyres are demanded jointly with vehicles and mileage.   In the first connection, the proportionate expenditure on tyres is not often more than 5 per cent., and in the second, the proportion of running cost assignable to the wear of tyres is not usually greater than 10 per cent.   Accordingly the demand for tyres is inelastic.   It does not follow necessarily that the demand for raw rubber is inelastic, since it competes with reclaimed. The proportion of reclaimed to raw rubber used by manufacturers has varied between 20 per cent. and 50 per cent., according to the price of raw rubber and the technique of reclamation.   Had technique been stationary it might have been possible to conclude from the statistics that the elasticity of demand for raw rubber was ·2, but since the technique of reclamation has been advancing, coincidently with the cheapening of raw rubber, the elasticity of demand for the latter is almost certainly greater than ·2, though probably not greater than unity, since the substitutability of the two types is far from perfect.

It is possible to obtain some idea of relative elasticities of demand as between types of commodities by comparing the degree in which consumption falls off during a slump.   Dr. Kuznets (*Cyclical Fluctuations*) [1] finds the standard deviations in retail sales by values in the United States during 1919–25 as stated on opposite page (Table 23).

At the top of the list come branches of trade patronised particularly by farmers (mail-order houses) and expensive

[1] Pp. 37, 41, 102 and 114.

TABLE 23.—STANDARD DEVIATIONS IN U.S. RETAIL SALES,
1919–25

Business.	Standard Deviation.	Business.	Standard Deviation.
Mail-order houses	16·4	Music stores	11·8
Dry goods	11·5	Groceries	10·6
Shoes	9·6	Tobacco	7·9
Candy	7·9	Dept. stores	6·3
5- and 10-cent stores	5·1	Drug stores	4·4

luxuries (music and furnishings), and toward the end come cheap goods, whether luxurious or not, such as cigarettes and ice-cream sodas. It is of interest that groceries are as liable to depressions as these calculations show. The inflexibility of inelasticity of the demand for food, represented in groceries, cannot be very much greater than for clothing and comforts.

Corresponding statistics for Britain have only been collected since 1930 and are not published in a useful form. We may observe, however, by comparing the retail sales of February–December, 1931, with the corresponding period in 1930, that food and provisions suffered more than clothing and furnishing (5·2 per cent. decline compared to 4·3).

These various notes on the elasticity of demand for particular types of commodity can now be summed up. The following almost certainly have an inelastic demand : cereals, potatoes, cheap vegetables and fruit, milk and cheese, sugar, tea and coffee, tyres, minor articles of household use, and cheap comforts. The demand seems to be definitely elastic for expensive meats and fruits, beer, butter and eggs, and chocolate. Intermediate or uncertain are clothing, staple grades of meat, and tobacco. In the clothing group there are probably large gradations of elasticity, and the view that clothing as a whole has a decidedly elastic demand is not supported by studies of cyclical variability in consumption.

In all, a qualitative survey, eked out by such definite estimates as can occasionally be made, seems to show that the demand for agricultural produce is predominantly inelastic.

APPENDIX IV

MARKETING COSTS OF AGRICULTURAL PRODUCE

THIS appendix seeks to calculate the marketing, and in some cases processing and manufacturing, costs of several foods and raw materials. The sources are most scattered and fragmentary, and it is not possible to treat the commodities comparably, for levels of particular costs ruling at the same date. Nevertheless, it will be possible to show that for most commodities the essential cost of production is not the primary cost of creation, but the cost of distribution and preparation.

It is true that one might have arrived directly at this conclusion by the study of population statistics. More than one-half of the population of Australia, for instance, is located in six towns, and no adequate explanation is to be found in the existence of Australian urban industries which use imported material. On the contrary, a proportion of the processes of manufacture for the Australian market is performed outside Australia. The same preponderance of populations engaged in distributive and professional occupations is to be found in most food and raw material countries other than countries of peasant production.

The relative magnitudes of creative and distributive costs which the proportions of occupied population suggest will now be considered more precisely, commodity by commodity, first in detail, and then summarily.

Wheat.—(a) From farm to wholesale market or to mill as grain.—(i) Canada [1] to Liverpool, 1931.

TABLE 24.—PRIMARY DISTRIBUTION CHARGES OF WHEAT (a)
Percentages of Liverpool Price.

Country elevator charges	4·7
Rail from Saskatchewan point to Fort William	18
Lake shipper's charges at Fort William ; loading, inspection, weighing	2
Insurance, out-turn and brokerage at lake	1
Lake freight, Fort William to Montreal, including vessel brokerage and terminal unloading	12·7
Handling, brokerage, wharfage, etc., at Montreal	·7
Loading and freight, Montreal	8
Out-turn and marine insurance	1·3
Total	48·4
Growers' proportion	51·6
	100

[1] From *Marketing Agricultural Products* by Clark and Weld, 1931.

The proportion of wholesale receipts going to distributors is rather high in this example, since the 1931 prices were very depressed. At 1929 prices the proportion of distributive cost was nearer 35 per cent., and 65 per cent. is a fair estimate of the grower's proportion.

(ii) Rumania.—The costs are given as percentages of the c.i.f. price at a Rumanian port, which is nearly equal to an ordinary price quoted at wholesale.[1]

TABLE 25.—PRIMARY DISTRIBUTION CHARGES OF WHEAT (b)

	Per cent.
Producer to rail (f.o.r.)	2·9
F.o.r. to ship	22·5
Handling at port	6·6
Freight and insurance (f.o.b. to c.i.f.) . .	14·7
Total	46·7
Producer's share	53·3
	100

For earlier dates, such as 1929, the producer's share was again, as in Canada, nearer 65 per cent.

(b) Milling.—In Great Britain in 1929 the cost of milling [2] was 25 per cent. of the price of flour, or 30 per cent. of the price of grain ; or respectively 30 per cent. and 50 per cent. in 1931.

(c) Baking and Retail Distribution.—The costs of baking and retail distribution in Great Britain, taken item by item, are a mystery, which has baffled the Food Council. Nevertheless, a number of indirect but confirmatory evidences [3] show that these items in 1929 amounted to 25 per cent. of the cost of bread. (I have assumed that bread contains flour alone, and no water.) The same proportion appears to hold good for Finland, where detailed official estimates are available.[4]

Taking milling, baking and retail distribution together, we find that they cover about 45 per cent. of the price of grain. Apart from the item of wastage in the grain, it seems that the farmer consigning to the British market, who gets about 65 per cent. of the price of grain at wholesale, then gets 36 per cent. of the price of bread. Though the farmer is paid for a certain amount of husk, the consumer in turn pays for a quantity of water, so that if the allowances to be made for husk and water roughly cancel—and both are small—the final

[1] From League of Nations' *Agricultural Crisis*, Vol. II.
[2] Including wastage.
[3] Obtained by comparison of wheat, flour and bread prices, and their changes from time to time.
[4] *Agricultural Crisis*, Vol. II.

estimate of 36 per cent. should be approximately correct. That it is not too small is shown by the calculations of Doctors Warren and Pearson for New York State (1927) which showed the farmer to obtain 21 per cent.,[1] and by the official estimates for Rumania, which point to a proportion of 31 per cent.[2] Between 25 and 35 per cent. is probably a reasonable estimate for the trade as a whole.

Barley, Rye, Oats and Maize.—A part of the output of these cereals is used for more or less direct human consumption, but a greater part for animal feedingstuffs. As much as 75 per cent. of the American production of maize is taken for feed, and the marketing costs of this crop therefore tend to include the marketing costs of meat and dairy produce (but mainly of pig products). The marketing costs of animal products will be examined in greater detail below : here we shall take them as 50–60 per cent. of the final value. Now since it is extremely rare to find feedstuffs accounting for more than 15 per cent. of farm costs—eight to ten per cent. being the typical proportion— we can safely say that the complete marketing costs of cereals fed to stock amount to at least 90 per cent. In the case of oats, which is very largely fed to horses, horses being auxiliaries rather than final farm products, the marketing costs are even greater than 90 per cent.

That part of the output of barley, rye, oats or maize which is used as a human foodstuff has marketing costs which approximate to the marketing costs of wheat used for bread. The final costs, baking, milling and so forth, are less than with wheat, but the costs of primary distribution are higher in relation to the value of the commodity (barley to wheat : 4 as to 3). Taking all the uses of the four cereals together, and noticing that the more important uses are as animal foodstuffs, we must conclude that the average complete marketing cost is not less than 70 per cent., and probably verges on 80–85 per cent.

Meat.—There is a wide variety of marketing costs for meat from country to country, but in general we may say that primary distribution costs 15–20 per cent. of the final price, and retail distribution, 20–25 per cent. Table 26 shows calculations that have been made in separate markets, most of them protected.

In respect of some of the European markets I feel doubtful whether the wholesale price has been sufficiently well distinguished from the producer's price, since imported and home-produced meats are occasionally amalgamated for purposes of

[1] Quoted by Clark and Weld, *Marketing Agricultural Products.*
[2] Compiled from data in *Agricultural Crisis*, Vol. II.

TABLE 26.—DISTRIBUTION COSTS OF MEAT [1]

1928	Norway	Beef Pork	41 per cent. of final price. 39 ,, ,, ,, ,, ,,
1930	Poland	Beef Pork	40 ,, ,, ,, ,, ,, 50 ,, ,, ,, ,, ,,
1929	Austria	Beef Pork	55 ,, ,, ,, ,, ,, 50 ,, ,, ,, ,, ,,
1929	Spain	Beef Pork Mutton	45 ,, ,, ,, ,, ,, 46 ,, ,, ,, ,, ,, 30 ,, ,, ,, ,, ,,
1929	Holland	Meat	60 ,, ,, ,, ,, ,, (about).
1927	New York [2] . . .	Beef Pork	58 ,, ,, ,, ,, ,, 62 ,, ,, ,, ,, ,,

compiling indexes. The proportions given for New York are probably more accurate, and that market, since much of the meat will have travelled some distance, gives a better idea of the costs that will be incurred by the important class of export meat.

For purposes of comparison it may be observed that the costs of marketing fish are 50 per cent. of the retail price in England.

Dairy Produce.—(a) Milk.—The following are the proportions of the final price absorbed by distributors : [1]

TABLE 27.—DISTRIBUTION COSTS OF MILK

1930	England (milk to London)	50 per cent.
1929	Holland	55 ,, ,, (about)
1928	Norway	34 ,, ,,
1929	Austria (milk to Vienna)	31 ,, ,,
1929	Finland [3]	9 ,, ,,
1929	Spain	43 ,, ,,
1929	Switzerland (milk and other dairy produce)	30 ,, ,,
1927	New York State [2]	63 ,, ,,

[1] Except for England, these estimates are compiled from *Agricultural Crisis*, Vol. II.

[2] Calculated by Drs. Warren and Pearson, quoted Clark and Weld, *Marketing Agricultural Products.*

[3] An example of co-operation.

Some explanation of these disparities is to be found in the use of different descriptions of standard milk and in the climatic conditions of the different areas. The low proportion given for New York State is probably due to the distances that the milk must travel. Handling and canning at country points as well as in towns is necessary, and the former accounts for about 20 per cent. of the final price.

(b) Butter.—The distribution costs amount to :

TABLE 28.—DISTRIBUTION COSTS OF BUTTER

1929	Holland [1]	20 per cent. of final price.
1929	Norway	11 ,, ,, ,, ,, ,,
1929	Austria	42 ,, ,, ,, ,, ,,
1927	New York [2]	21 ,, ,, ,, ,, ,,

(c) Eggs.—The distribution costs amount to :

TABLE 29.—DISTRIBUTION COSTS OF EGGS

1930	England	40 per cent. of final price.
1929	Holland [1]	20–30 ,, ,, ,, ,,
1929	Austria	45 ,, ,, ,, ,, ,,
1929	Spain	40 ,, ,, ,, ,, ,,
1927	New York [2]	36 ,, ,, ,, ,, ,,

Taking these estimates together we may suppose that the producer most commonly receives 50 per cent. of the price of milk, 80 per cent. of the price of butter, and 60 per cent. of the price of eggs.

Vegetables and Fruit.—(a) Potatoes.—Distributors absorb :

TABLE 30.—DISTRIBUTION COSTS OF POTATOES

1927	New York [2]	42 per cent. of final price.
1929	Spain [1]	55 ,, ,, ,, ,, ,,
1929	Holland	60 ,, ,, ,, ,, ,, (about).
1929	Norway	45 ,, ,, ,, ,, ,,

[1] Except for England the estimates are compiled from *Agricultural Crisis*, Vol. II.
[2] Estimated by Drs. Warren and Pearson.

(b) All Vegetables and Fruit.—The distributor takes :

TABLE 31.—DISTRIBUTION COSTS OF FRUIT AND VEGETABLES

Total	1929	Switzerland [1]	48 per cent. of final price (about).
	1929	Austria : fruit	72 per cent. of final price.
		vegetables	57 per cent. of final price.
	1923	Pacific States : fruit [2]	64–77 per cent. of final price.
Retail only	1924	New York	45 per cent. of final price.
	1925	St. Paul : fruit	20–25 per cent. of final price.
		vegetables	26–55 per cent. of final price.

The proportions received by grower for fruit and vegetables as a whole (including potatoes) run from 20 to 60 per cent., and in the examples given roughly average at 40 per cent.

Tea and Coffee.—The major part of the marketing cost of these commodities is incurred subsequent to the wholesale market, and in this area of distribution, in Great Britain, the secrets of the trade have been well kept. In respect of coffee, Mr. Rowe [3] accepts the view that Brazilian growers obtain about one-third of the final price. This is about right for coffee entering the British market. About 30 per cent. is absorbed in freight, insurance, duty, handling, brokerage and other charges prior to the wholesale market, and about 40 per cent. is taken by blenders, wholesalers and retailers. The total is 70 per cent., but the producer gets paid for some wastage, so that he is probably paid 35 per cent. of the final price.

The cost of getting tea to the London wholesale market is about 7 per cent. of the normal retail price (1928–9), and retail distribution including blending takes 32 per cent. Thus, apart from customs duties on tea, which in Great Britain come and go, the producer obtains 60 per cent.

Sugar.—The costs incurred by a consignment of Cuban sugar entering the British market in 1928 are summarised on next page (Table 32).

Of the 28 per cent. represented in the F.o.b. price the producer receives by no means the whole. In Mauritius in 1929 he received 88 per cent. This suggests that producers in general receive about 20–25 per cent. of the final price.

[1] European data from *Agricultural Crisis.*
[2] American data from *Marketing Agricultural Products.*
[3] *Studies in the Artificial Control of Raw Material Supplies,* No. 3.

TABLE 32.—DISTRIBUTION COSTS OF SUGAR, 1928

	Per Cent. of Retail Price.
F.o.b. Cuba	28
Delivery to London	4
Duty [1]	26
Landing and refining	17
Wholesale distribution and transport . .	14
Retailing	11
	100

Cotton.—Between 1919 and 1929 the proportion of the Liverpool price of raw cotton obtained by American farmers has varied between 70 and 90 per cent. At the levels of price that have ruled in the latter portion of the decade, 70 per cent. reflects the average farmer's proportion better than 90 per cent., and we shall take 75 per cent. as a reasonable estimate. But the bulk of the supplementary costs incurred in supplying fabrics to the final consumer are incurred subsequent to the wholesale market, in spinning, weaving, finishing, and final distribution. I submit below, as percentages of the final price in English provincial towns, these various costs calculated for 1929 and 1931 by a large well-integrated Lancashire firm :

TABLE 33.—DISTRIBUTION AND PROCESSING COSTS OF COTTON, 1929 AND 1931

	Overall Cloth. American Cotton.		Voile Cloth. Egyptian Cotton.	
	1929.	1931.	1929.	1931.
Raw cotton	15·52	9·57	6·83	3·67
Spinning and weaving . .	12·40	11·04	22·80	20·24
Finishing (printing and making up)	21·87	26·60	15·97	17·60
Selling and distribution (expenses and margins of merchant and retailer) .	50·21	52·79	54·40	58·49
	100	100	100	100

[1] The level of duty in Britain, which closely corresponds to the American duties of the same period, is fairly well representative for the world as a whole.

I accept 12 per cent. as a rough average of the 1929 pro-portion for raw cotton, and relating this to the costs of primary distribution, we may conclude that the farmer obtains 9 per cent. of the final retail price.

Wool.—The various uses of wool, even within the one cate-gory of clothing, are so various and different that it is almost impossible to obtain an idea of the sheep-farmer's share. We shall attempt only to consider the limits within which it probably lies.

In the wool manufacturing industry, the cost of raw material generally varies within 10 and 40 per cent. of the wholesale selling price.[1] Of this cost of raw material about 80 per cent. goes to the farmer, which means that he gets 8–32 per cent. of the wholesale price. In the case of cotton we found that the wholesale price was less than a half of the retail price, and though the ratio must be greater for wool (since the values are higher) it is likely to be at least 30–40 per cent. Therefore the farmer's proportion falls to 3–12 per cent. It is probably larger than this for woollen blankets, but is negligible for tailored suits, so that the all-round average cannot be much greater than 10 per cent.

Rubber.—The price of rubber has varied within six years from 55 cents to three or four, so that the following calculations must be confined to one particular year, for which alone are they relevant. The year chosen is 1929 when the price (at New York) was 19 cents. In that year the cost of transport to New York, with landing, brokerage, etc., was about 6 cents. By far the greater costs are incurred in the manufacturing stage, which is the manufacture of tyres, to which about 80 per cent. of raw rubber is devoted. The value of rubber at that date in medium-weight tyres of moderate quality was 10 per cent. of the selling price at retail. Accordingly we may say that the grower obtained about 8 per cent. of final value.

Now having considered a number of commodities separately by aggregating intermediate costs, we shall attempt to corrobo-rate the result by making some deductions from the relative movements of prices at particular stages in the completion and journey of the product. For instance, if we have the whole-sale and retail prices of the same commodity for a number of years, and if the movement in the wholesale series is double the movement in the retail, it is a fair deduction that the value at retail is double of the corresponding value at wholesale, provided that we are dealing with conditions of competition and that the only constituent of the retail price that has changed is the wholesale price. For the period 1928–30 this last requirement

---

[1] Cf. Du Plessis, *The Marketing of Wool*, p. 306.

was very well fulfilled in Great Britain, for neither wages nor other costs of distribution were at all seriously disturbed. We have available price lists of the Co-operative Wholesale Society and of the Co-operative Union, from which the following conclusions can be drawn :

TABLE 34.—DISTRIBUTION COSTS IN GREAT BRITAIN, 1928–30

	Costs between Importer or Manufacturer and Retailer.
Danish bacon	30 per cent. of retail price.
Butter	35–40 ,, ,, ,, ,, ,,
Eggs	55 ,, ,, ,, ,, ,, (of which 35 per cent. in retail section).
Cheese	30 per cent. of retail price.
Woollen vests	45–60 ,, ,, ,, ,, ,,

Some similar indications are available for other countries, but the descriptions of the produce and their condition and situation are not precise, so that no hard and fast conclusions can be drawn.[1]

TABLE 35.—DISTRIBUTION COSTS IN GENERAL

Canada.	Cost between Stage of Raw, Partly Manufactured and Fully or Chiefly Manufactured.
Field crops	60 per cent. of wholesale price.
Animal products . .	25 ,, ,, ,, ,, ,,
Marine produce . . .	43 ,, ,, ,, ,, ,,
Forest produce . . .	30 ,, ,, ,, ,, ,,
Italy.	Cost between Raw and Finished Stages.
Domestic produce ex food .	32 per cent. of wholesale price.
Germany.	Cost between Raw or Semi-finished and Finished.
Domestic produce . . .	44 per cent. of wholesale price.
United States.	Cost between Raw and Finished Stages.
Domestic produce . . .	40 per cent. of wholesale price.

The proportions of marketing cost shown by this method, since they mostly work out at between 40 and 60 per cent., seem to be in general accord with the proportions given by adding individual items of cost. Our general conclusions as to the weight of marketing costs can now be summarised in a table based on the earlier method of calculation. In the first column are placed figures indicating the proportion of the final price obtained by the producer, and in the second, the pro-

[1] Compiled from *Agricultural Crisis*, Vol. II.

portionate fall in price registered between 1929 and 1931, as percentages.

TABLE 36.—SUMMARY OF DISTRIBUTION COSTS

	A. Producer's Proportion.	B. Price Fall.
Wheat	25–35	40
Other cereals	20	40–60
Meat	40	15–30
Dairy produce :		
Milk	60	
Butter	80	
Eggs	60	
Vegetables and fruit :		
Potatoes	50	
Other	25–55	
Coffee	35	60
Tea	60	30
Sugar	20–25	35
Cotton	10	60
Wool	10 ?	45
Rubber	8	70

The correlation between a low proportion of the final price to the producer and a large variation in wholesale price seems to be reasonably close.

CARRYING COSTS OF STOCKS OF RAW PRODUCE

SOME indication of the carrying costs is obtainable from the comparison of spot and future quotations in "organised" produce markets, and in others less organised but also dealing in commodities sold by description.

This method of discovering the costs was set forth by Mr. Keynes (*Treatise*, Vol. II, p. 142). We may take it that the carrying costs are at least equal to the spread between future and spot prices where futures are the higher—the spread being called contango—for if the carrying costs were greater it would pay to sell spot and buy forward rather than hold the stocks for the period. It does not follow, however, that the carrying costs are no more than the contango. They will usually exceed the contango by an amount equal to the latent backwardation appropriate to the circumstances. The backwardation—an excess of spot over future prices—reflects the convenience to producers of being able to sell at a date before they are prepared to supply. Although the backwardation may be overlaid by a contango when surplus stocks are present, it nevertheless exists at all times, usually reaching its maximum shortly before new crops are expected.

In setting forth a list of contangoes designed to indicate the minima of carrying costs, I have chosen three dates, 4th January, 1932, 1st July (or 13th July), 1932, and 4th January, 1933. At the January dates, when the bulk of the preceding autumn crops will have been marketed, the backwardations are mainly low : at the July dates, a number of the quotations are reflecting the prospect of coming autumn crops. But the relations between the quotations for the January and July dates are not uniform throughout, since the statistical positions of the commodities— apart from seasonal considerations—have all altered unevenly. The spreads between future and spot prices are greater in markets nearer the source of supply, particularly at markets near to places where stocks are held, and where these stocks are potential supplies.

The items in the list are expressed as percentages per annum for the sake of comparisons, but in only one case is twelve months the actual period for which quotations were obtained. The quoted periods are stated, and it will be noticed that the assumed annual charges rise rapidly as the period lengthens (unless it lengthens out into a harvest season), so that the rate for twelve months may well be double the rate for six months. It is not possible to make any deductions as to the rate for such periods as three years.

TABLE 37.—CONTANGO QUOTATIONS FOR RAW PRODUCE

		January, 1932.		July, 1932.	January, 1933.
Wheat	London	3 months . . . — 4 ,, . . . 8 6 ,, . . . 8		7·6 — 9·4	3·7 — —
	Liverpool	3 months . . 21 (March–July) 5 months . . . —		— 8·4	— —
	New York	3 months . . . —		25	—
	Chicago	3 months . . 12 (March–July) 6 months . . . 6 (March–September) 5 months . . . —		— — 29	— — —
	Winnipeg	5 months . . . —		20	—
Maize	London	3 months . . . —		7·6	5·5
	Liverpool	3 months . . . 21		8·4	—
	Chicago	5 months . . . — 6 ,, . . . 20 (March–September)		9·6 —	— —
Oats	Chicago	5 months . . . —		24	—
Rye	Chicago	5 months . . . —		5̇0	—
American Cotton	Liverpool	12 months . . . 1·2		4·8	2·6
	New York	6 months . . . 12 10 ,, . . . 13		10 14	11·7 11·7
Egyptian Cotton	Liverpool	4 months . . . 24 6 ,, . . . —		12 14	69 6·6

		January, 1932.		July, 1932.	January, 1933.
	London .	3 months . . .	—	7·2	—
		4 ,, . . .	16·5	—	23
		10 ,, . . .	—	15	—
		11 ,, . . .	14	—	19
Sugar	Liverpool .	10 months . . .	—	20	—
		11 ,, . . .	13	—	20
	New York	6 months . . .	28	9	41
		10 ,, . . .	—	16	—
		11 ,, . . .	28	—	28
	Liverpool .	10 months . . .	7·8	3·4	—
Cocoa	London .	11 months . . .	—	—	7·3
	New York .	6 months . . .	18	8	20
	London .	6 months . . .	20	13·8	7·7
Rubber		9 ,, . . .	24	18·4	10·3
	New York	6 months . . .	14	22	9·9
Coffee	New York .	5 months . . .	14	—	—
		11 ,, . . .	10	—	—
Jute	London .	3 months . . .	18.	—	12
Linseed	London .	3 months . . .	—	13	3
Ground-nuts	London .	3 months . . .	—	10·4	4
		5 ,, . . .	8	—	—

Some of these recorded spreads are extraordinary and need individual explanation. Most of them fall between 10 and 20 per cent.

INDEX

Acreage history : of seven crops, 1927–30, 30 ; of American crops, 1927–31, 31

Activity : definition of, 186 ; ratio of primary to secondary, 9 *n.*, 185

Ad valorem taxes, 52

Aftalion, Professor, 135 *n.*, 140

Agrarian reform, 107

Agriculture - trade correlations, 210

American Telephone and Telegraph Co., 147 *n.*, 165, 233

Animal Produce : price declines in, 80 ; proportionate value of, 157, 169

Argentina, investment and crop receipts in, 197

Australia : economic history during depression, 83, 86, 87 ; investment and crop receipts in, 196

Bagging material, 53

Banking policy for stabilisation, 237

Belshaw, Professor, 16 *n.*

Beverages, elasticity of demand for, 251

Botanical advances in farming, 106

Bowley, A. L., 39

Brazil, 126, 259

Broomhall, F. C., 95 *n.*

Budgets of agricultural countries, 195, 208

Canada : costs of handling wheat in, 254 ; investment and crop receipts in, 196

Capacity, curtailment of, 125

Capital : costs of farming, 21, 22, 245 ; expenditure on farming, 28 ; issues on long term, 194 ; wearing out of fixed, 145

Carrying costs, 64, 264

China, and price of silver, 88

Clark, C. G., 236 *n.*

Clark and Weld, 254 *n.*

Coffee, marketing, costs of, 259

Combines, 108

Compensations : inter-crop, 151, 170 ; inter-local, 151, 171 ; inter-temporal, 174

Confidence theories of trade cycle, 137, 147

Consumer : budgets in Great Britain, 39 ; fixed outgoings of, 42 ; gain on low food prices, 9, 113

Consumers' goods, oversupply of, 140

Consumption, measurement of physical, 34

Contango quotations in produce markets, 264

Contraction of farm activity, 19, 23, 109

Co-operation among farmers, 93

Costs : cost level of farm requisites, 28 ; decline of farm costs, 77 ; distribution of, in farming, 214 ; " cost relation " in storage projects, 67

Cotton : description of marketing, 50 ; costs of marketing, 260

Credit : financing of farm expansion by, 105, 190, 192 ; issued by merchants, 21 ; prolonged during depression, 93